THE Eminence IN Shadow

2

Art **Anri Sakano**

Original Story **Daisuke Aizawa**

Character Design **Touzai**

Episode.5

Episode.6

Episode.7

Episode.8

Episode.5

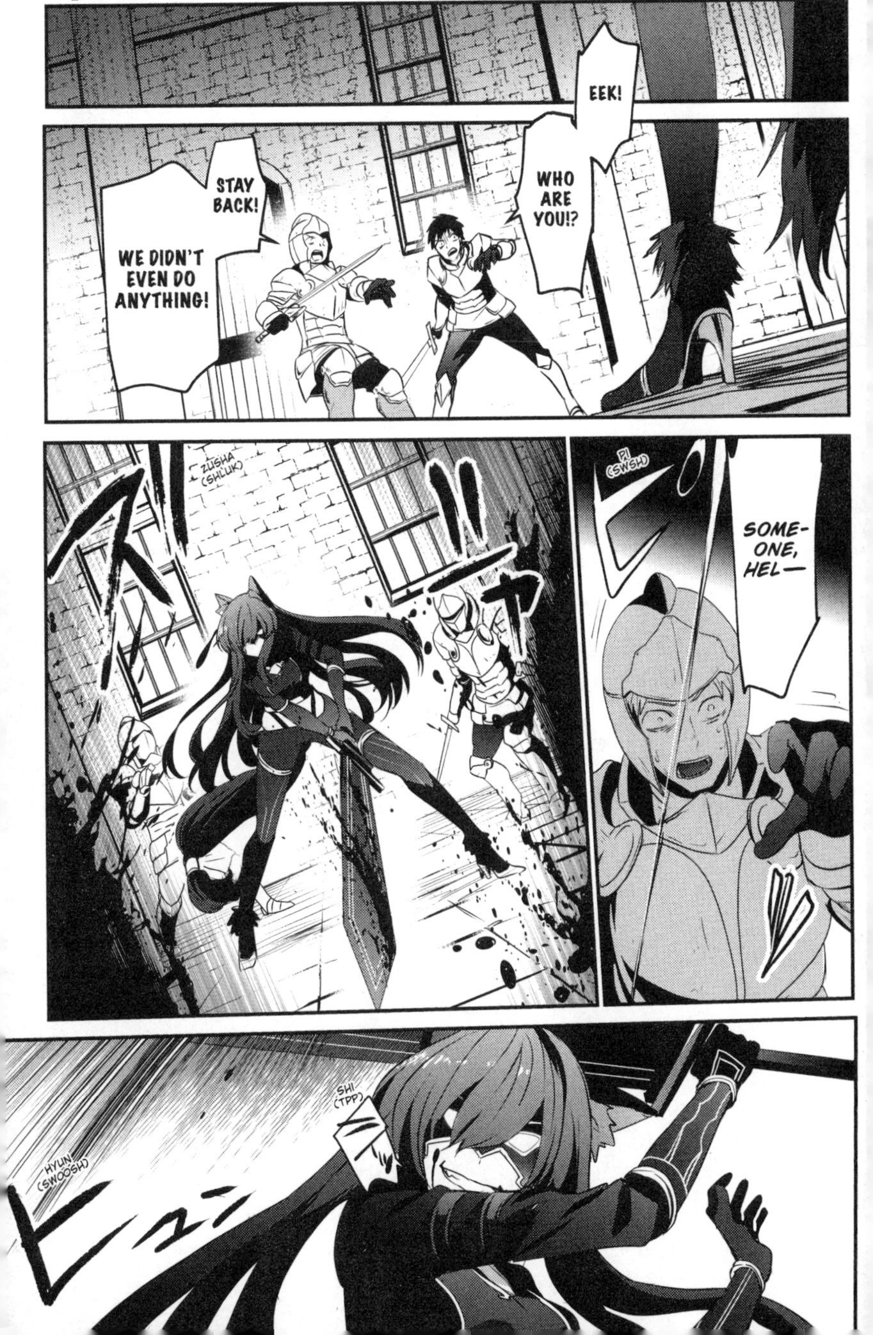
EEK!
WHO ARE YOU!?
STAY BACK!
WE DIDN'T EVEN DO ANYTHING!
PI (SWSH)
SOME-ONE, HEL—
ZUSHA (SHLUK)
SHI (TPP)
HYUN (SWOOSH)

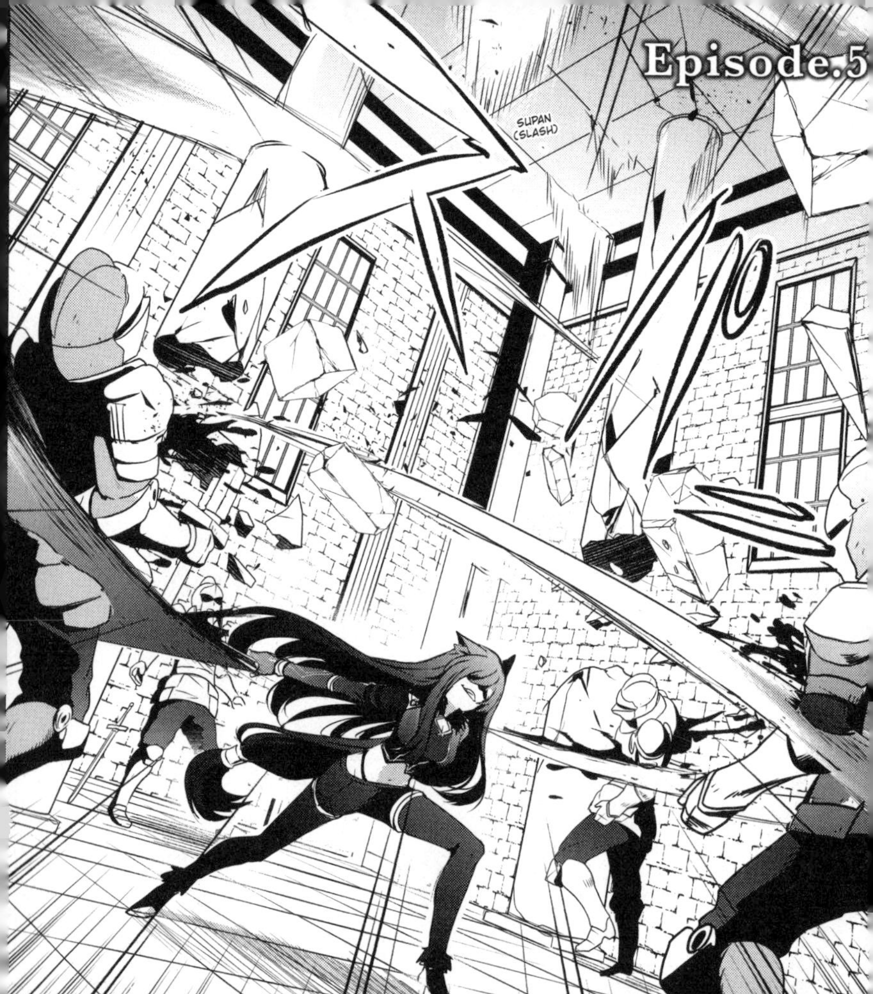
Episode.5
SUPAN
(SLASH)

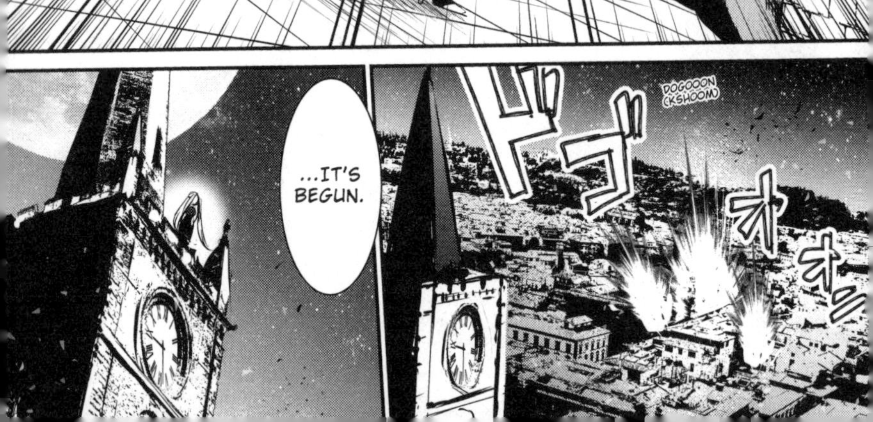
DOGOOON
(KSHOOM)
...IT'S BEGUN.

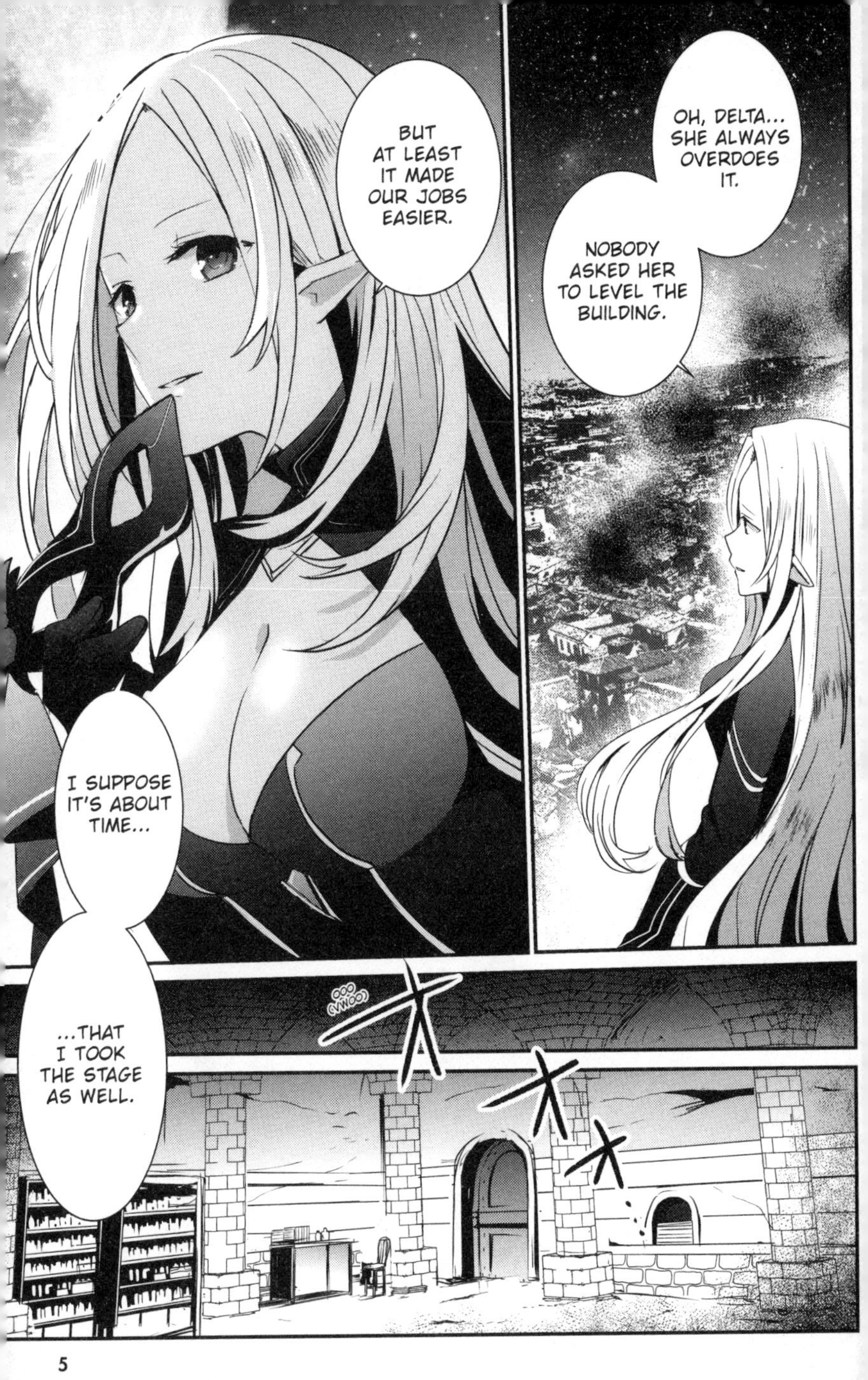
OH, DELTA... SHE ALWAYS OVERDOES IT.
NOBODY ASKED HER TO LEVEL THE BUILDING.
BUT AT LEAST IT MADE OUR JOBS EASIER.
I SUPPOSE IT'S ABOUT TIME...
...THAT I TOOK THE STAGE AS WELL.
(VWOOOOO)

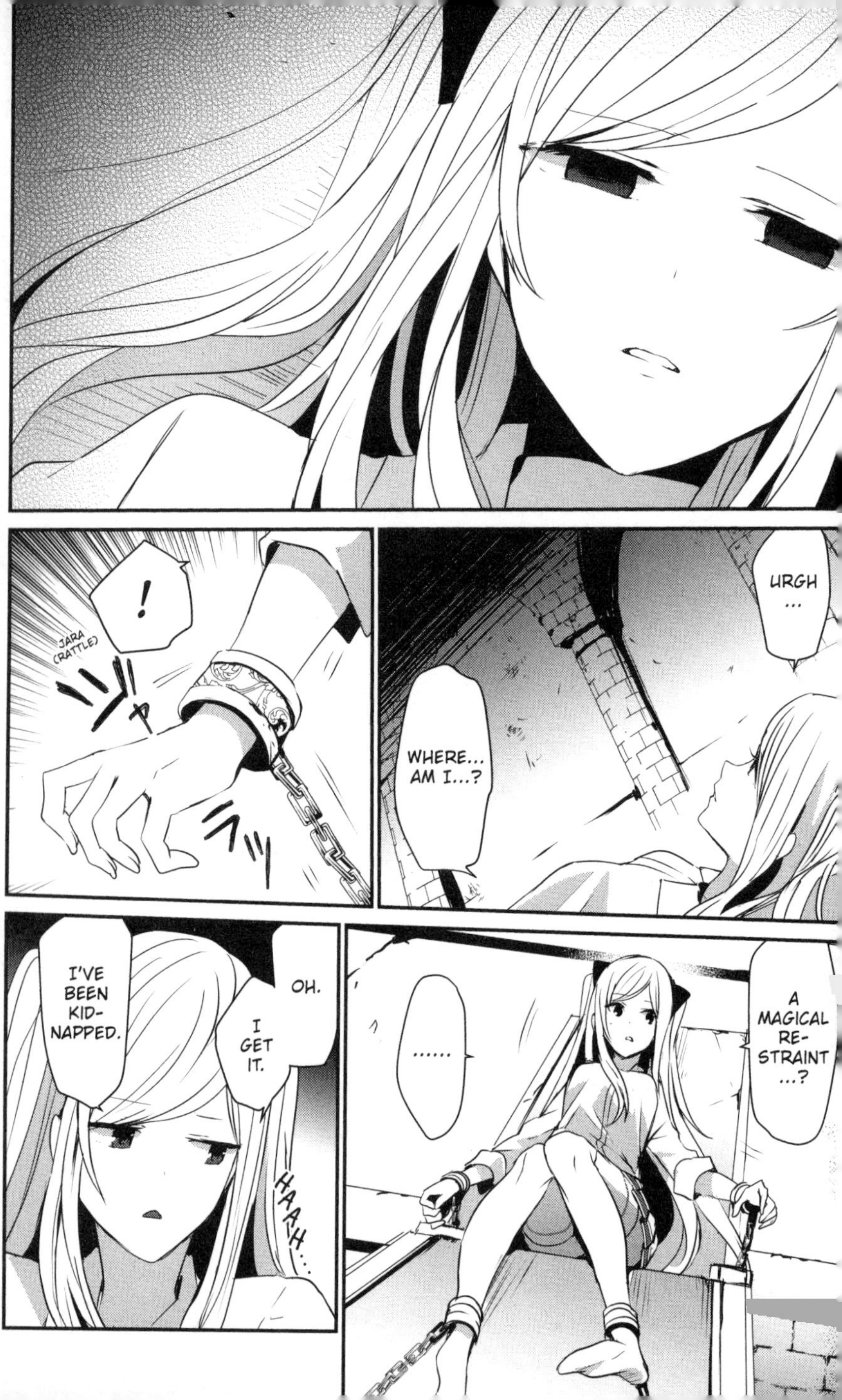
URGH...
WHERE... AM I...?
!
JARA (RATTLE)
A MAGICAL RE-STRAINT...?
......
OH.
I GET IT.
I'VE BEEN KID-NAPPED.
HAAAH...

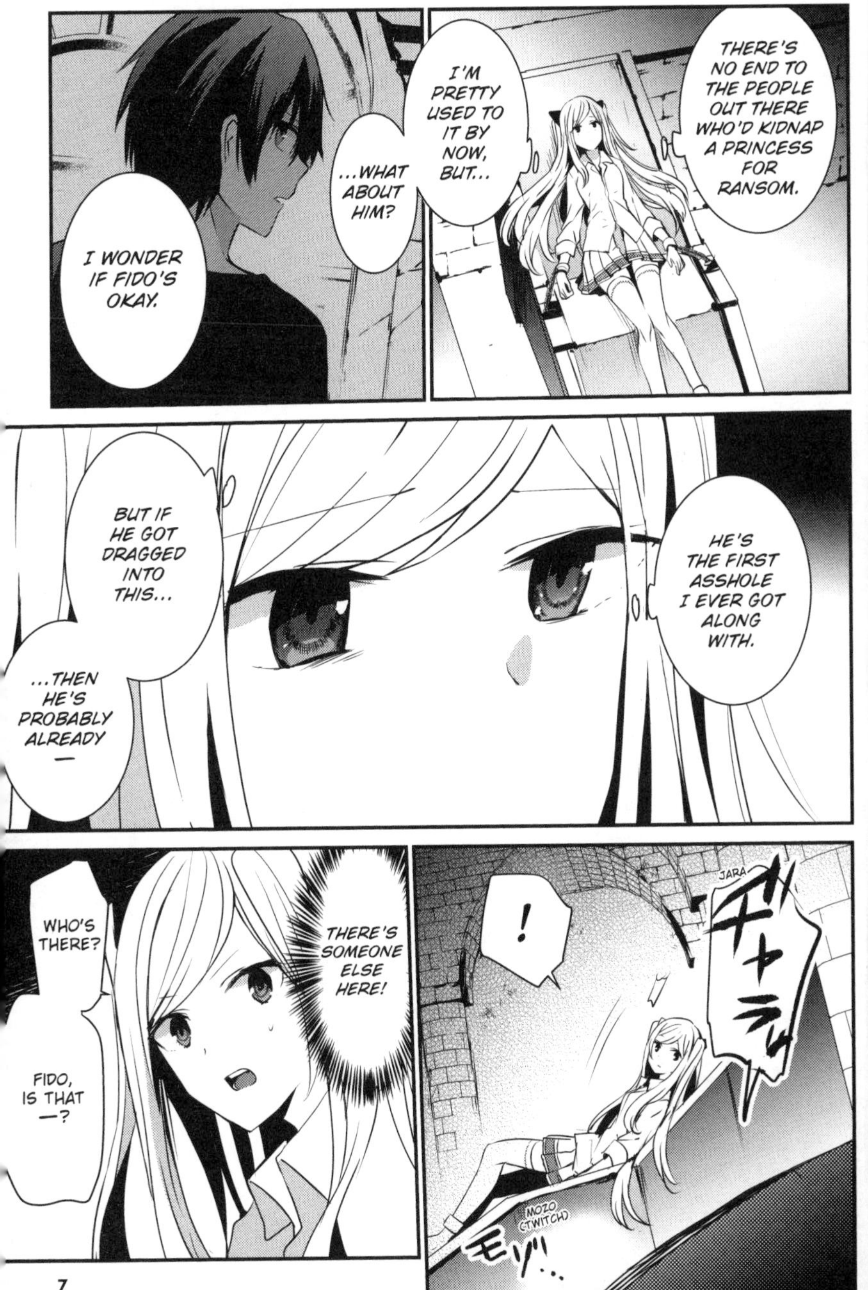
THERE'S NO END TO THE PEOPLE OUT THERE WHO'D KIDNAP A PRINCESS FOR RANSOM.
I'M PRETTY USED TO IT BY NOW, BUT...
...WHAT ABOUT HIM?
I WONDER IF FIDO'S OKAY.
HE'S THE FIRST ASSHOLE I EVER GOT ALONG WITH.
BUT IF HE GOT DRAGGED INTO THIS...
...THEN HE'S PROBABLY ALREADY—
!
JARA
MOZO (TWITCH)
THERE'S SOMEONE ELSE HERE!
WHO'S THERE?
FIDO, IS THAT—?

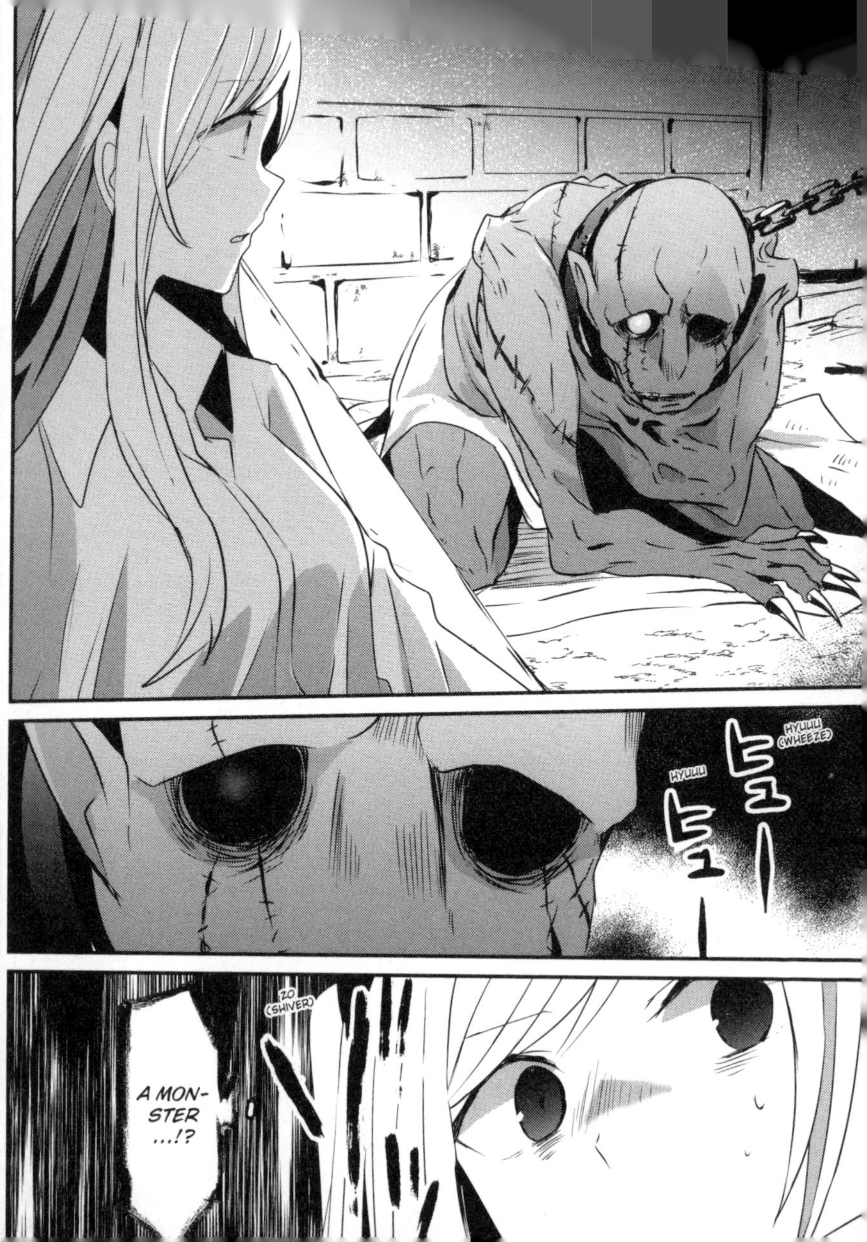
ヒュー
HYUUU (WHEEZE)
ヒュー
HYUUU
ZO (SHIVER)
A MON-
STER
...!?

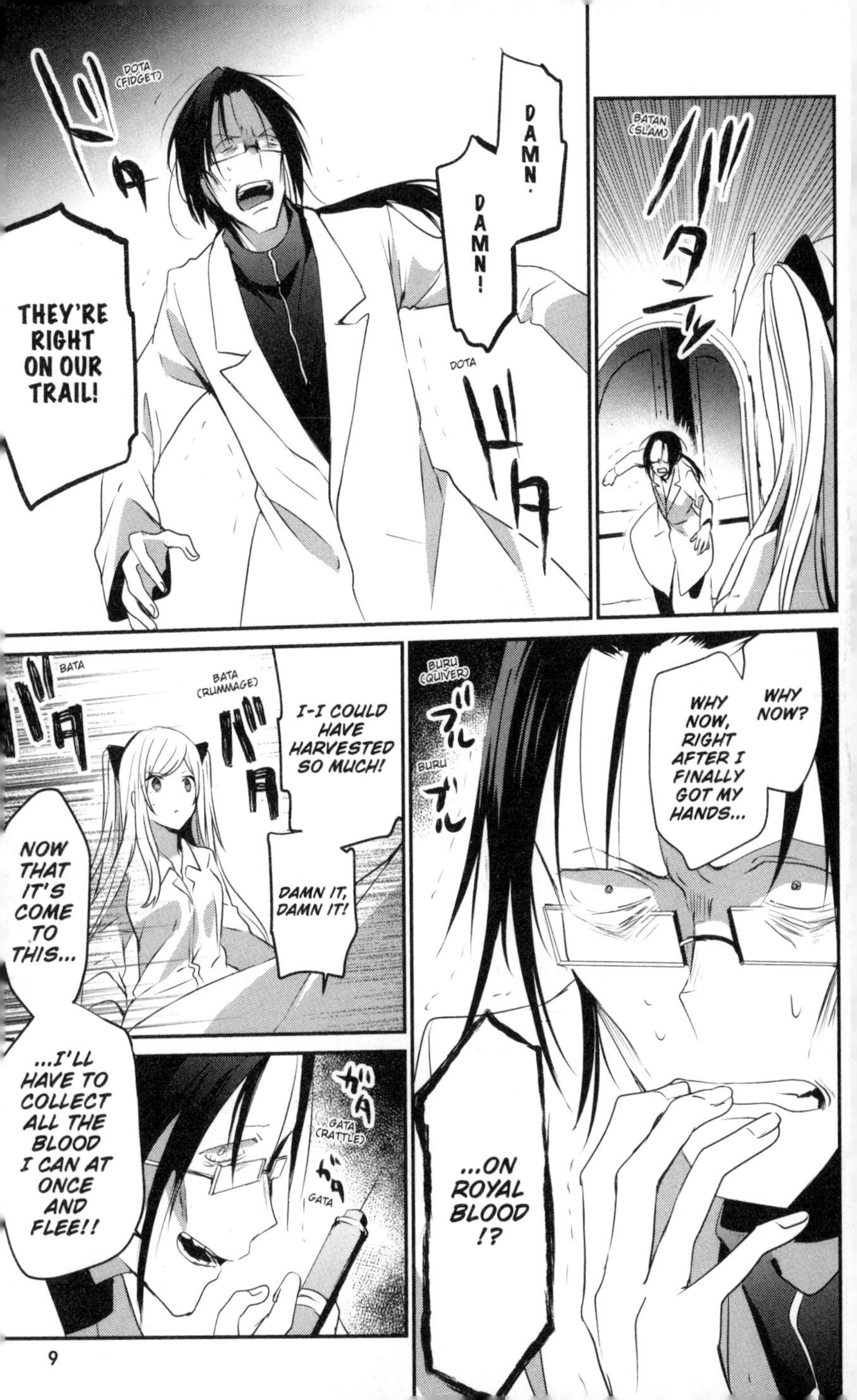
BATAN (SLAM)
DAMN. DAMN!
DOTA (FIDGET)
DOTA
THEY'RE RIGHT ON OUR TRAIL!
WHY NOW?
BURU (QUIVER)
BURU
WHY NOW, RIGHT AFTER I FINALLY GOT MY HANDS...
...ON ROYAL BLOOD!?
I-I COULD HAVE HARVESTED SO MUCH!
BATA (RUMMAGE)
BATA
DAMN IT, DAMN IT!
NOW THAT IT'S COME TO THIS...
GATA (RATTLE)
GATA
...I'LL HAVE TO COLLECT ALL THE BLOOD I CAN AT ONCE AND FLEE!!

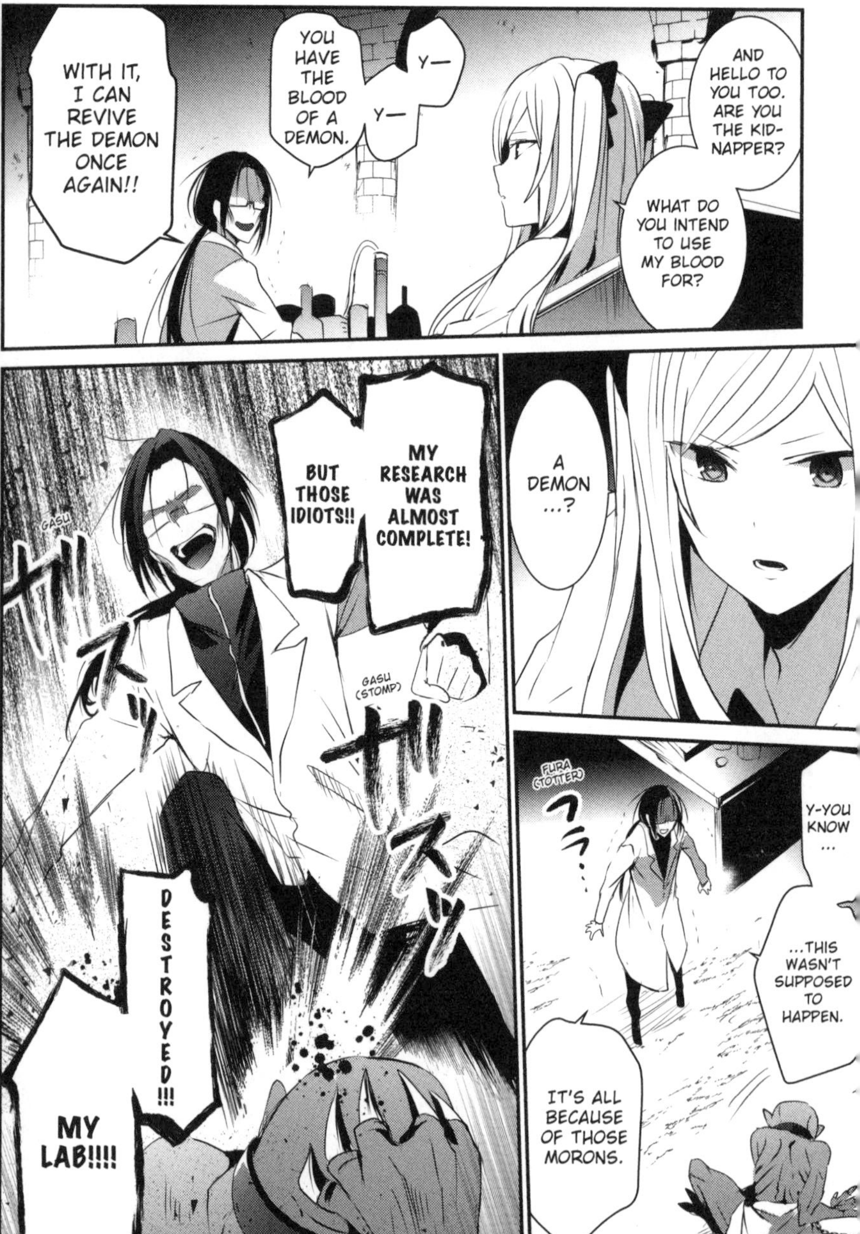
AND HELLO TO YOU TOO. ARE YOU THE KID-NAPPER?
WHAT DO YOU INTEND TO USE MY BLOOD FOR?
Y—
Y—
YOU HAVE THE BLOOD OF A DEMON.
WITH IT, I CAN REVIVE THE DEMON ONCE AGAIN!!
A DEMON ...?
FURA (STOTTER)
Y-YOU KNOW ...
...THIS WASN'T SUPPOSED TO HAPPEN.
IT'S ALL BECAUSE OF THOSE MORONS.
MY RESEARCH WAS ALMOST COMPLETE!
BUT THOSE IDIOTS!!
GASU
GASU (STOMP)
DESTROYED!!!
MY LAB!!!!

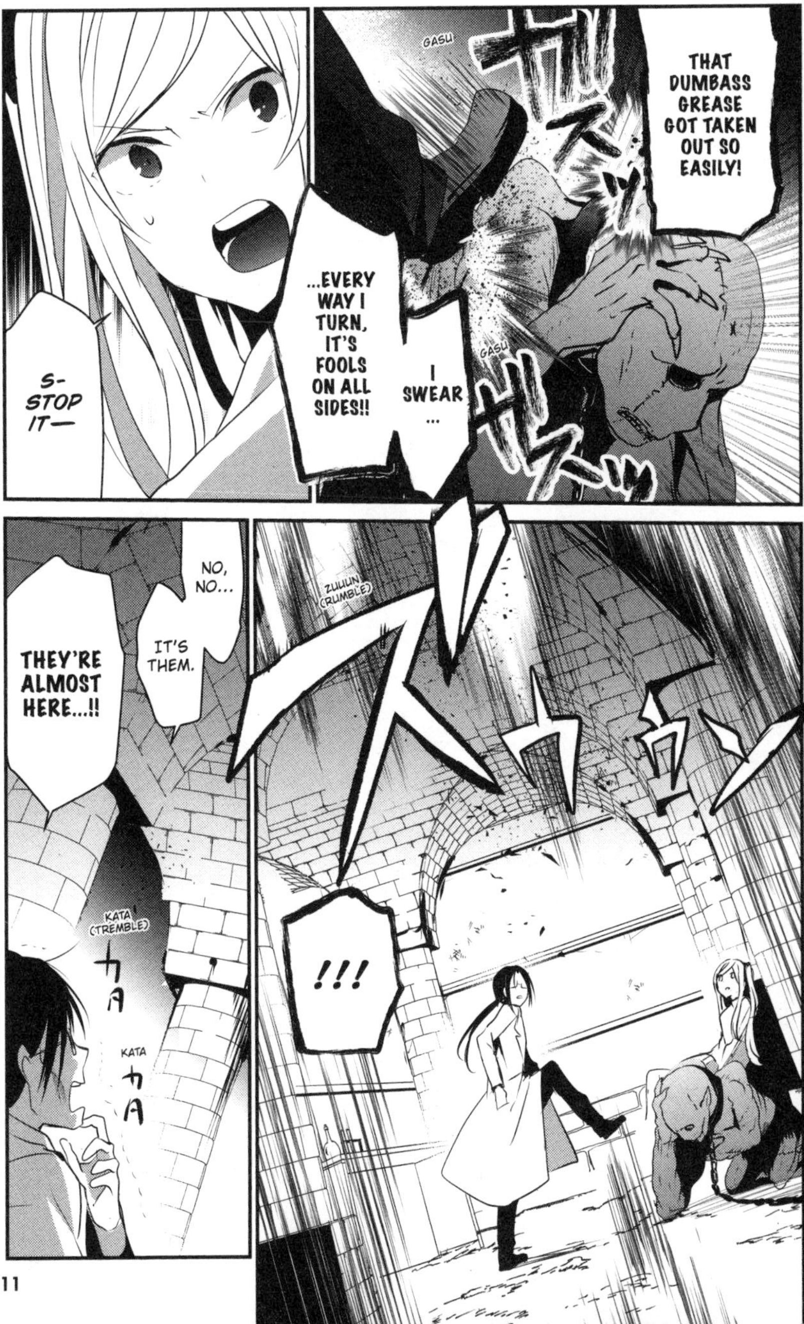
GASU
THAT DUMBASS GREASE GOT TAKEN OUT SO EASILY!
GASU
I SWEAR...
...EVERY WAY I TURN, IT'S FOOLS ON ALL SIDES!!
S-STOP IT—
ZUUUN (RUMBLE)
!!!
NO, NO...
IT'S THEM.
THEY'RE ALMOST HERE...!!
KATA (TREMBLE)
KATA

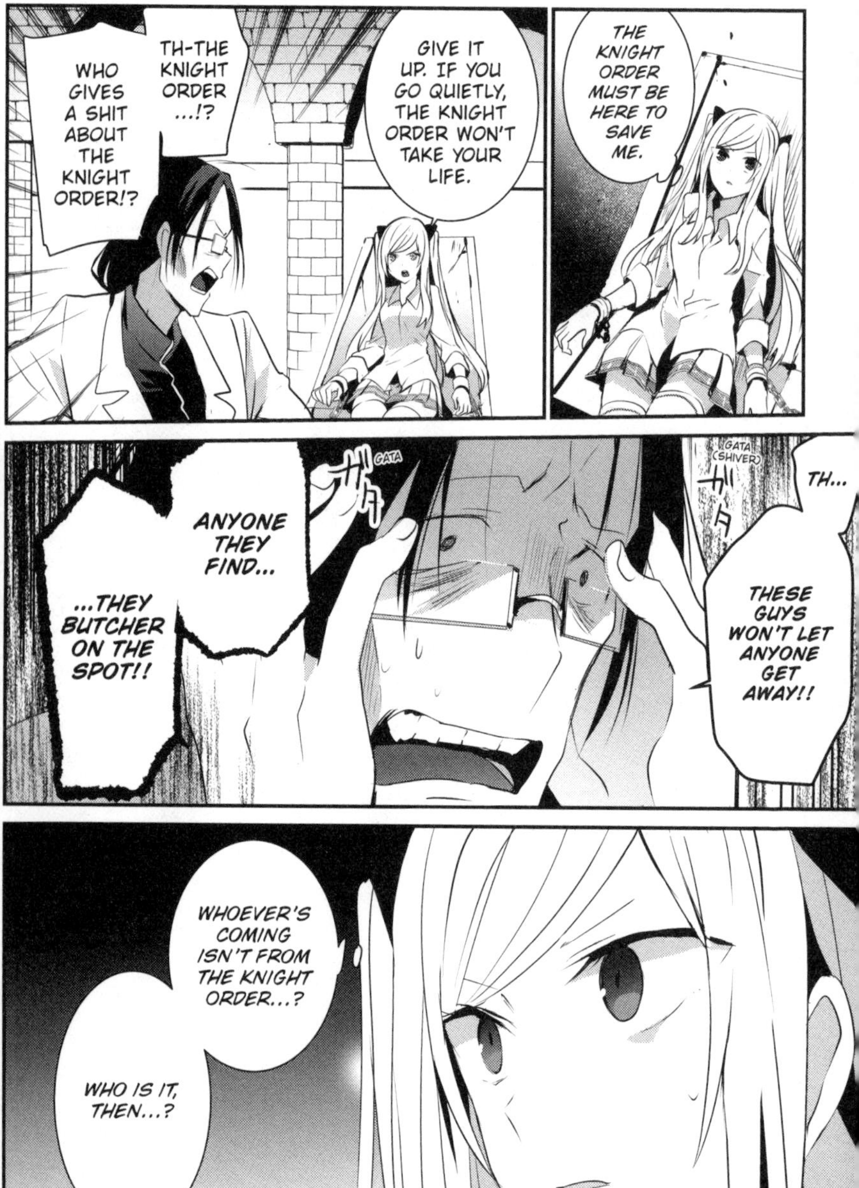
THE KNIGHT ORDER MUST BE HERE TO SAVE ME.
GIVE IT UP. IF YOU GO QUIETLY, THE KNIGHT ORDER WON'T TAKE YOUR LIFE.
TH-THE KNIGHT ORDER ...!?
WHO GIVES A SHIT ABOUT THE KNIGHT ORDER!?
GATA (SHIVER)
TH...
THESE GUYS WON'T LET ANYONE GET AWAY!!
GATA
ANYONE THEY FIND...
...THEY BUTCHER ON THE SPOT!!
WHOEVER'S COMING ISN'T FROM THE KNIGHT ORDER...?
WHO IS IT, THEN...?

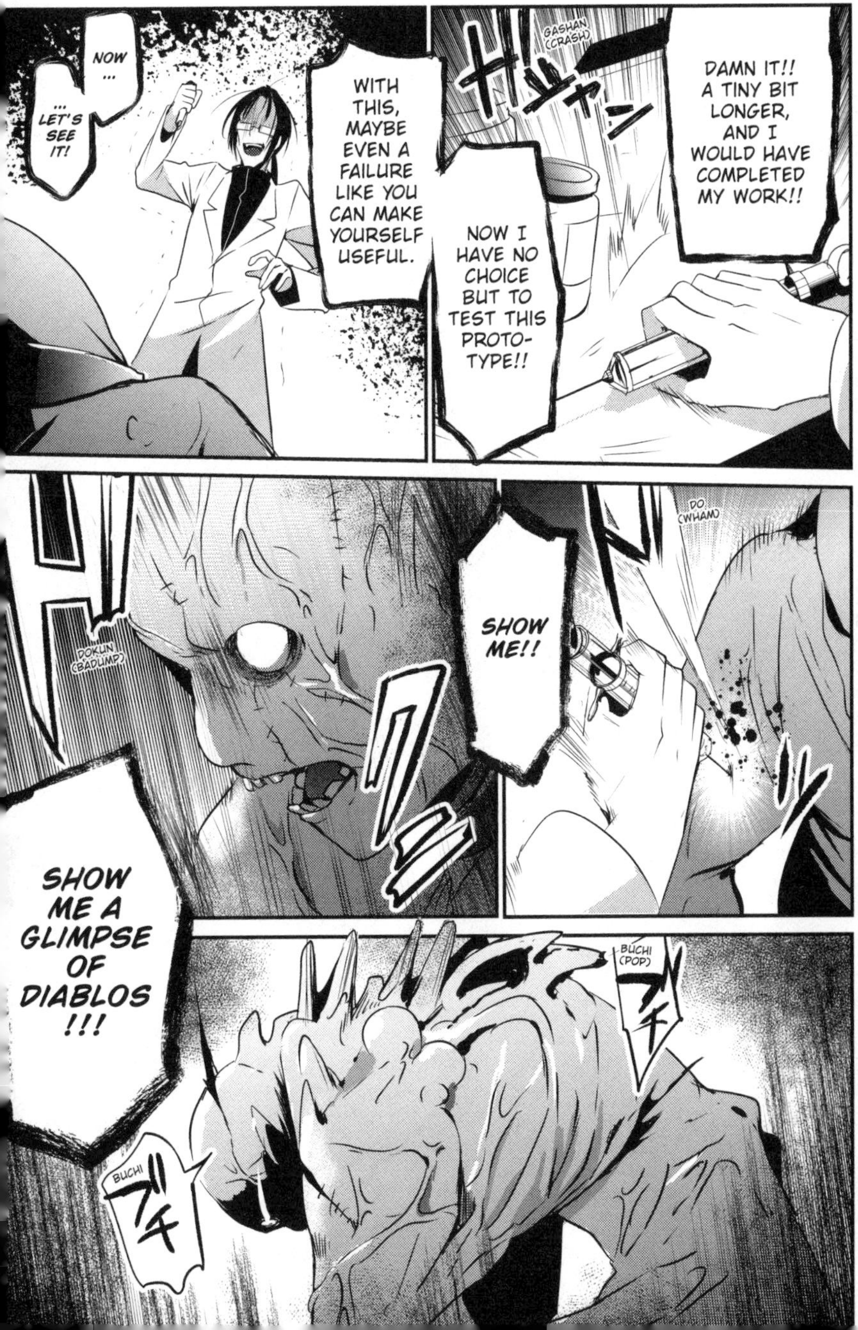
GASHAN (CRASH)
DAMN IT!! A TINY BIT LONGER, AND I WOULD HAVE COMPLETED MY WORK!!
NOW I HAVE NO CHOICE BUT TO TEST THIS PROTO-TYPE!!
WITH THIS, MAYBE EVEN A FAILURE LIKE YOU CAN MAKE YOURSELF USEFUL.
NOW...
...LET'S SEE IT!
DO (WHAM)
SHOW ME!!
DOKUN (BADUMP)
BUCHI (POP)
SHOW ME A GLIMPSE OF DIABLOS!!!
BUCHI

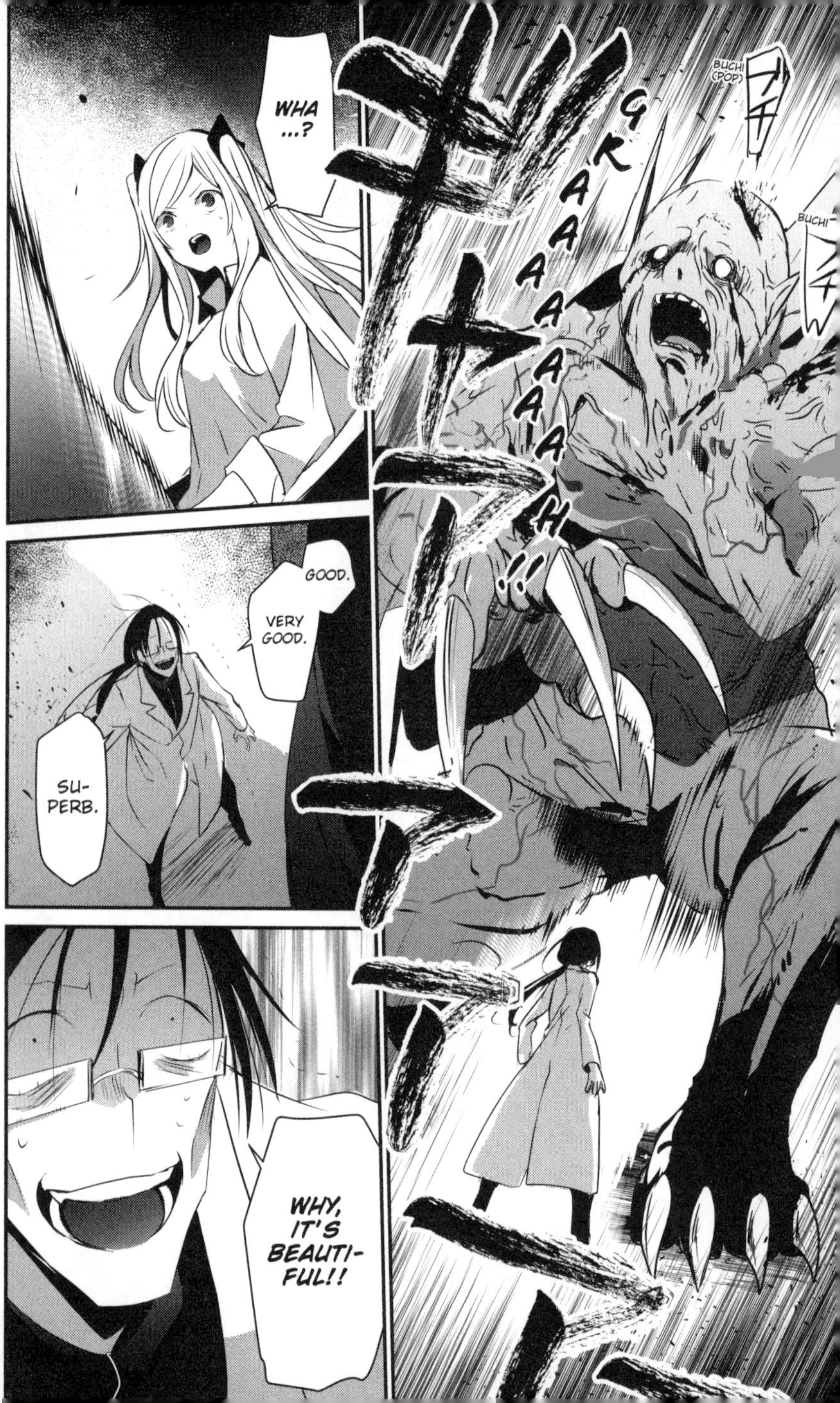
BUCHI (POP)
BUCHI
GRAAAAAAAAAH!!
WHA...?
GOOD.
VERY GOOD.
SU-PERB.
WHY, IT'S BEAUTI-FUL!!

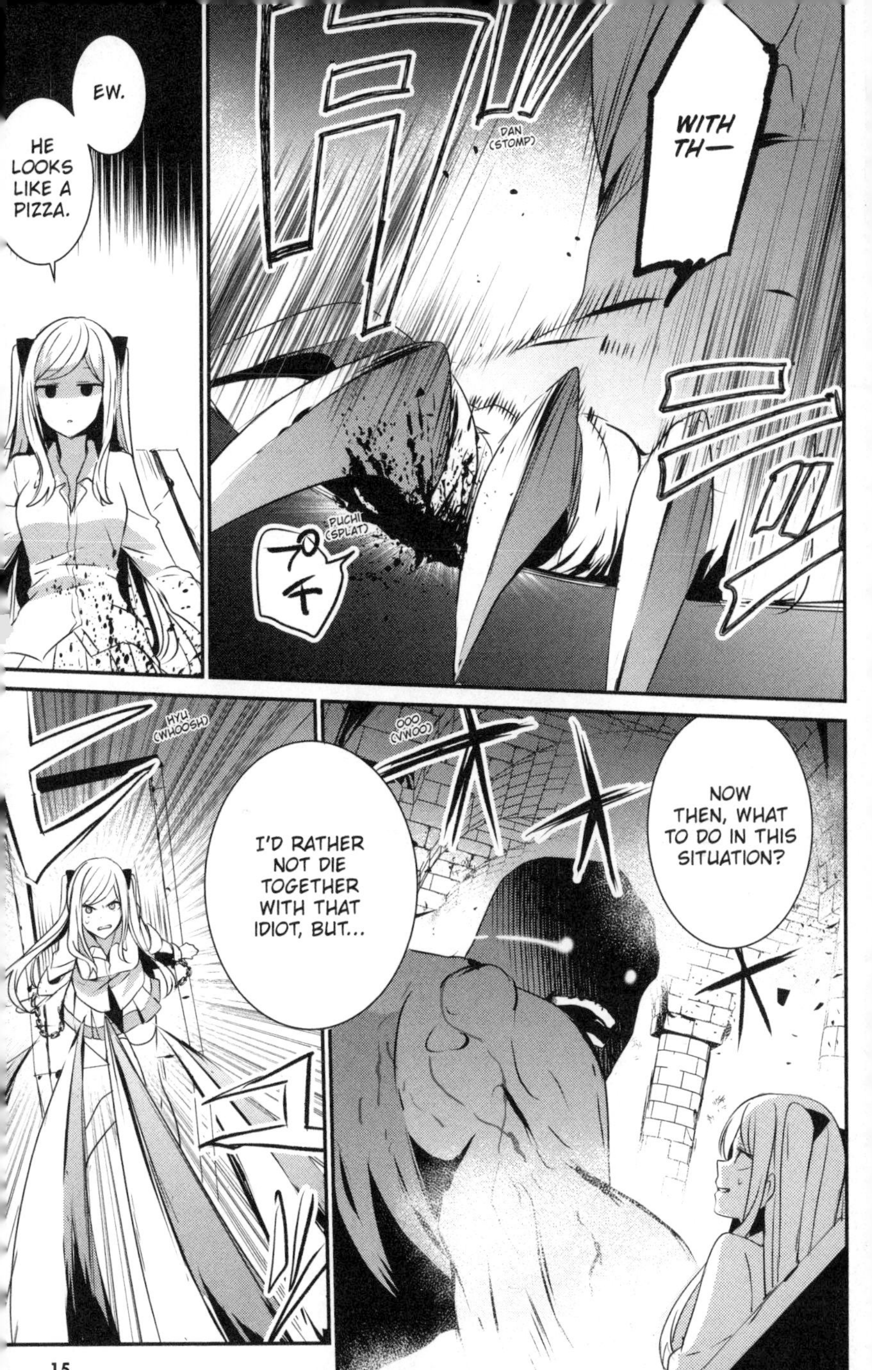
WITH TH—
DAN (STOMP)
PUCHI (SPLAT)
EW.
HE LOOKS LIKE A PIZZA.
NOW THEN, WHAT TO DO IN THIS SITUATION?
OOO (VWOO)
I'D RATHER NOT DIE TOGETHER WITH THAT IDIOT, BUT...
HYU (WHOOSH)

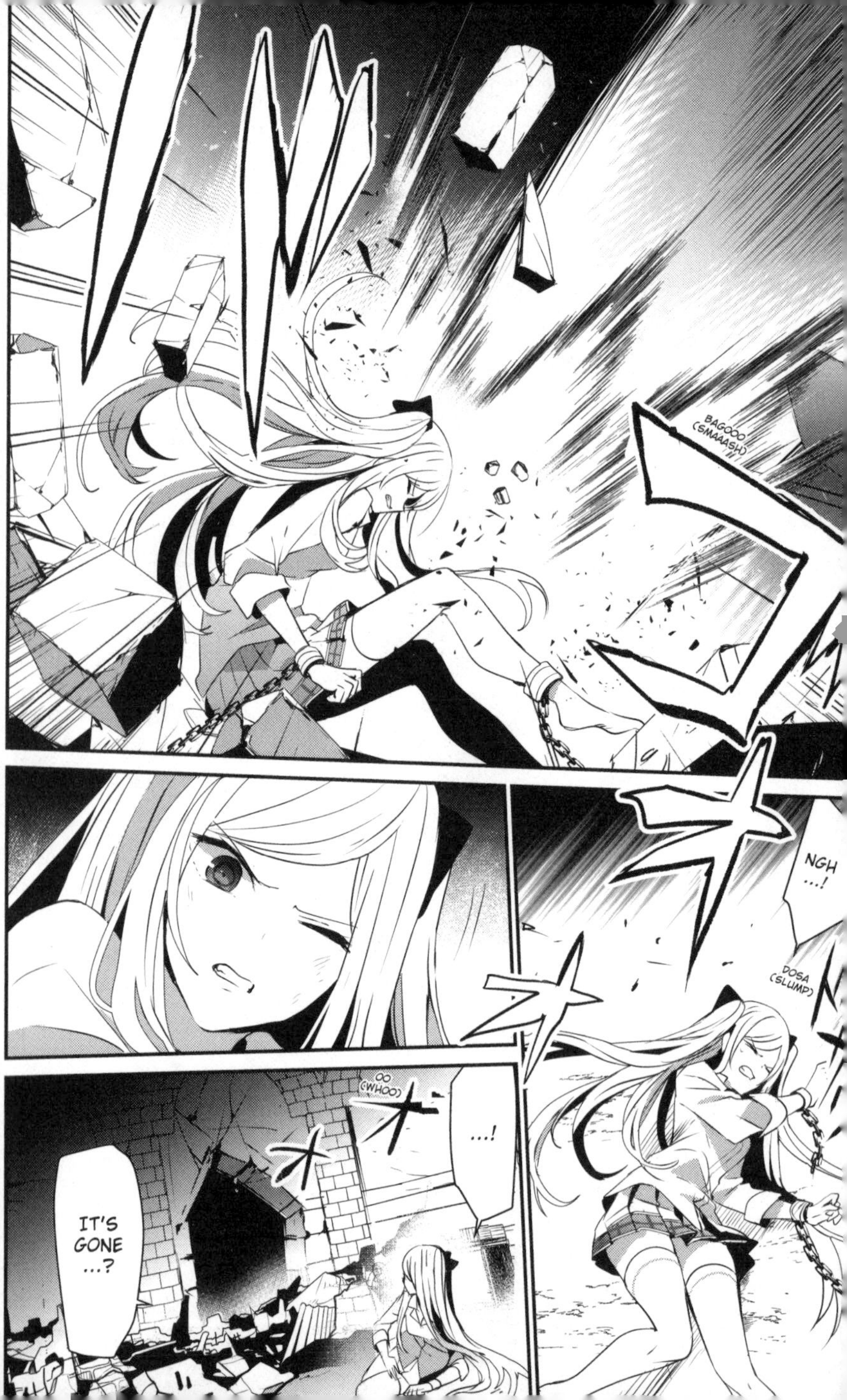
BAGOOO (SMAAASH)
NGH ...!
DOSA (SLUMP)
OO (WHOO)
...!
IT'S GONE ...?

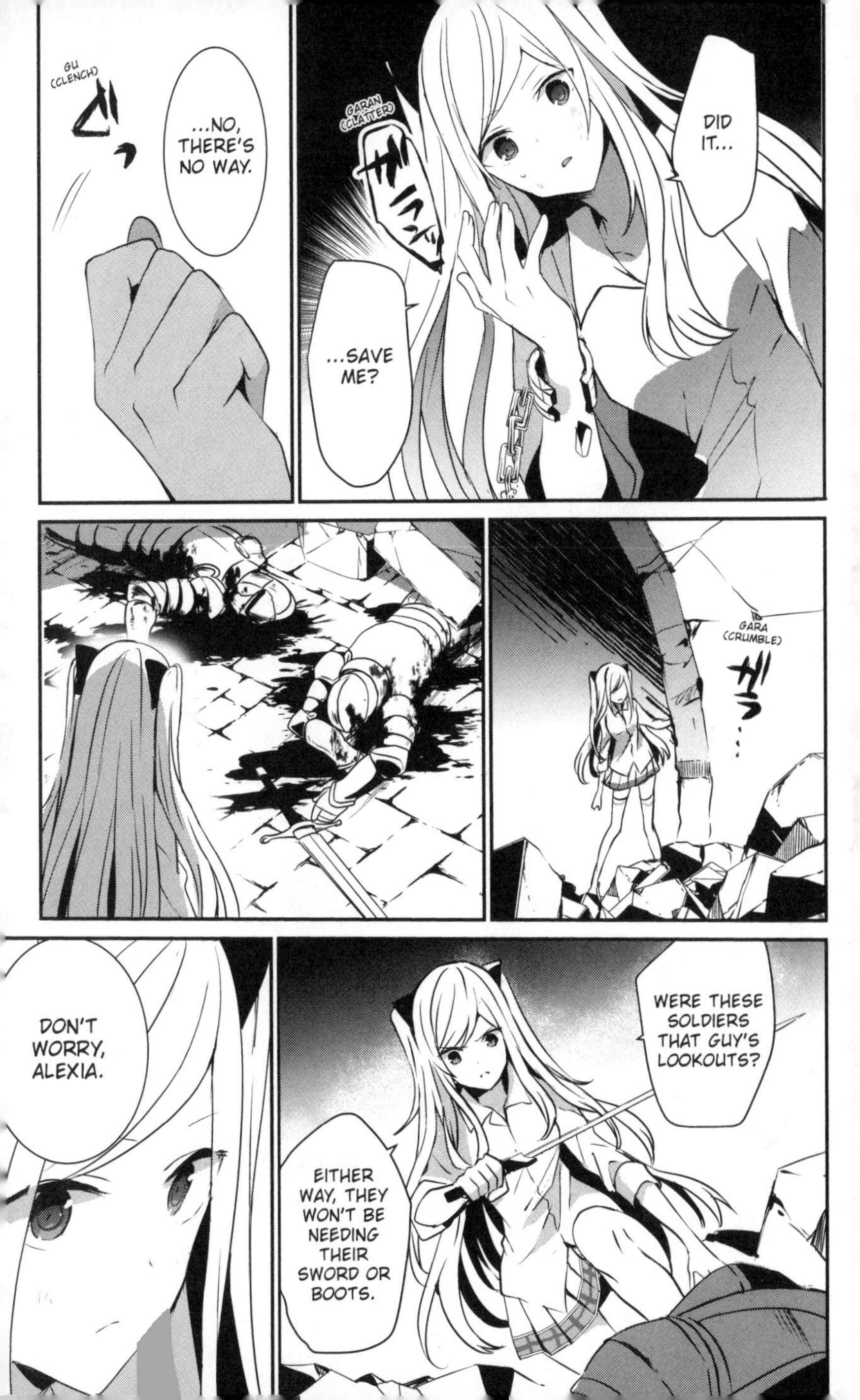
DID IT...
GARAN (CLATTER)
...SAVE ME?
...NO, THERE'S NO WAY.
GU (CLENCH)
GARA (CRUMBLE)
WERE THESE SOLDIERS THAT GUY'S LOOKOUTS?
EITHER WAY, THEY WON'T BE NEEDING THEIR SWORD OR BOOTS.
DON'T WORRY, ALEXIA.

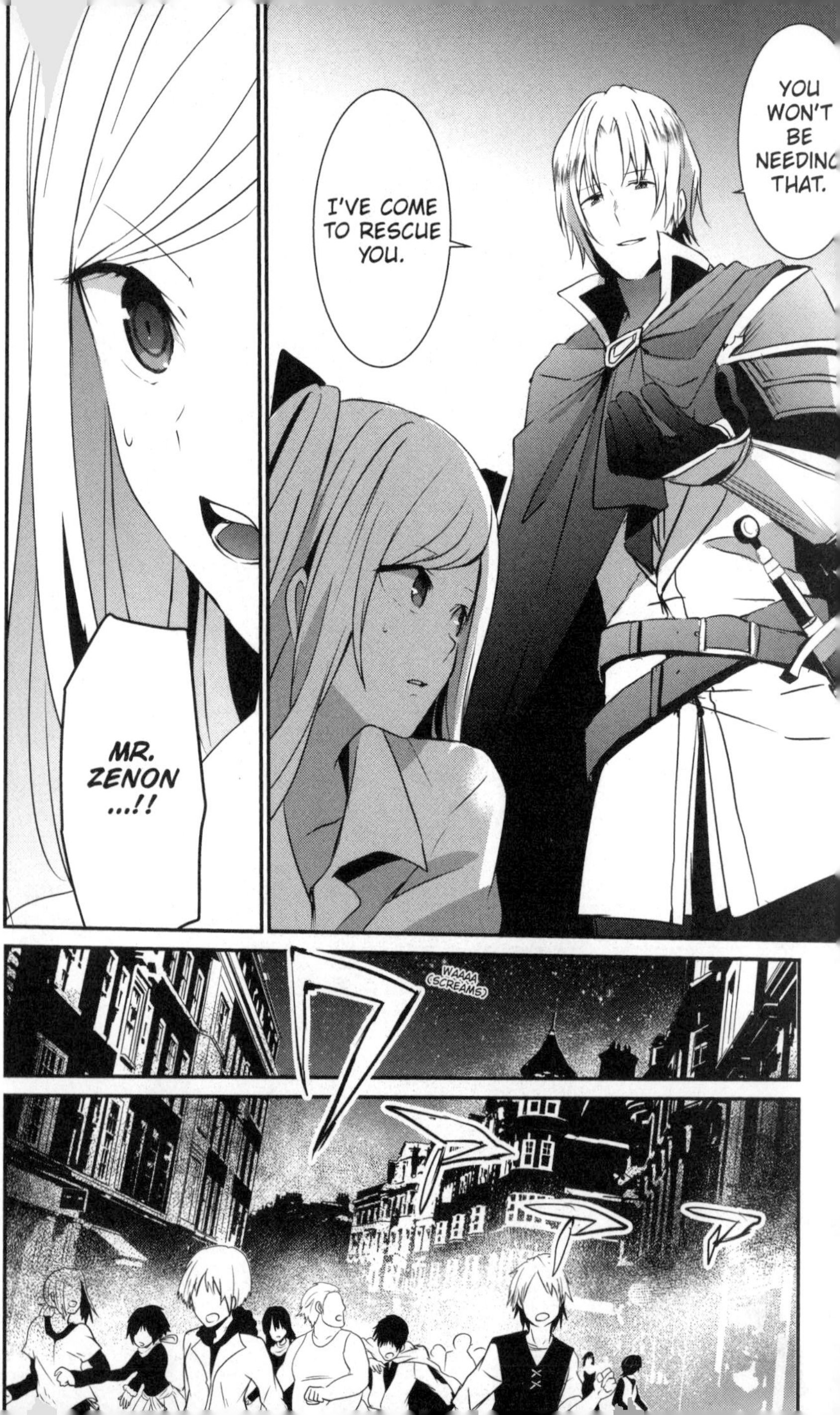
YOU WON'T BE NEEDING THAT.
I'VE COME TO RESCUE YOU.
MR. ZENON ...!!
WAAAA (SCREAMS)

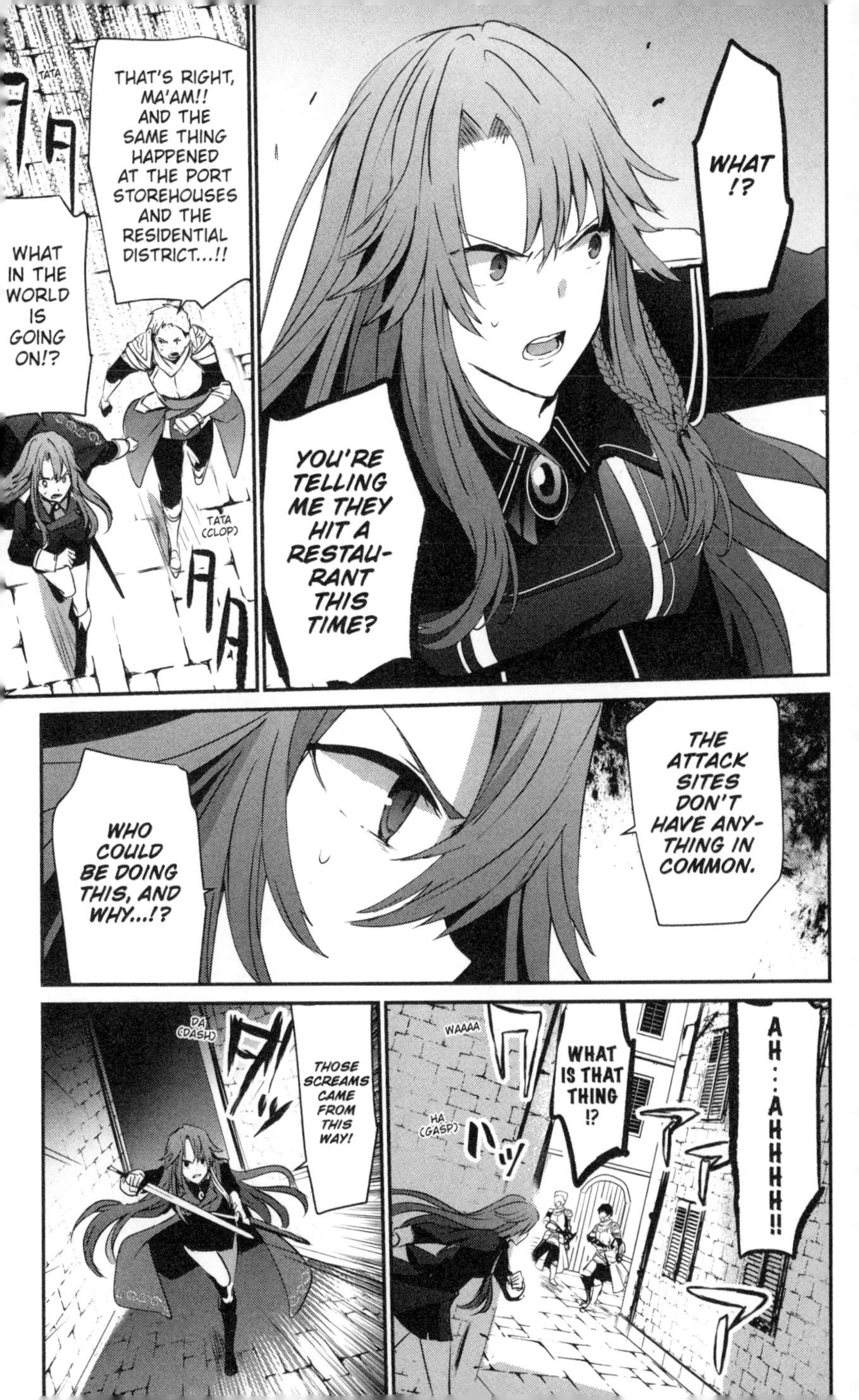
WHAT!?
YOU'RE TELLING ME THEY HIT A RESTAU-RANT THIS TIME?
TATA
THAT'S RIGHT, MA'AM!! AND THE SAME THING HAPPENED AT THE PORT STOREHOUSES AND THE RESIDENTIAL DISTRICT...!!
WHAT IN THE WORLD IS GOING ON!?
TATA (CLOP)
THE ATTACK SITES DON'T HAVE ANY-THING IN COMMON.
WHO COULD BE DOING THIS, AND WHY...!?
AH...AHHHH!!
WAAAA
WHAT IS THAT THING!?
HA (GASP)
DA (DASH)
THOSE SCREAMS CAME FROM THIS WAY!

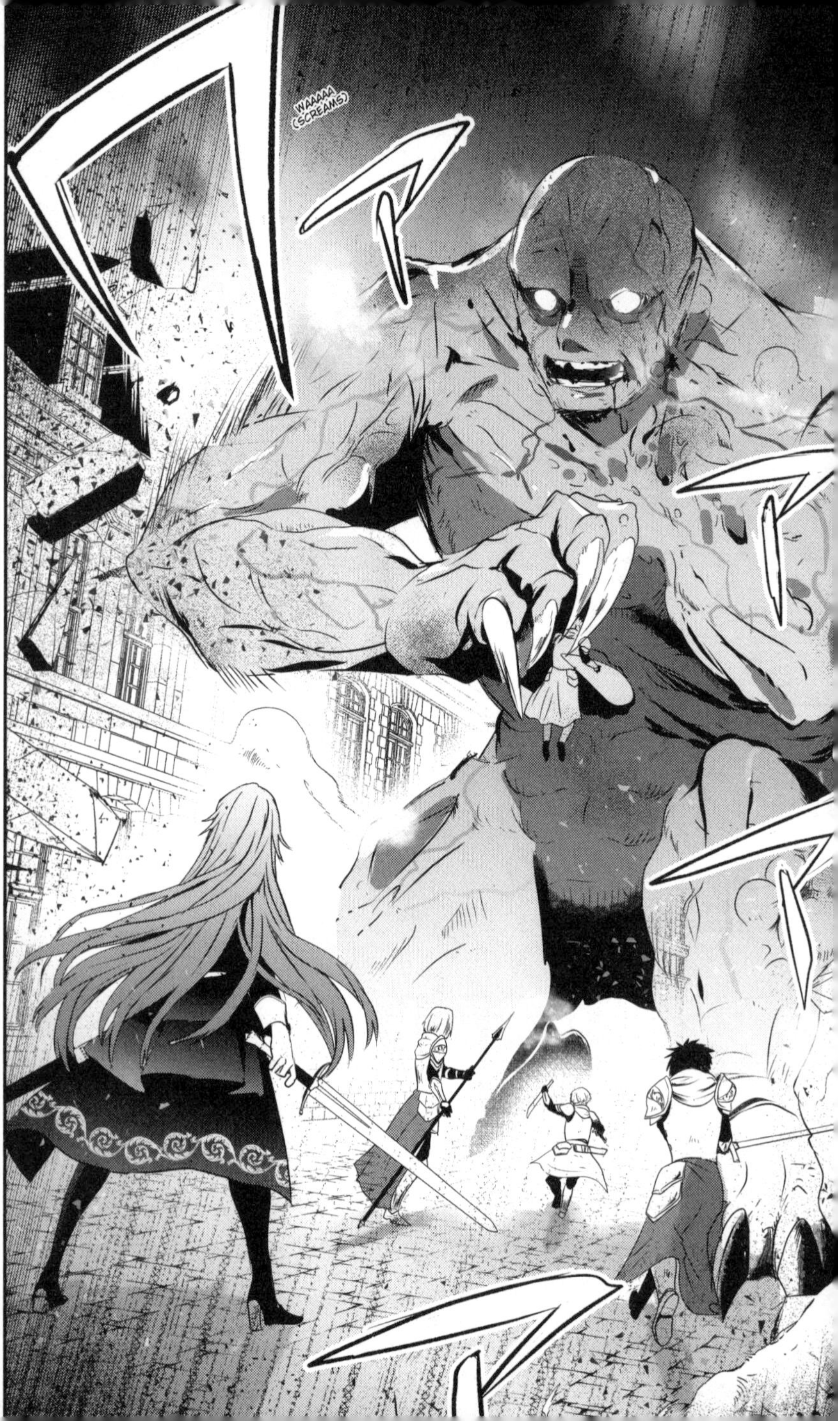
WAAAAA (SCREAMS)

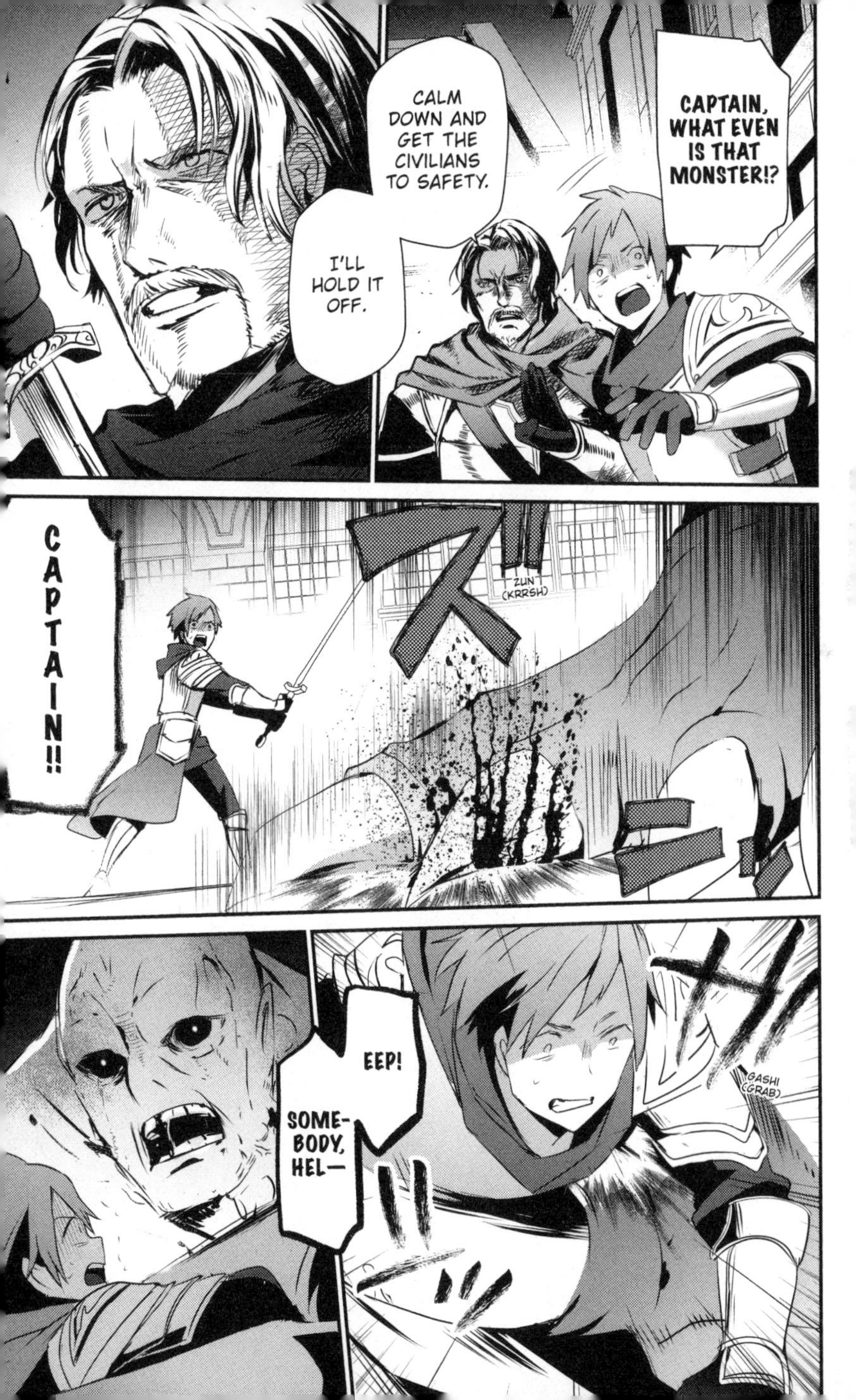
CAPTAIN, WHAT EVEN IS THAT MONSTER!?
CALM DOWN AND GET THE CIVILIANS TO SAFETY.
I'LL HOLD IT OFF.
ZUN (KRRSH)
CAPTAIN!!
GASHI (GRAB)
EEP!
SOME-BODY, HEL—

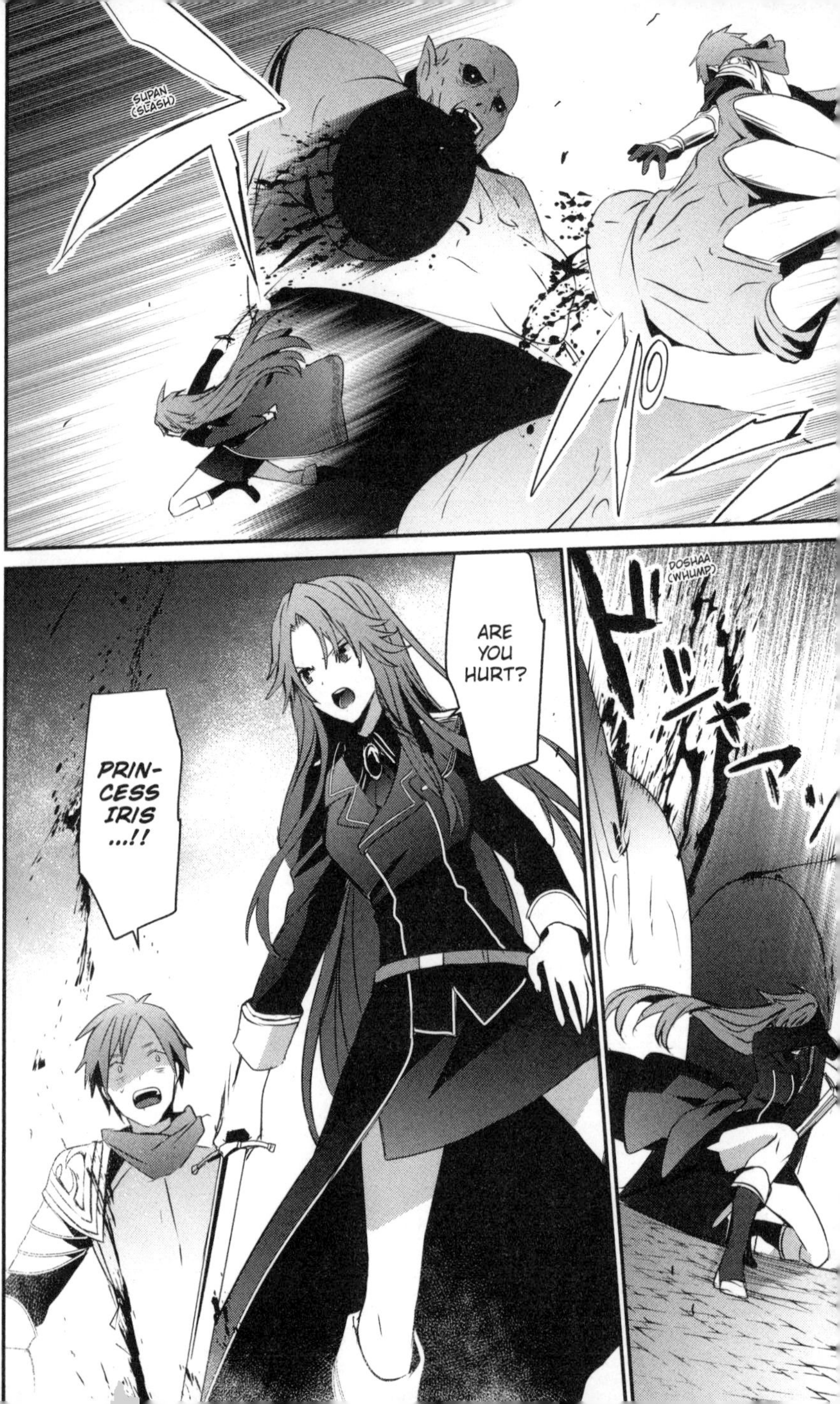
SUPAN (SLASH)
DOSHAA (WHUMP)
ARE YOU HURT?
PRIN-CESS IRIS ...!!

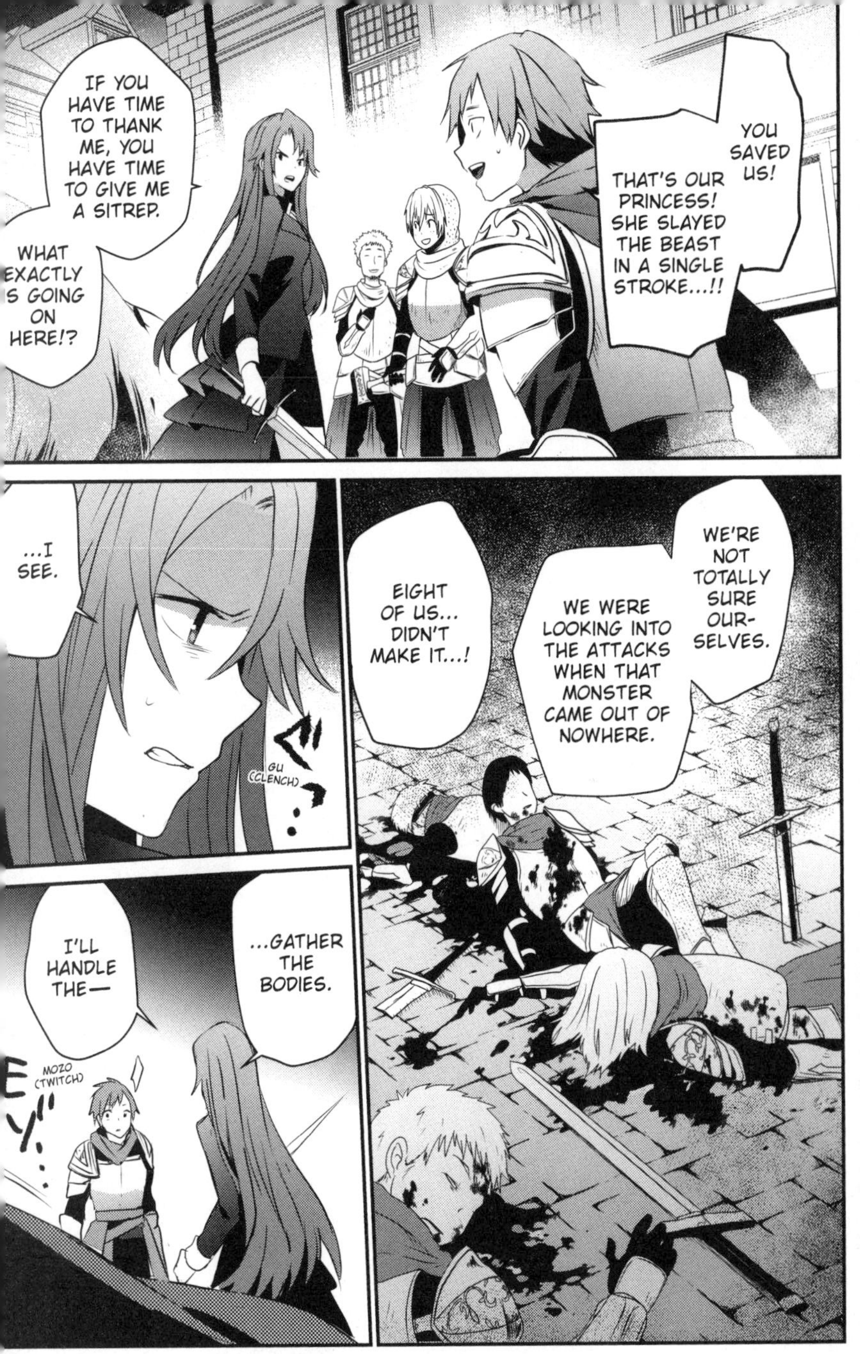
YOU SAVED US!
THAT'S OUR PRINCESS! SHE SLAYED THE BEAST IN A SINGLE STROKE...!!
IF YOU HAVE TIME TO THANK ME, YOU HAVE TIME TO GIVE ME A SITREP.
WHAT EXACTLY S GOING ON HERE!?
WE'RE NOT TOTALLY SURE OUR-SELVES.
WE WERE LOOKING INTO THE ATTACKS WHEN THAT MONSTER CAME OUT OF NOWHERE.
EIGHT OF US... DIDN'T MAKE IT...!
...I SEE.
GU (CLENCH)
...GATHER THE BODIES.
I'LL HANDLE THE—
MOZO (TWITCH)

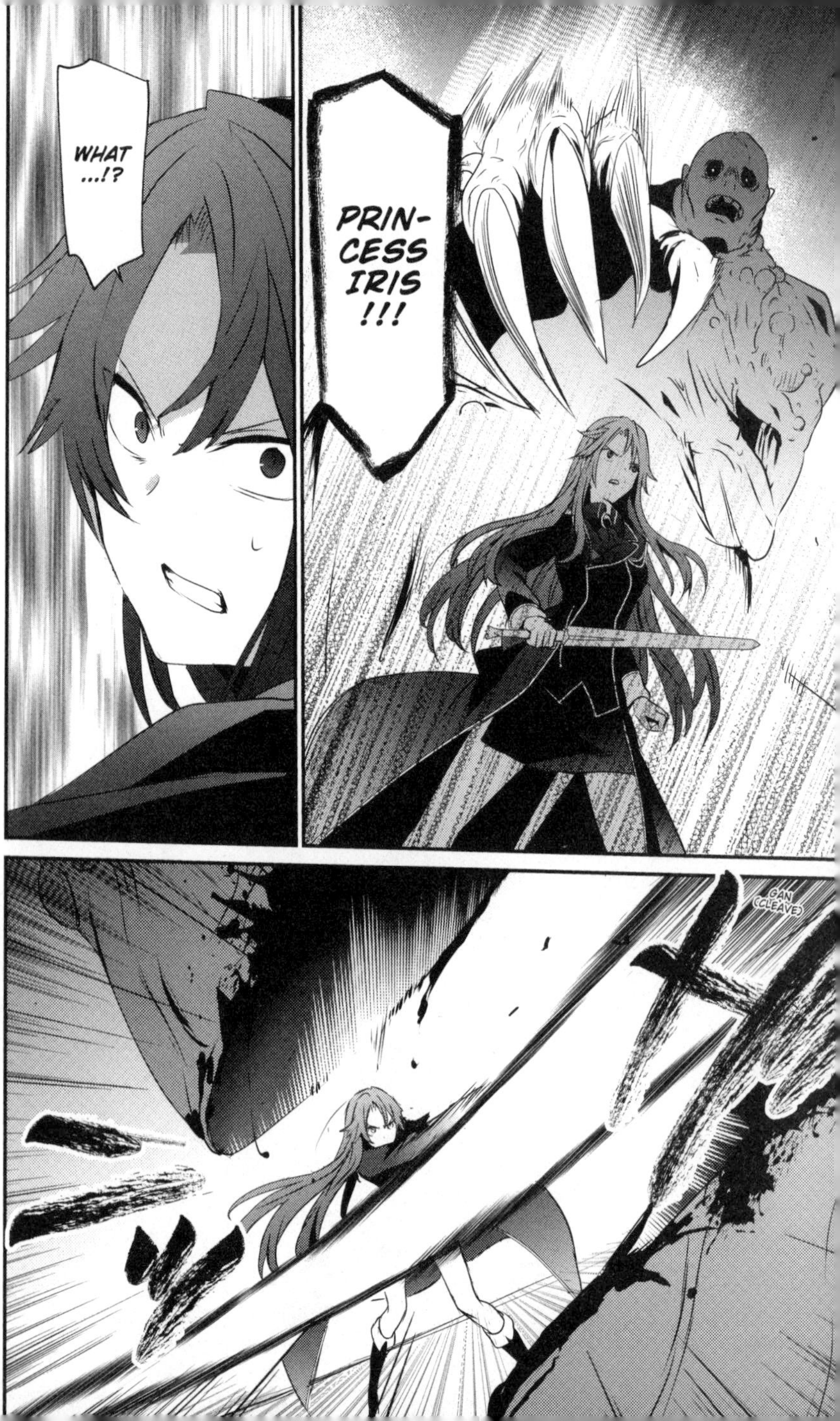
PRIN-CESS IRIS !!!
WHAT ...!?
GAN (CLEAVE)

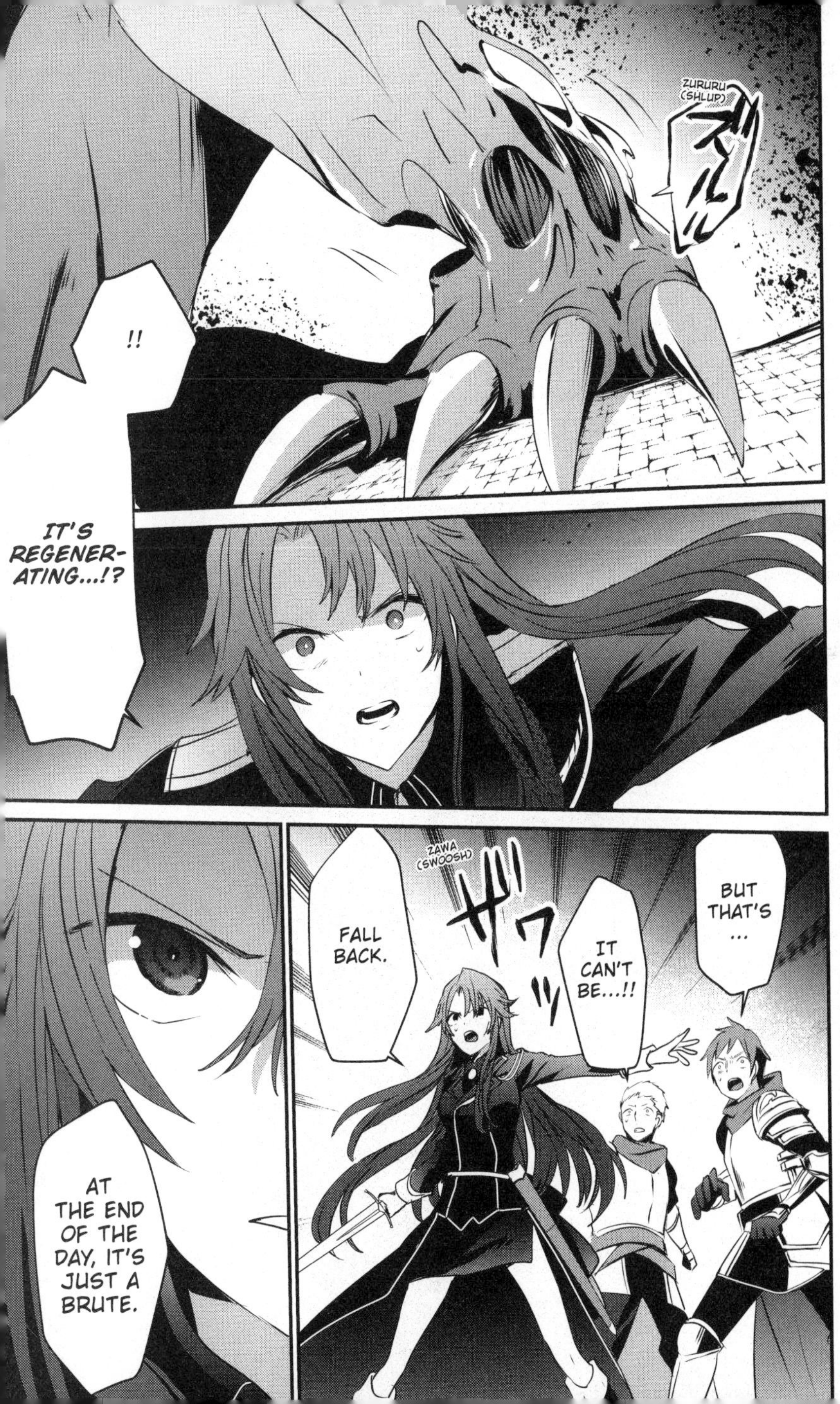
ZURURU (SHLUP)
!!
IT'S REGENER-ATING...!?
BUT THAT'S ...
ZAWA (SWOOSH)
IT CAN'T BE...!!
FALL BACK.
AT THE END OF THE DAY, IT'S JUST A BRUTE.

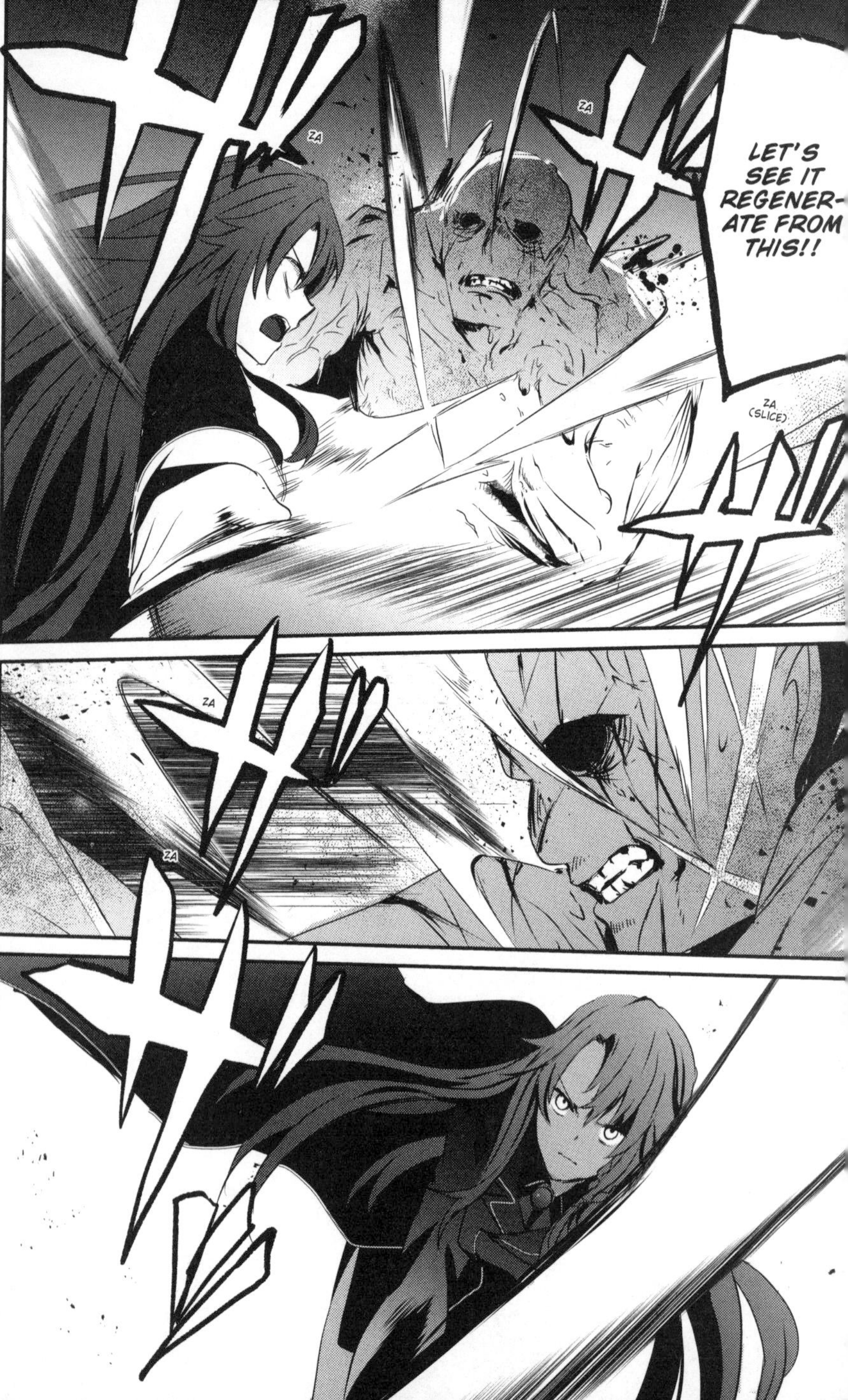
ZA
LET'S SEE IT REGENERATE FROM THIS!!
ZA (SLICE)
ZA
ZA
ZA

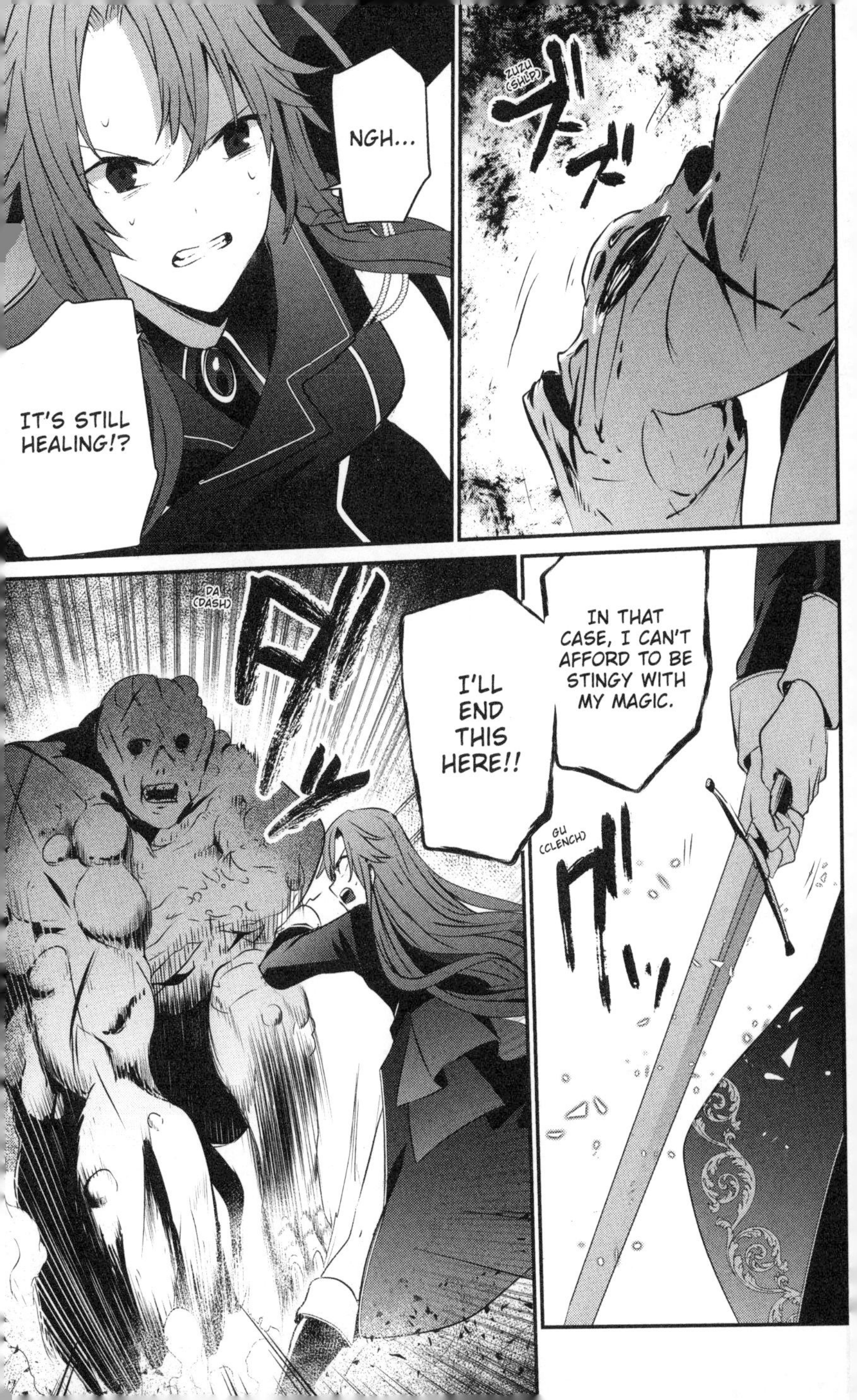
ZUZU (SHLP)
NGH...
IT'S STILL HEALING!?
IN THAT CASE, I CAN'T AFFORD TO BE STINGY WITH MY MAGIC.
GU (CLENCH)
DA (DASH)
I'LL END THIS HERE!!

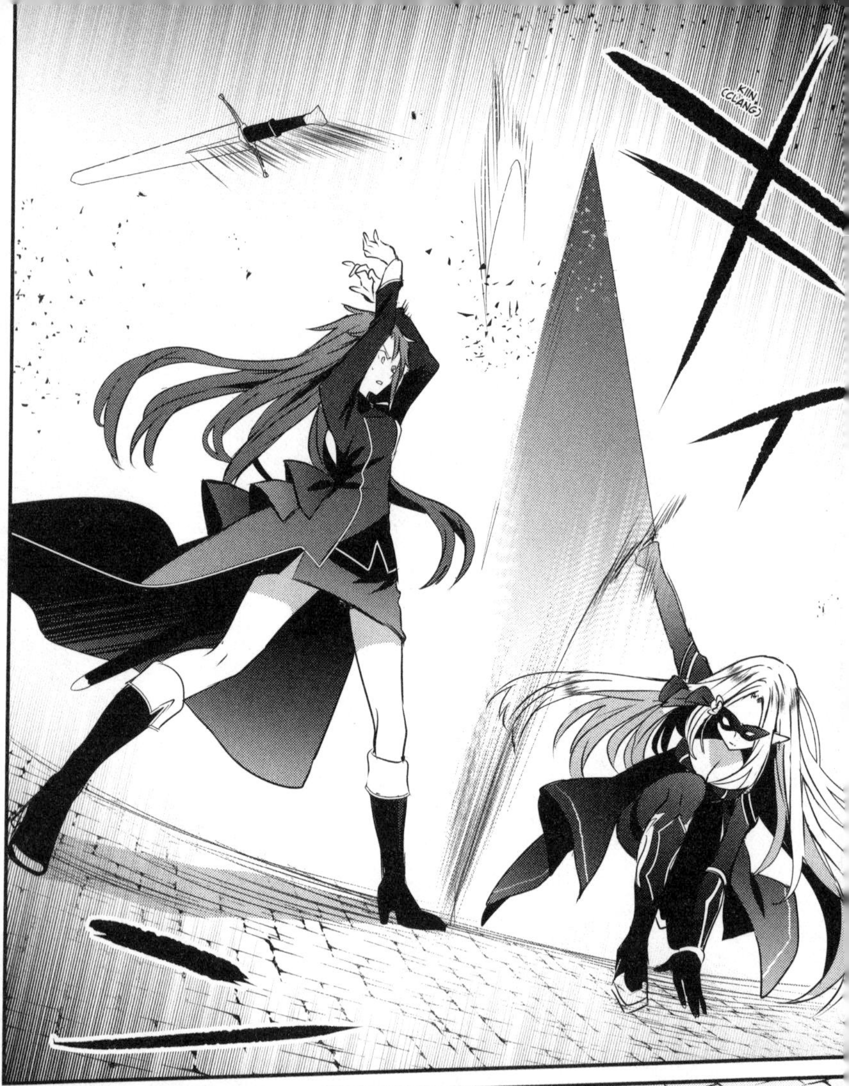
KIIN
(CLANG)

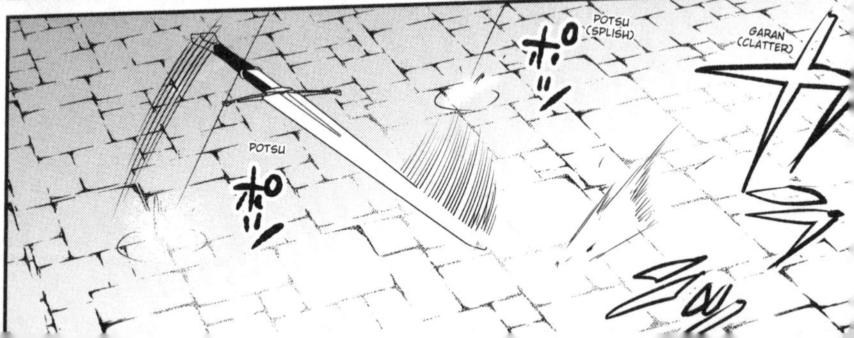
GARAN
(CLATTER)
POTSU
(SPLISH)
POTSU

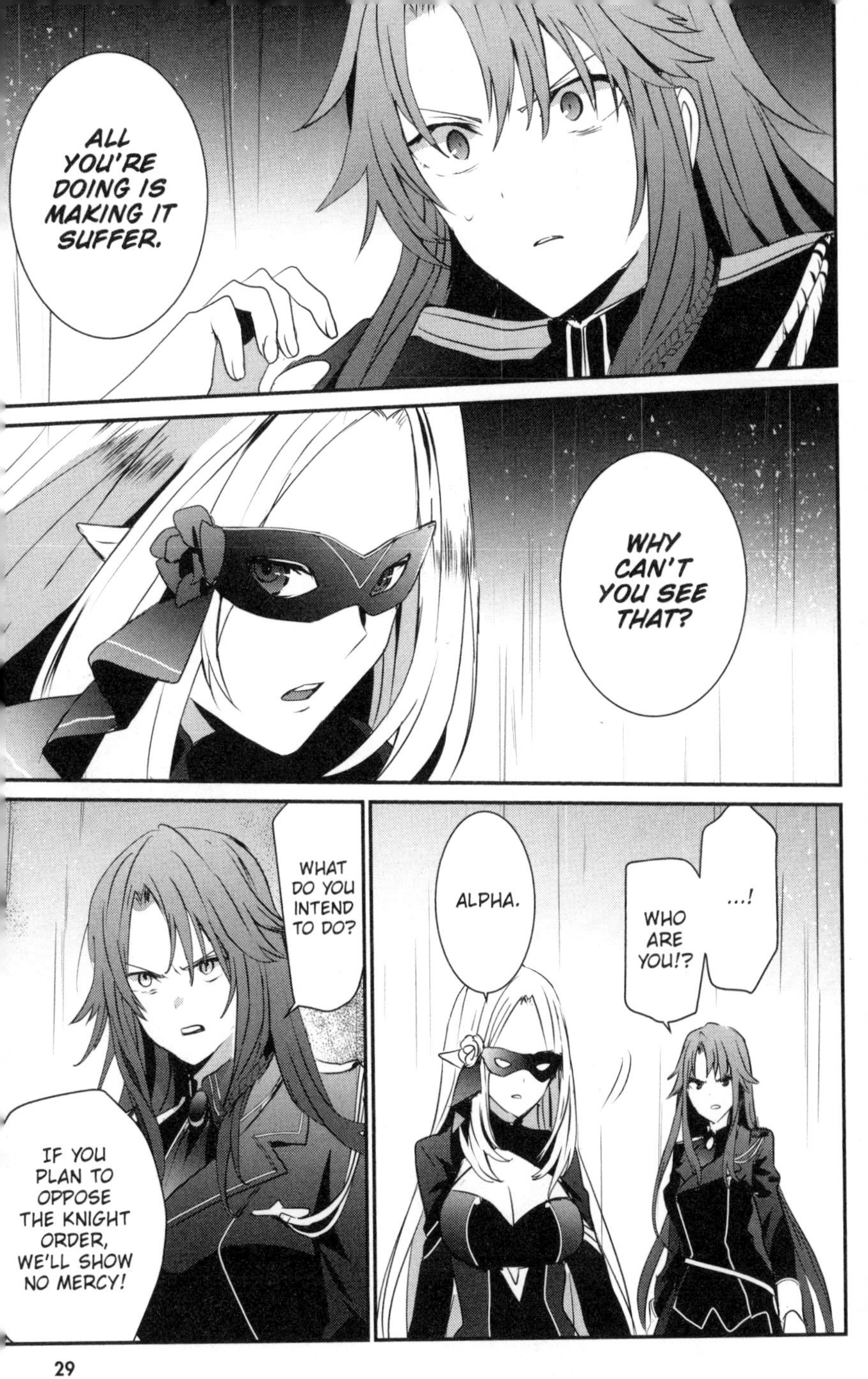
ALL YOU'RE DOING IS MAKING IT SUFFER.
WHY CAN'T YOU SEE THAT?
...!
WHO ARE YOU!?
ALPHA.
WHAT DO YOU INTEND TO DO?
IF YOU PLAN TO OPPOSE THE KNIGHT ORDER, WE'LL SHOW NO MERCY!

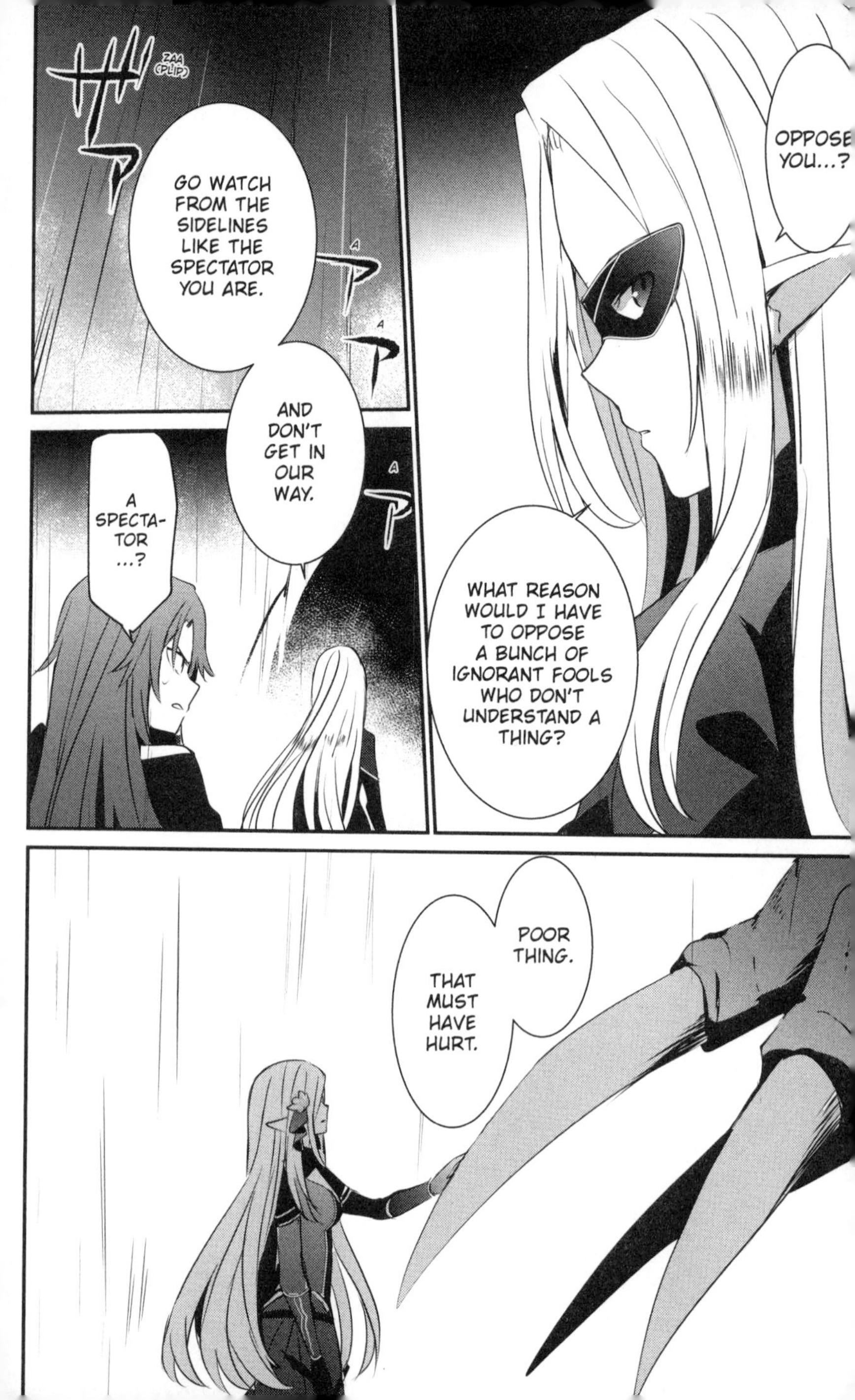
OPPOSE YOU...?
WHAT REASON WOULD I HAVE TO OPPOSE A BUNCH OF IGNORANT FOOLS WHO DON'T UNDERSTAND A THING?
ZAA (PLIP)
GO WATCH FROM THE SIDELINES LIKE THE SPECTATOR YOU ARE.
A
A
AND DON'T GET IN OUR WAY.
A
A SPECTA-TOR ...?
POOR THING.
THAT MUST HAVE HURT.

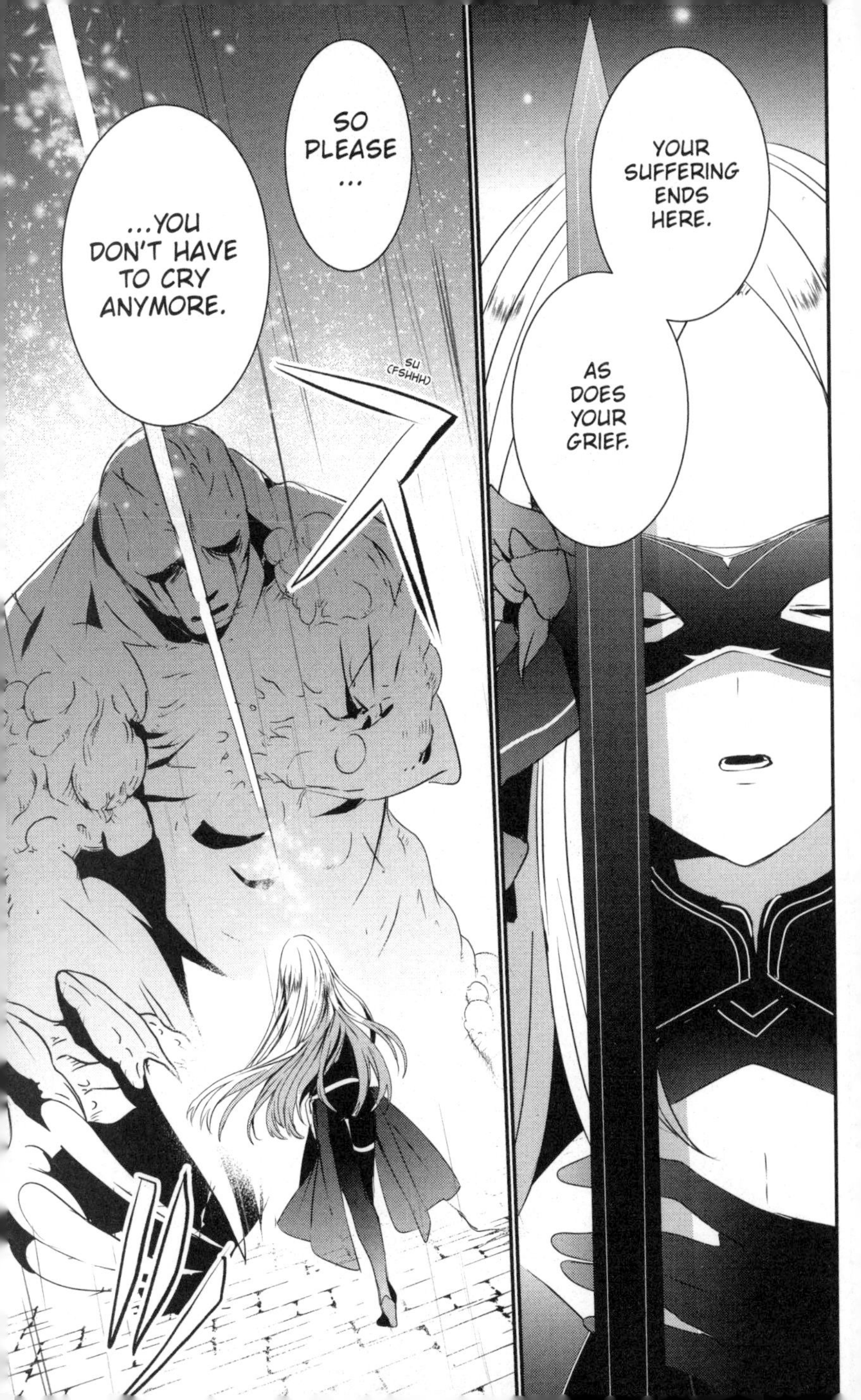
YOUR SUFFERING ENDS HERE.
AS DOES YOUR GRIEF.
SO PLEASE ...
...YOU DON'T HAVE TO CRY ANYMORE.
SU (FSHHH)

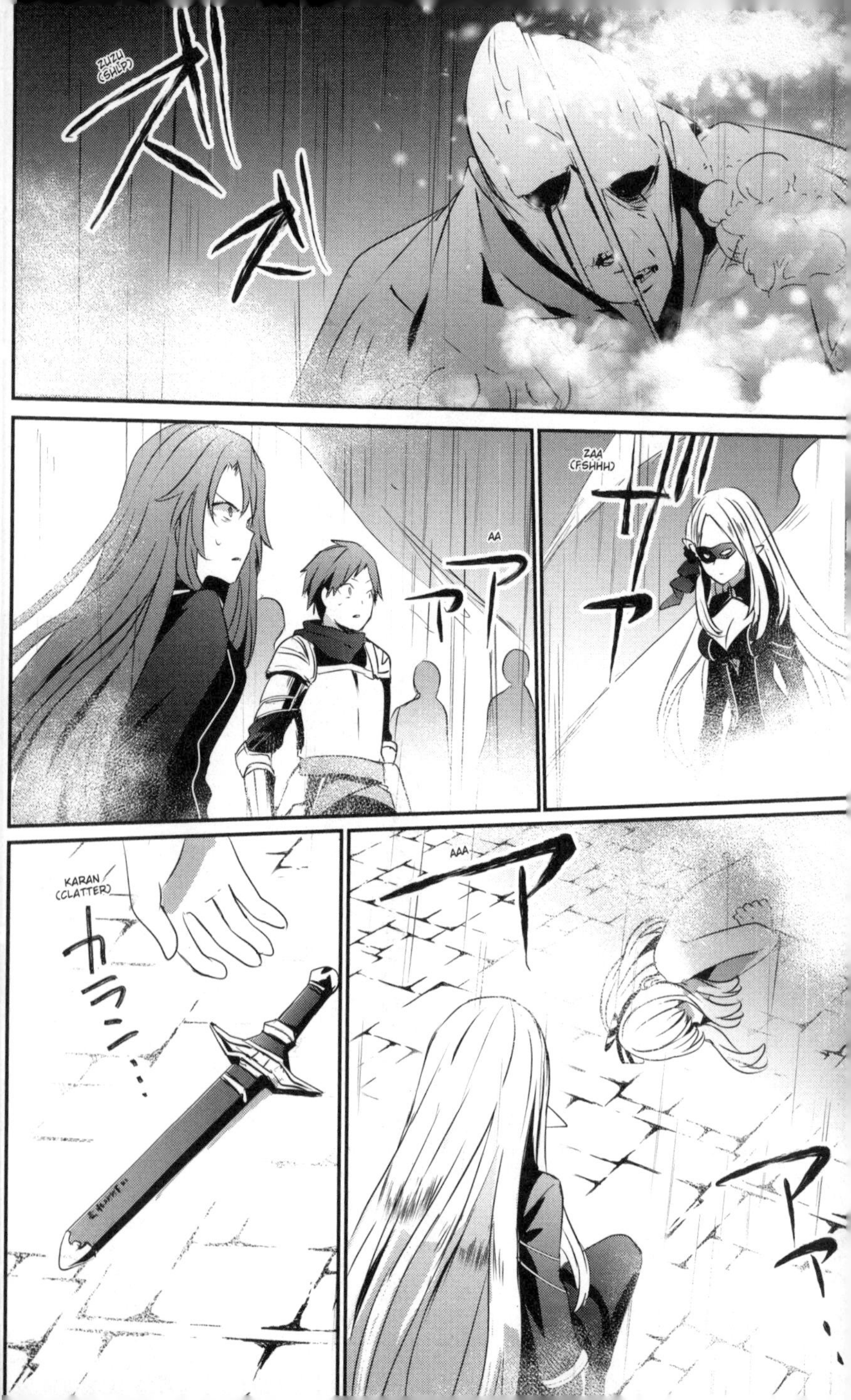
ZUZU
(SHLP)
ZAA
(FSHHH)
AA
AAA
KARAN
(CLATTER)

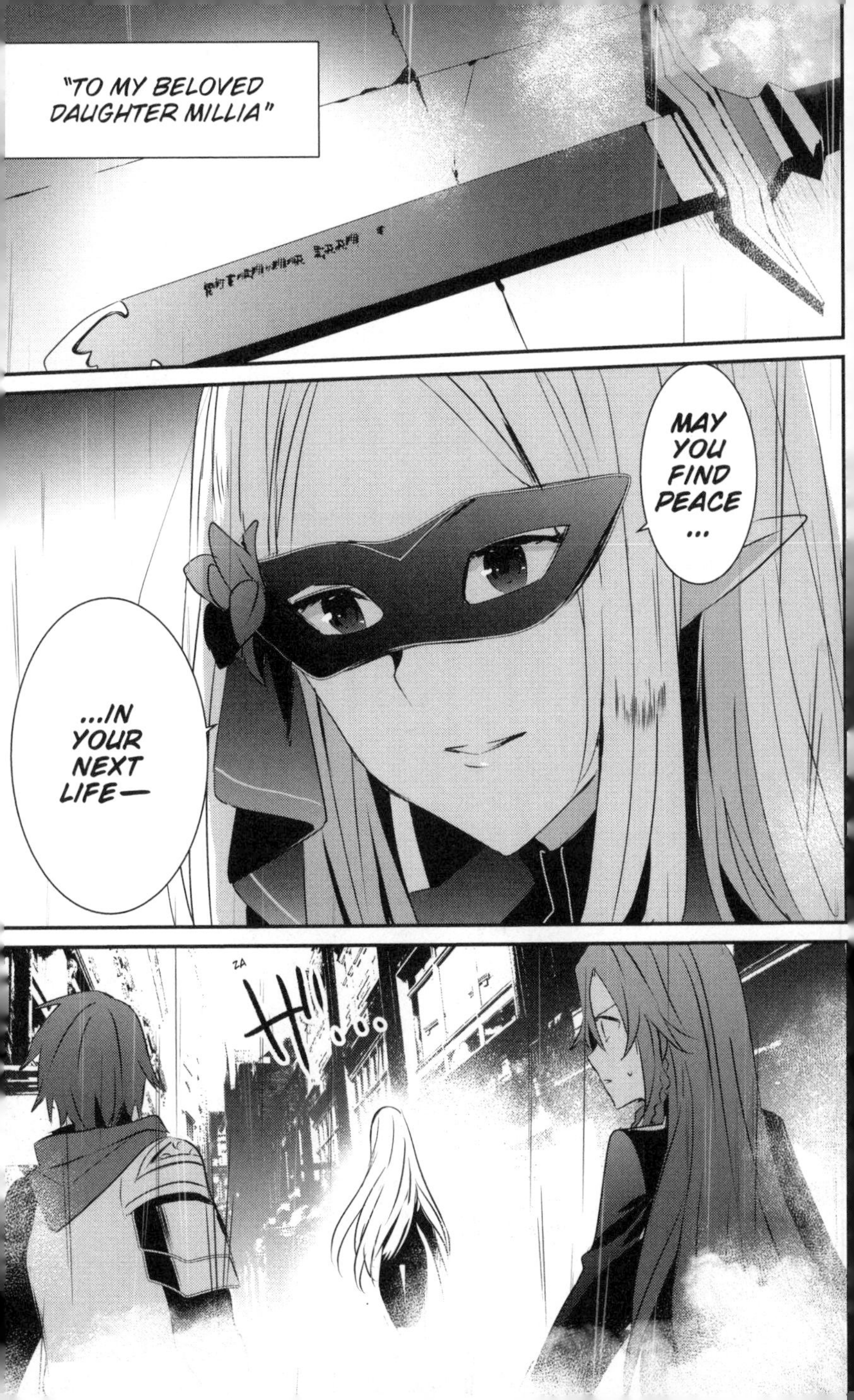
"TO MY BELOVED DAUGHTER MILLIA"
MAY YOU FIND PEACE...
...IN YOUR NEXT LIFE—
ZA

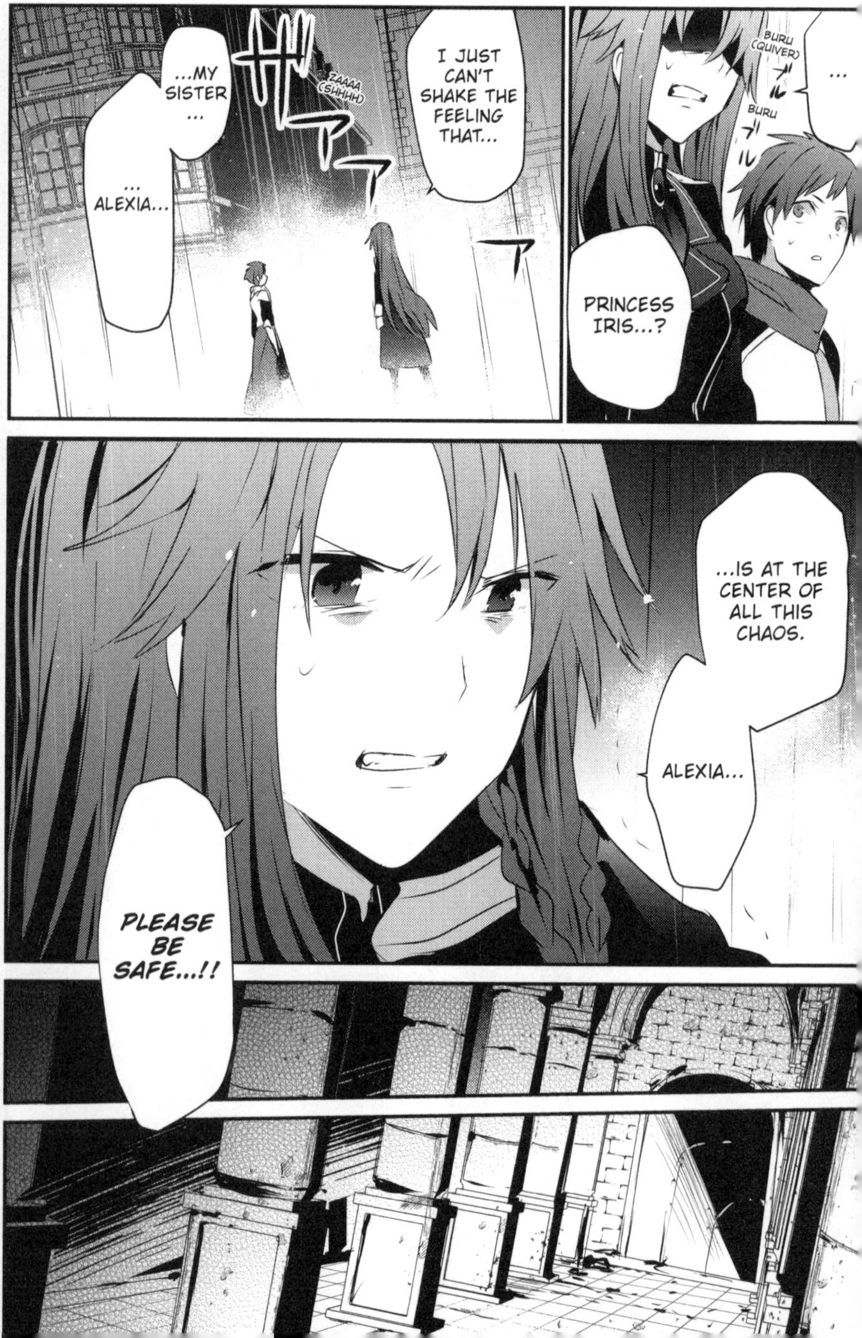
...
BURU (QUIVER)
BURU
PRINCESS IRIS...?
I JUST CAN'T SHAKE THE FEELING THAT...
ZAAAA (SHHHH)
...MY SISTER ...
... ALEXIA...
...IS AT THE CENTER OF ALL THIS CHAOS.
ALEXIA...
PLEASE BE SAFE...!!

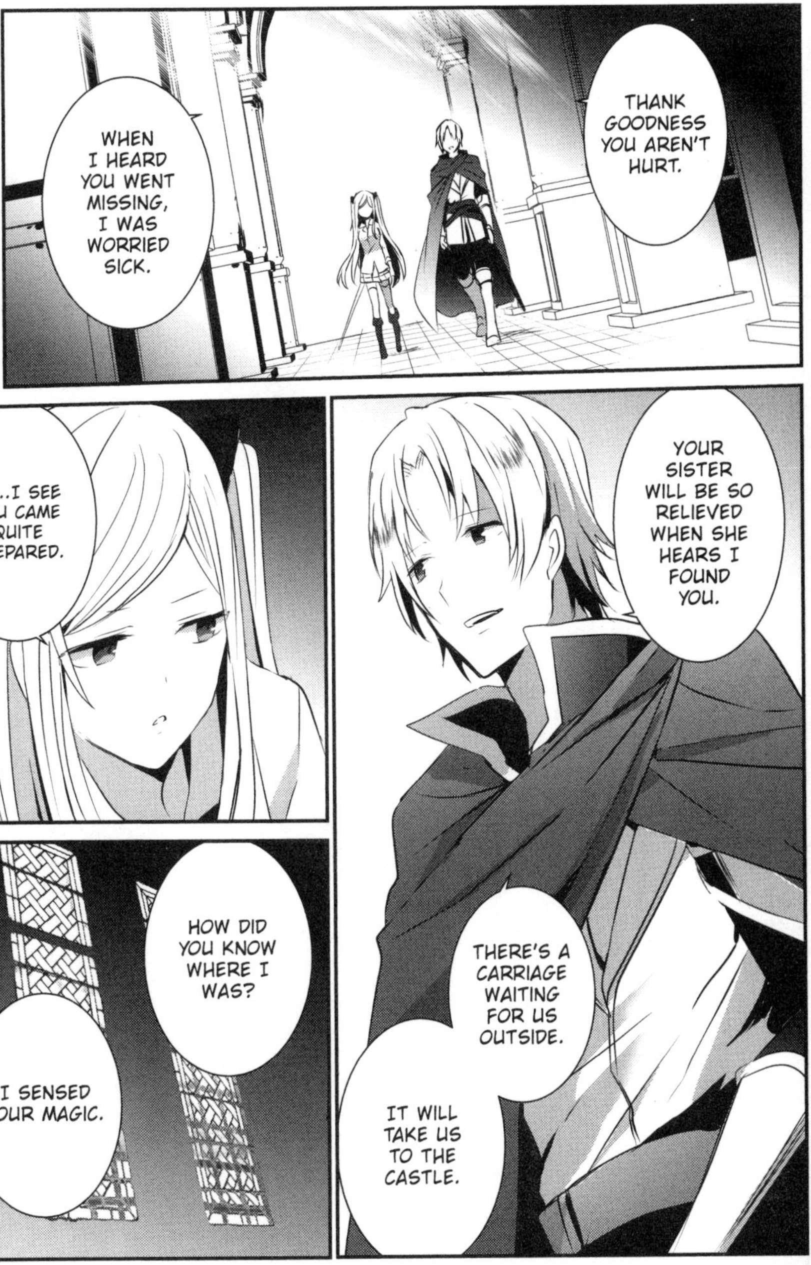
THANK GOODNESS YOU AREN'T HURT.
WHEN I HEARD YOU WENT MISSING, I WAS WORRIED SICK.
YOUR SISTER WILL BE SO RELIEVED WHEN SHE HEARS I FOUND YOU.
......I SEE YOU CAME QUITE PREPARED.
HOW DID YOU KNOW WHERE I WAS?
I SENSED YOUR MAGIC.
THERE'S A CARRIAGE WAITING FOR US OUTSIDE.
IT WILL TAKE US TO THE CASTLE.

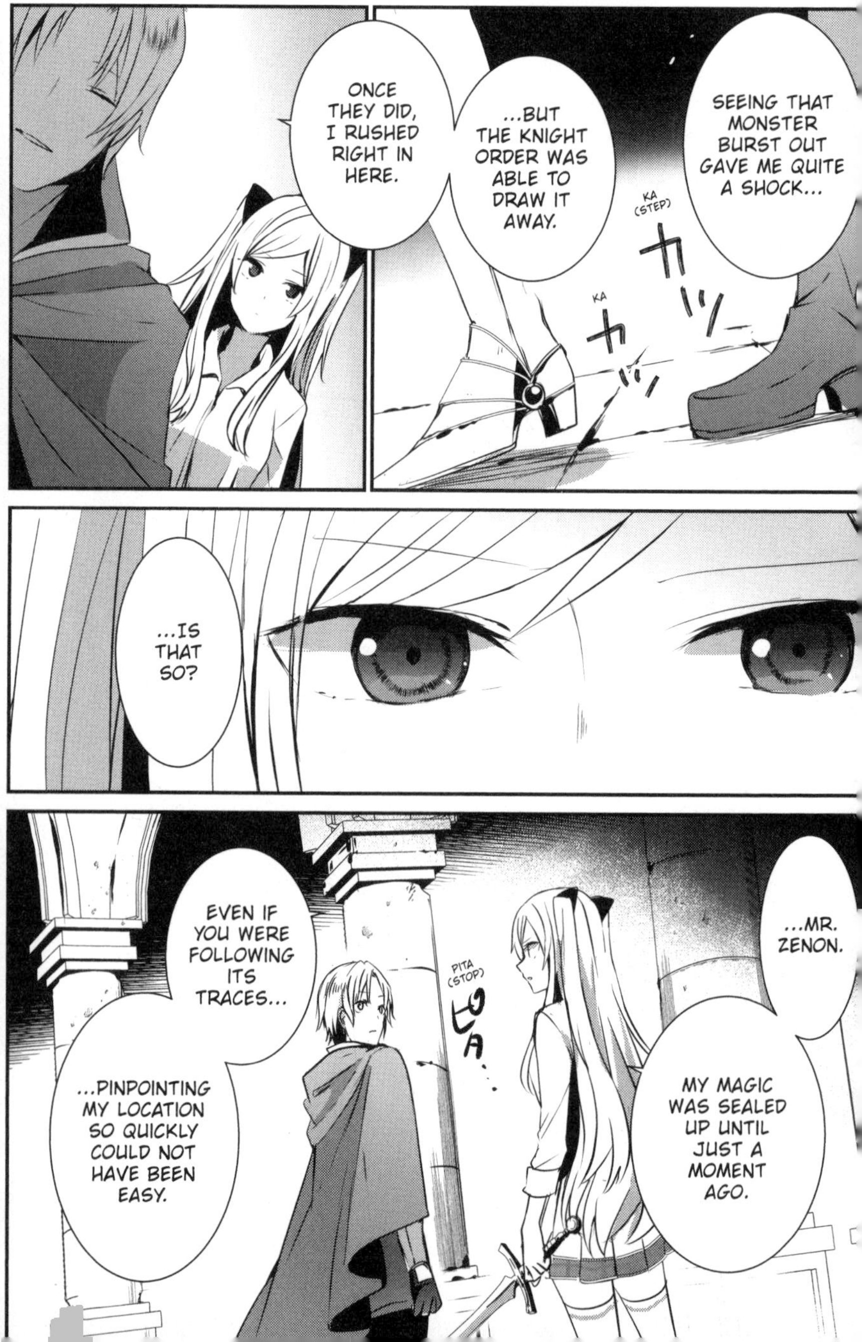
SEEING THAT MONSTER BURST OUT GAVE ME QUITE A SHOCK...
KA (STEP)
カッ
KA
カッ
...BUT THE KNIGHT ORDER WAS ABLE TO DRAW IT AWAY.
ONCE THEY DID, I RUSHED RIGHT IN HERE.
...IS THAT SO?
...MR. ZENON.
MY MAGIC WAS SEALED UP UNTIL JUST A MOMENT AGO.
PITA (STOP)
ピタ...
EVEN IF YOU WERE FOLLOWING ITS TRACES...
...PINPOINTING MY LOCATION SO QUICKLY COULD NOT HAVE BEEN EASY.

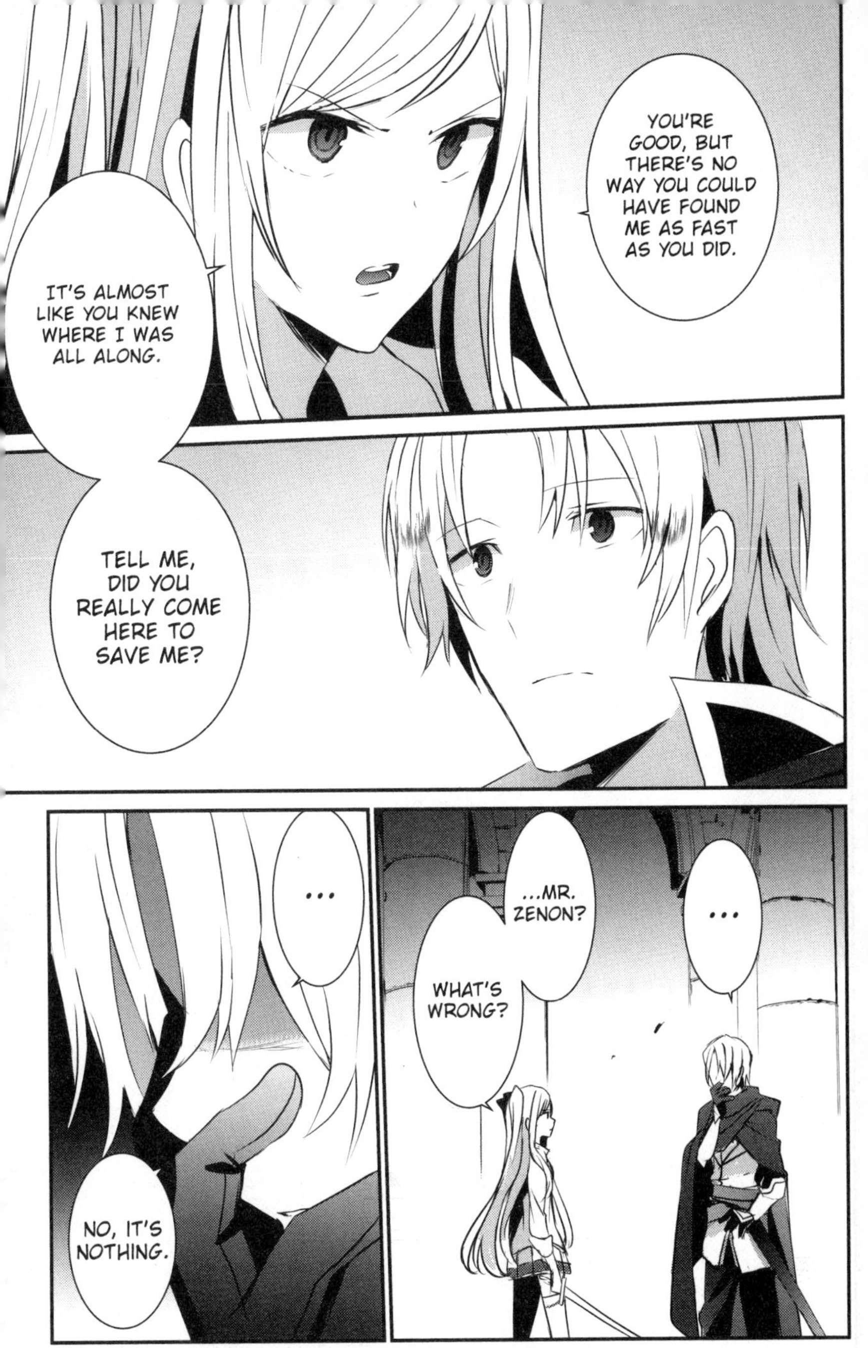
YOU'RE GOOD, BUT THERE'S NO WAY YOU COULD HAVE FOUND ME AS FAST AS YOU DID.
IT'S ALMOST LIKE YOU KNEW WHERE I WAS ALL ALONG.
TELL ME, DID YOU REALLY COME HERE TO SAVE ME?
...
...MR. ZENON?
WHAT'S WRONG?
...
NO, IT'S NOTHING.

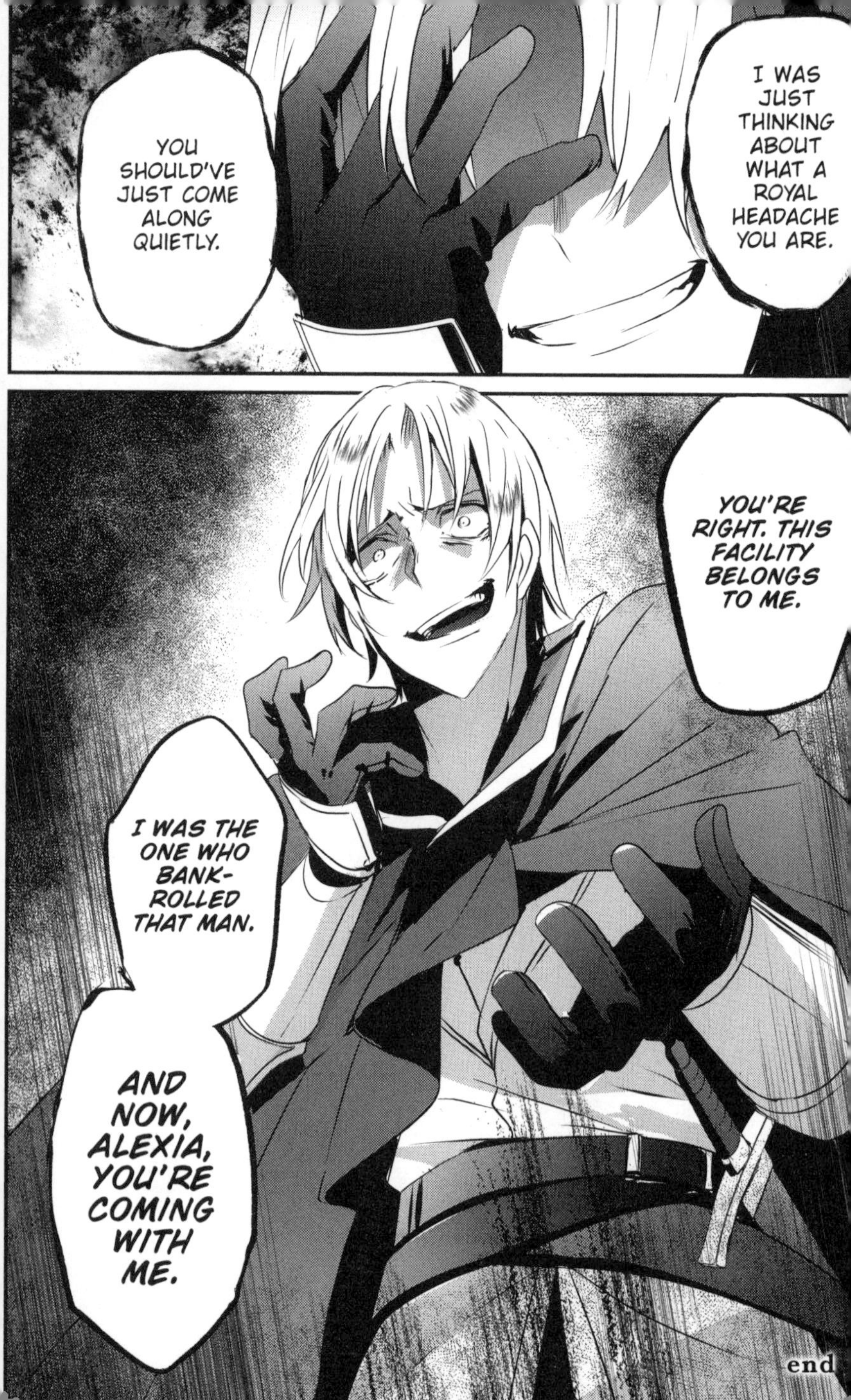
I WAS JUST THINKING ABOUT WHAT A ROYAL HEADACHE YOU ARE.
YOU SHOULD'VE JUST COME ALONG QUIETLY.
YOU'RE RIGHT. THIS FACILITY BELONGS TO ME.
I WAS THE ONE WHO BANK-ROLLED THAT MAN.
AND NOW, ALEXIA, YOU'RE COMING WITH ME.
end

Episode.6

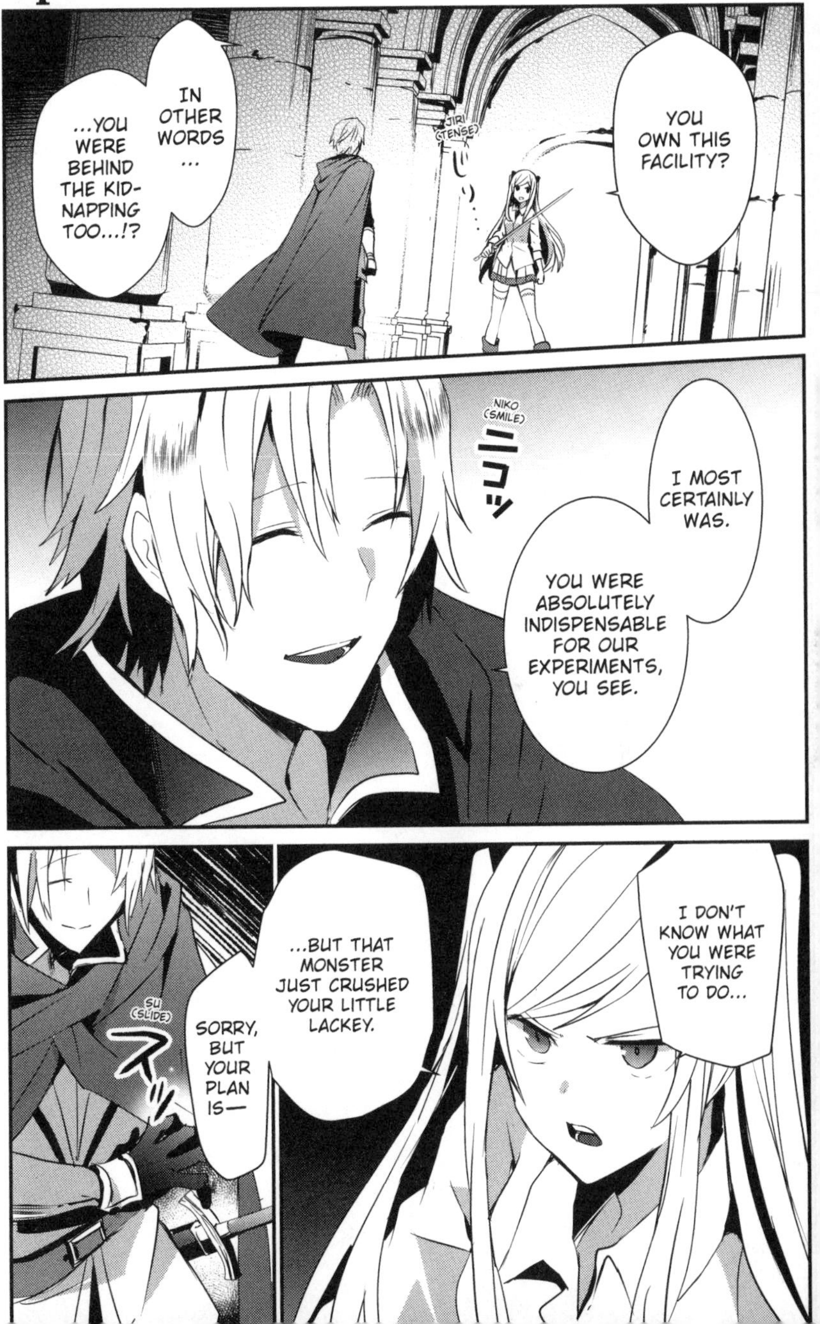
YOU OWN THIS FACILITY?
JIRI (TENSE)
じり…
IN OTHER WORDS...
...YOU WERE BEHIND THE KID-NAPPING TOO...!?
NIKO (SMILE)
ニコッ
I MOST CERTAINLY WAS.
YOU WERE ABSOLUTELY INDISPENSABLE FOR OUR EXPERIMENTS, YOU SEE.
I DON'T KNOW WHAT YOU WERE TRYING TO DO...
...BUT THAT MONSTER JUST CRUSHED YOUR LITTLE LACKEY.
SORRY, BUT YOUR PLAN IS—
SU (SLIDE)
スッ

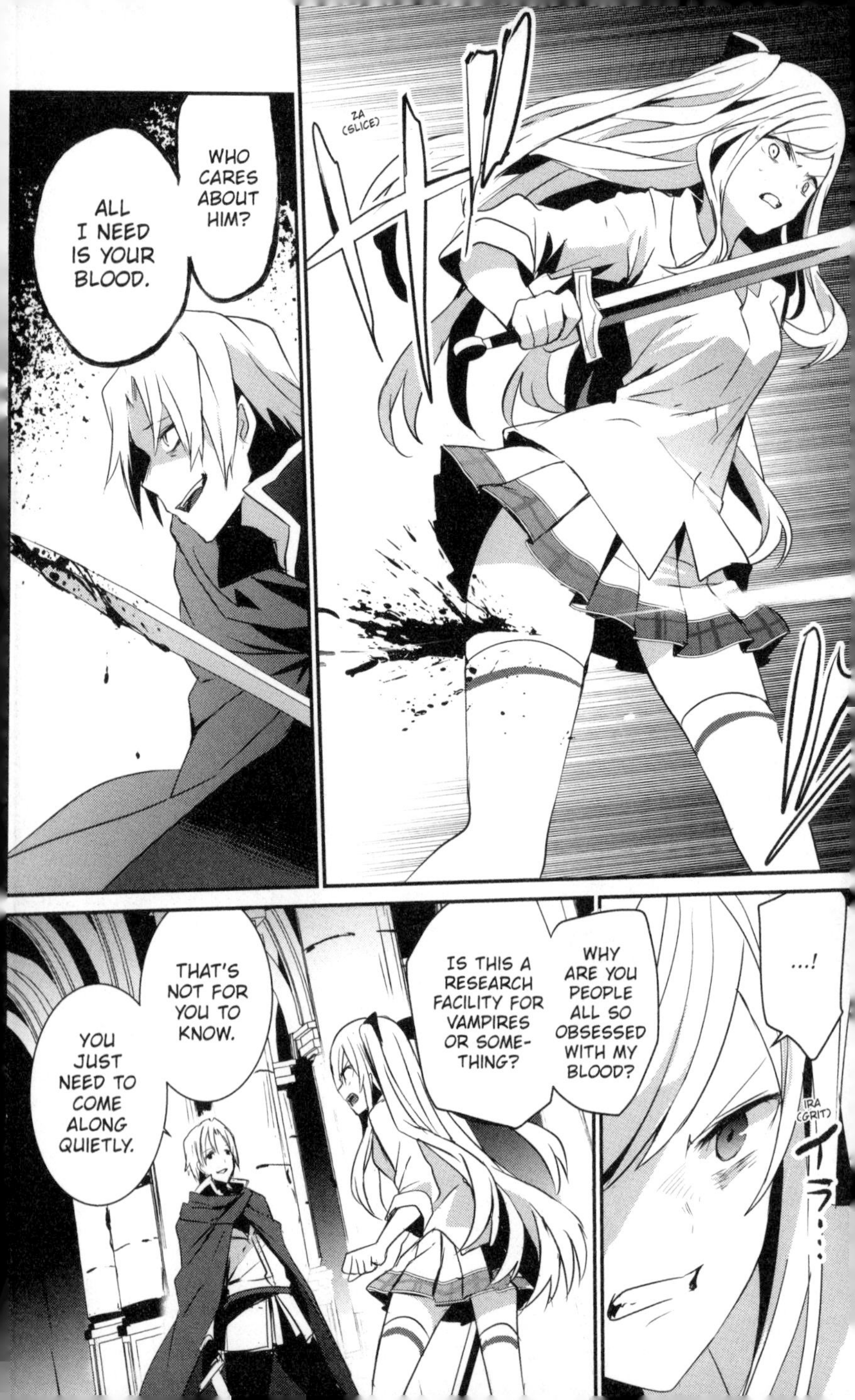
ZA (SLICE)
WHO CARES ABOUT HIM?
ALL I NEED IS YOUR BLOOD.
...!
IRA (GRIT)
イラ…
WHY ARE YOU PEOPLE ALL SO OBSESSED WITH MY BLOOD?
IS THIS A RESEARCH FACILITY FOR VAMPIRES OR SOME-THING?
THAT'S NOT FOR YOU TO KNOW.
YOU JUST NEED TO COME ALONG QUIETLY.

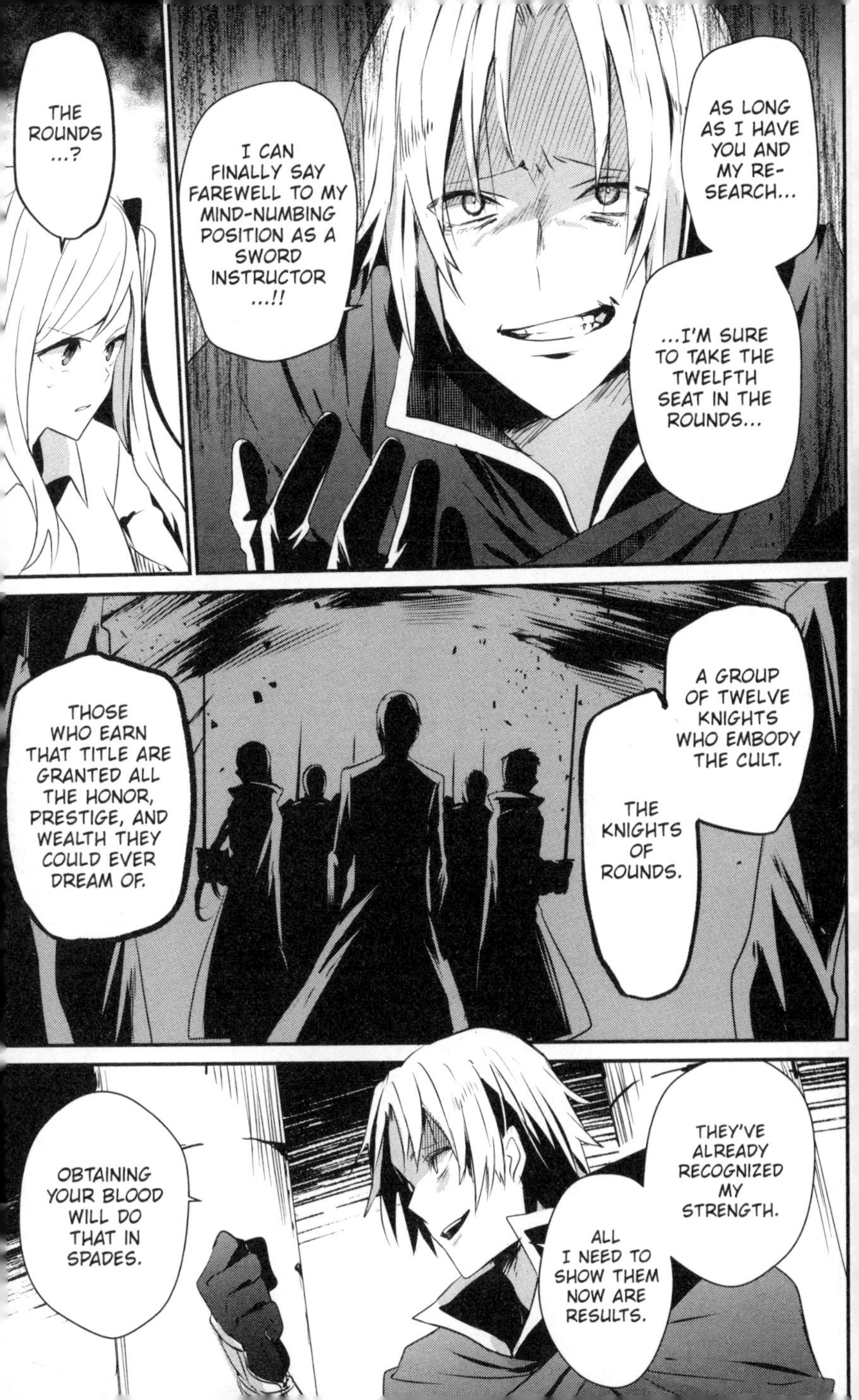
AS LONG AS I HAVE YOU AND MY RE-SEARCH...
...I'M SURE TO TAKE THE TWELFTH SEAT IN THE ROUNDS...
I CAN FINALLY SAY FAREWELL TO MY MIND-NUMBING POSITION AS A SWORD INSTRUCTOR ...!!
THE ROUNDS ...?
A GROUP OF TWELVE KNIGHTS WHO EMBODY THE CULT.
THE KNIGHTS OF ROUNDS.
THOSE WHO EARN THAT TITLE ARE GRANTED ALL THE HONOR, PRESTIGE, AND WEALTH THEY COULD EVER DREAM OF.
THEY'VE ALREADY RECOGNIZED MY STRENGTH.
ALL I NEED TO SHOW THEM NOW ARE RESULTS.
OBTAINING YOUR BLOOD WILL DO THAT IN SPADES.

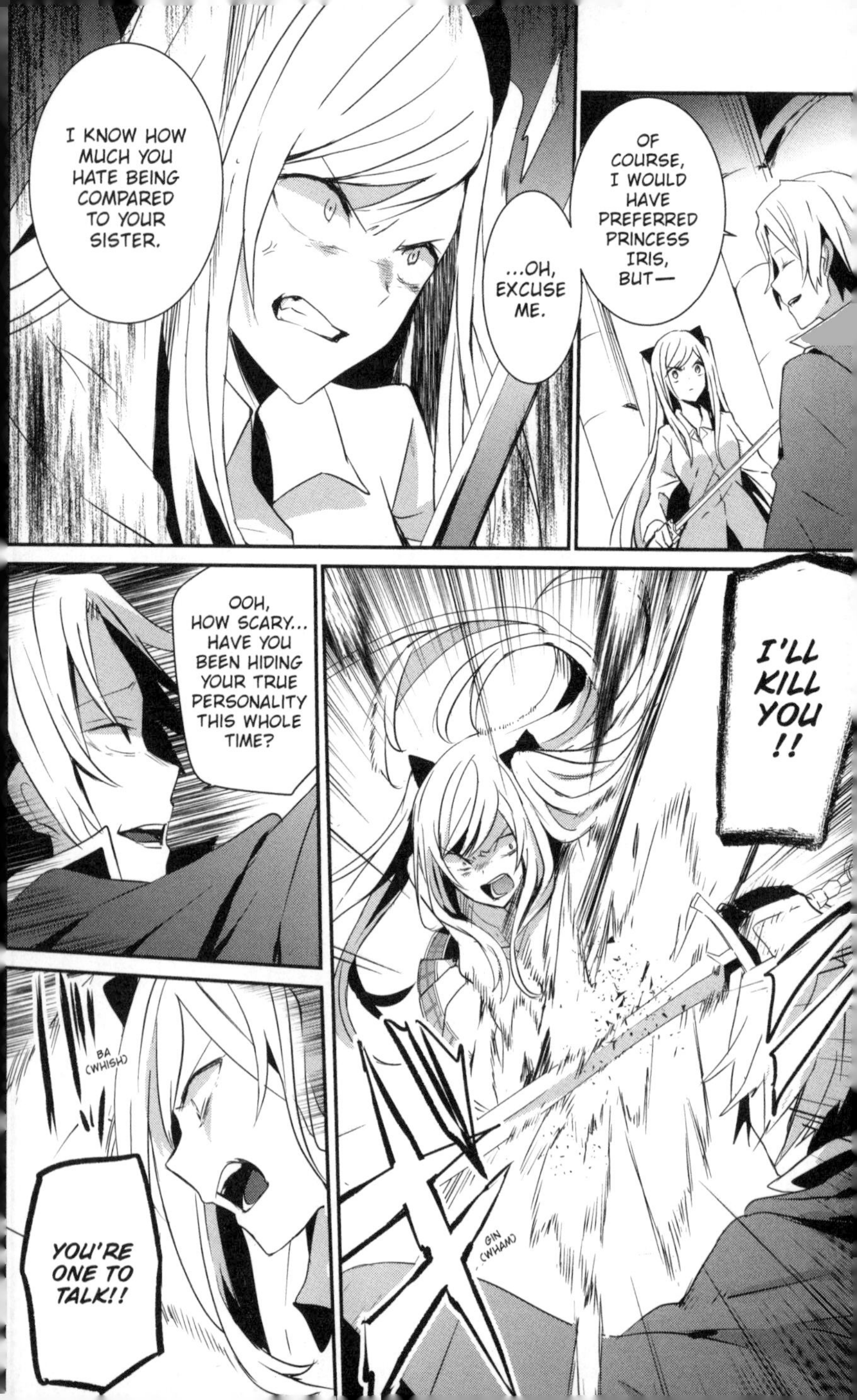
OF COURSE, I WOULD HAVE PREFERRED PRINCESS IRIS, BUT—
…OH, EXCUSE ME.
I KNOW HOW MUCH YOU HATE BEING COMPARED TO YOUR SISTER.
I'LL KILL YOU!!
GIN (WHAM)
OOH, HOW SCARY… HAVE YOU BEEN HIDING YOUR TRUE PERSONALITY THIS WHOLE TIME?
BA (WHISH)
YOU'RE ONE TO TALK!!

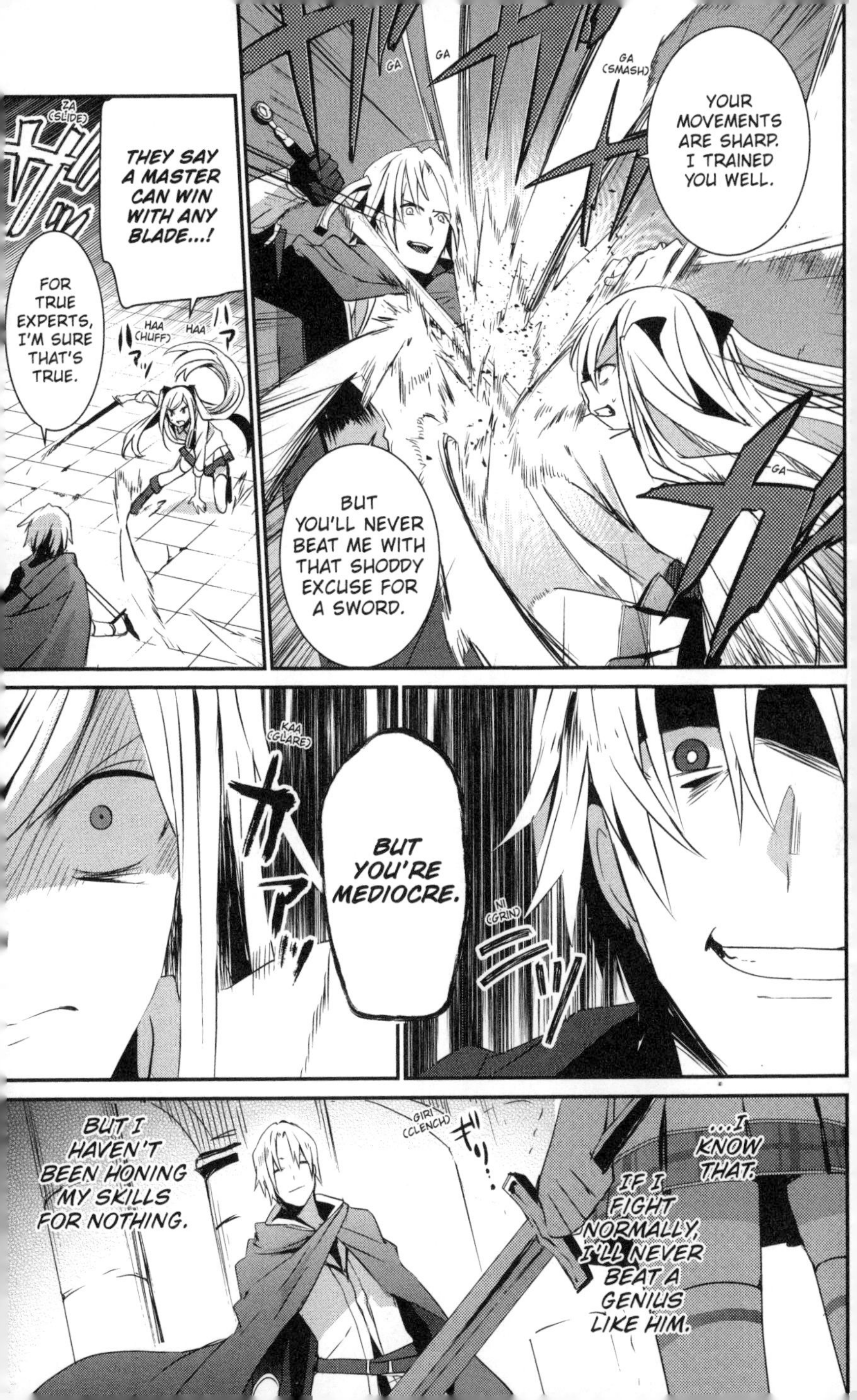
GA
GA
GA (SMASH)
YOUR MOVEMENTS ARE SHARP. I TRAINED YOU WELL.
GA
BUT YOU'LL NEVER BEAT ME WITH THAT SHODDY EXCUSE FOR A SWORD.
ZA (SLIDE)
THEY SAY A MASTER CAN WIN WITH ANY BLADE...!
HAA HAA (HUFF)
FOR TRUE EXPERTS, I'M SURE THAT'S TRUE.
NI (GRIN)
KAA (GLARE)
BUT YOU'RE MEDIOCRE.
...I KNOW THAT.
IF I FIGHT NORMALLY, I'LL NEVER BEAT A GENIUS LIKE HIM.
GIRI (CLENCH)
BUT I HAVEN'T BEEN HONING MY SKILLS FOR NOTHING.

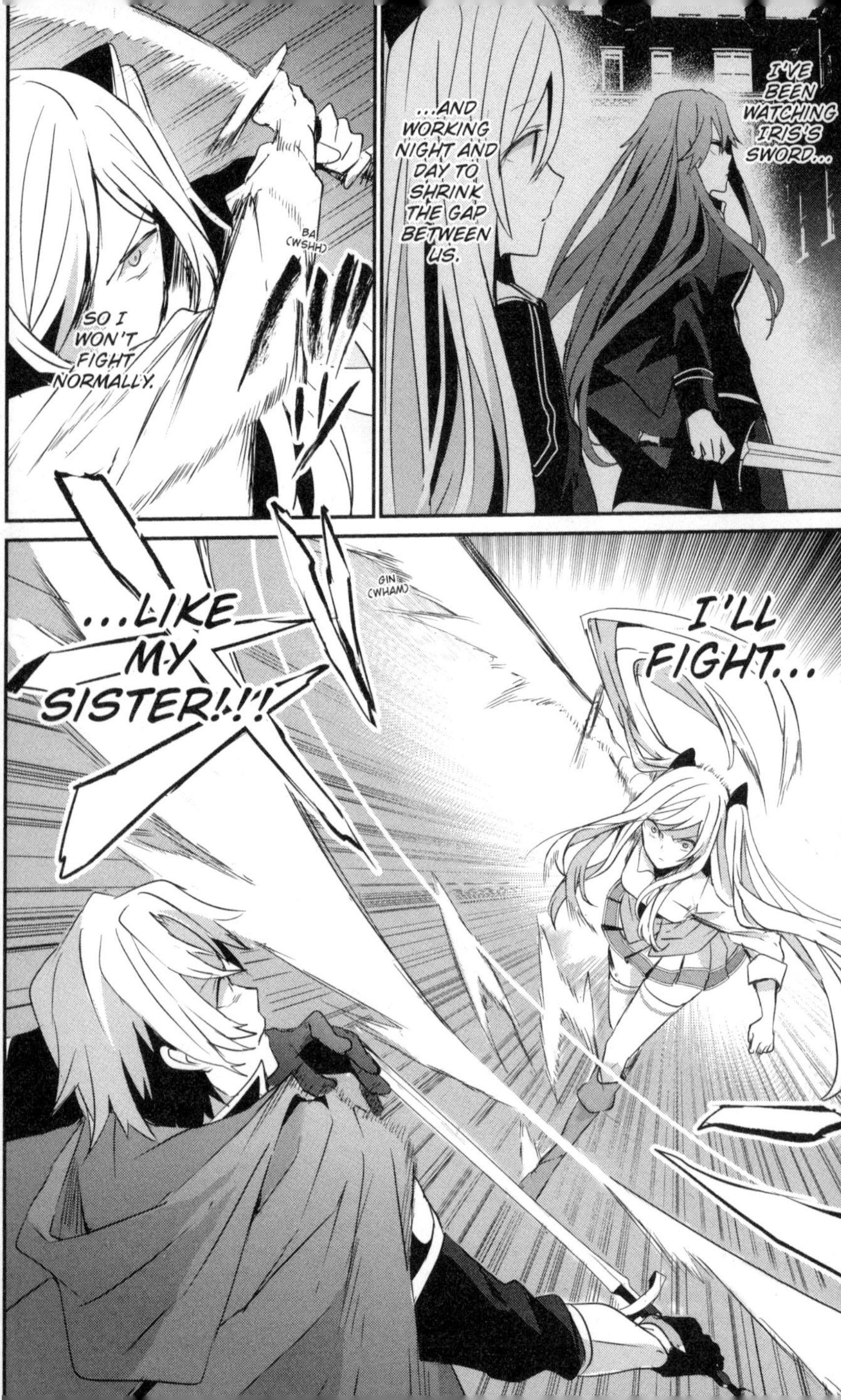
I'VE BEEN WATCHING IRIS'S SWORD...
...AND WORKING NIGHT AND DAY TO SHRINK THE GAP BETWEEN US.
BA (WSHH)
SO I WON'T FIGHT NORMALLY.
I'LL FIGHT...
GIN (WHAM)
...LIKE MY SISTER!!!

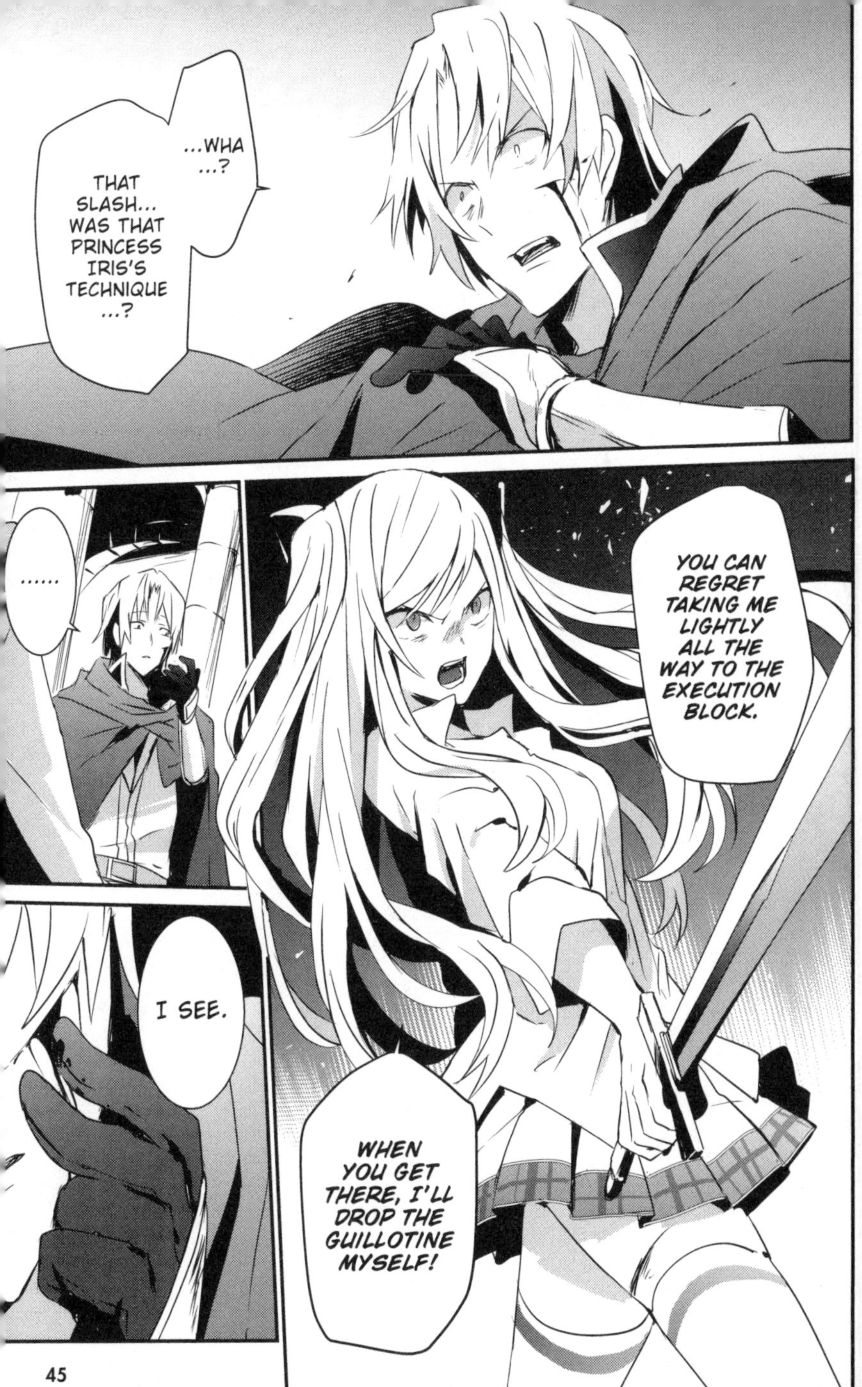

...WHA ...?
THAT SLASH... WAS THAT PRINCESS IRIS'S TECHNIQUE ...?
YOU CAN REGRET TAKING ME LIGHTLY ALL THE WAY TO THE EXECUTION BLOCK.
WHEN YOU GET THERE, I'LL DROP THE GUILLOTINE MYSELF!
......
I SEE.

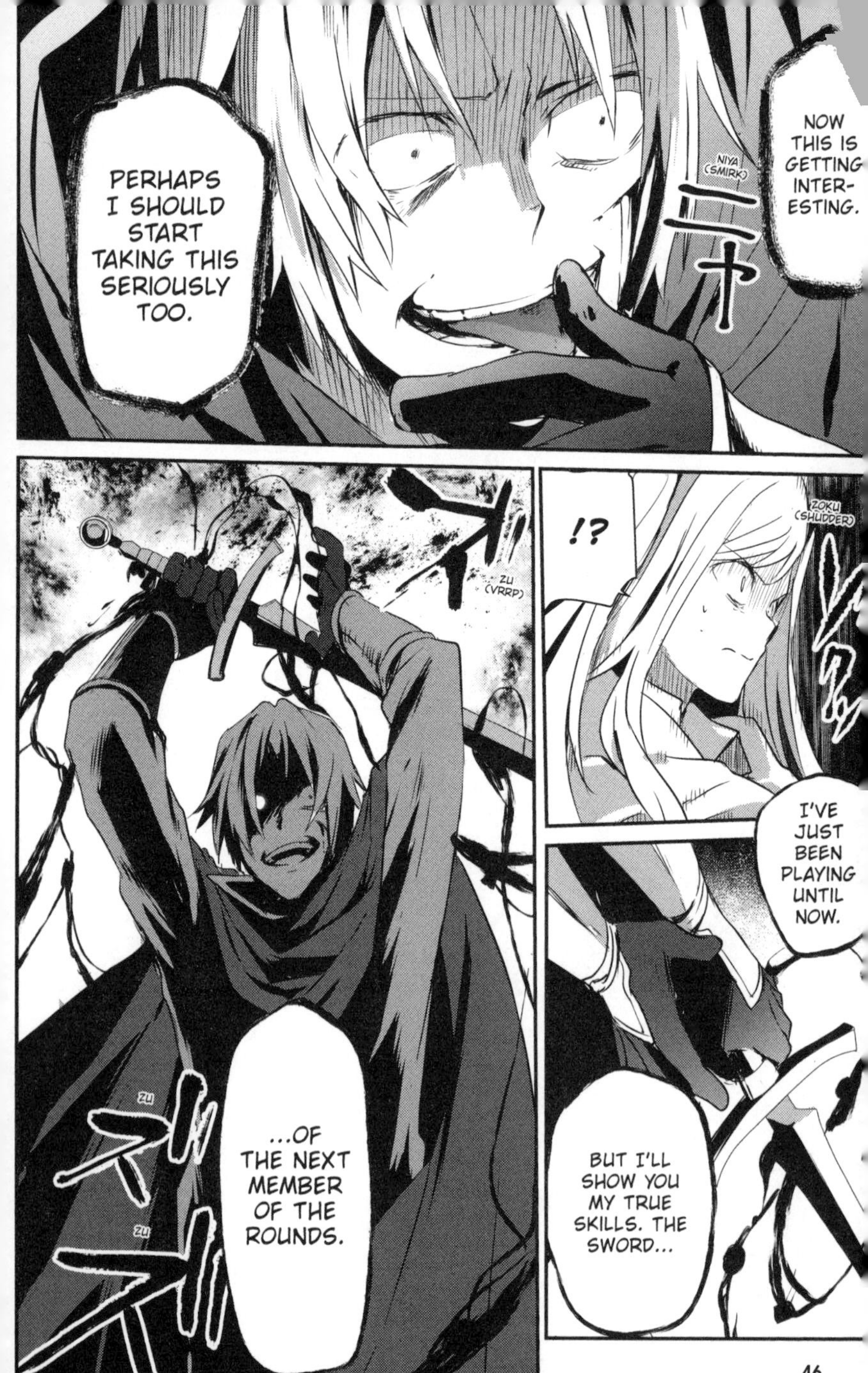

NOW THIS IS GETTING INTER-ESTING.
NIYA (SMIRK)
PERHAPS I SHOULD START TAKING THIS SERIOUSLY TOO.
ZOKU (SHUDDER)
!?
I'VE JUST BEEN PLAYING UNTIL NOW.
BUT I'LL SHOW YOU MY TRUE SKILLS. THE SWORD...
ZU (VRRP)
...OF THE NEXT MEMBER OF THE ROUNDS.
ZU
ZU

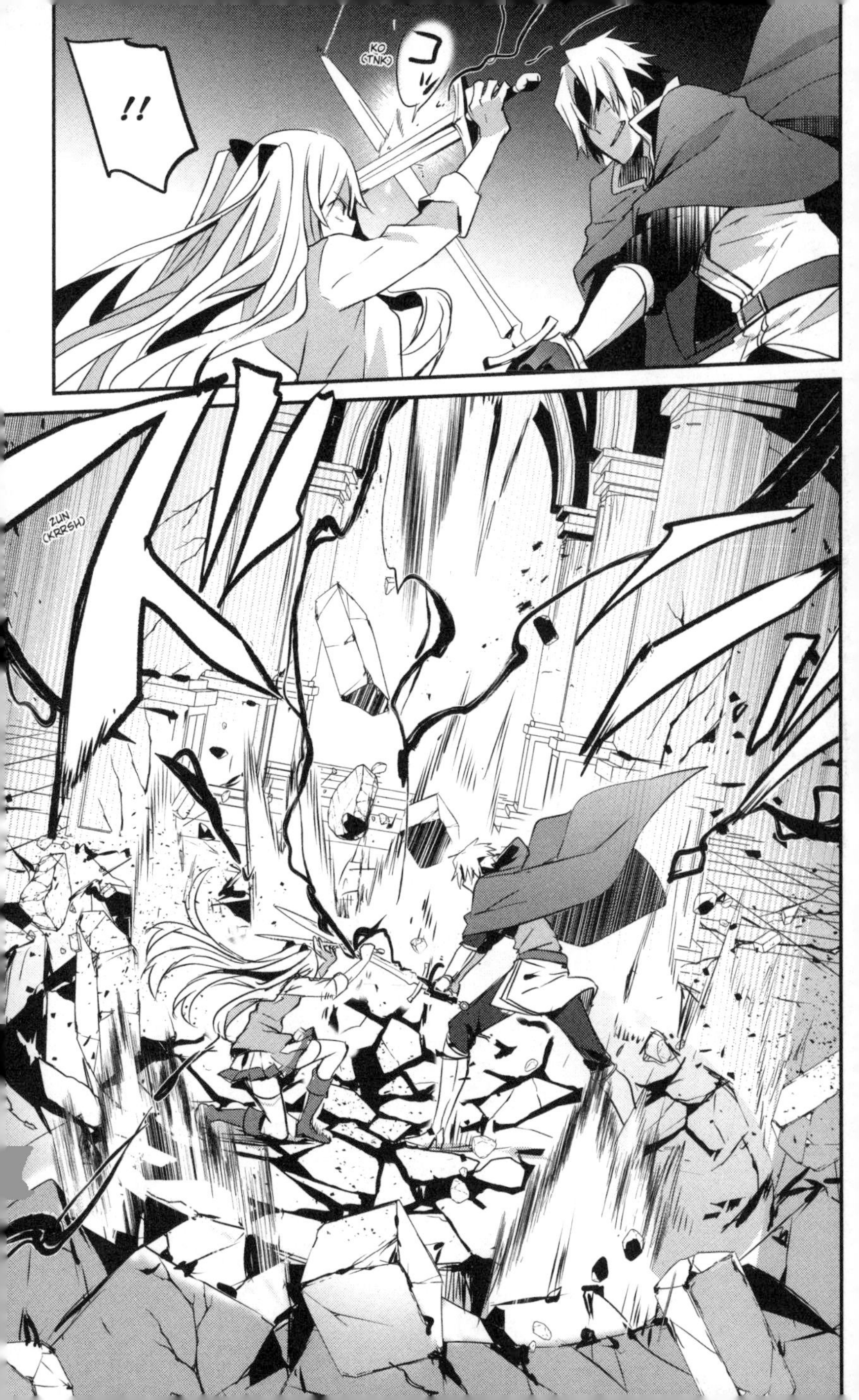
KO (TNK)
!!
ZUN (KRRSH)

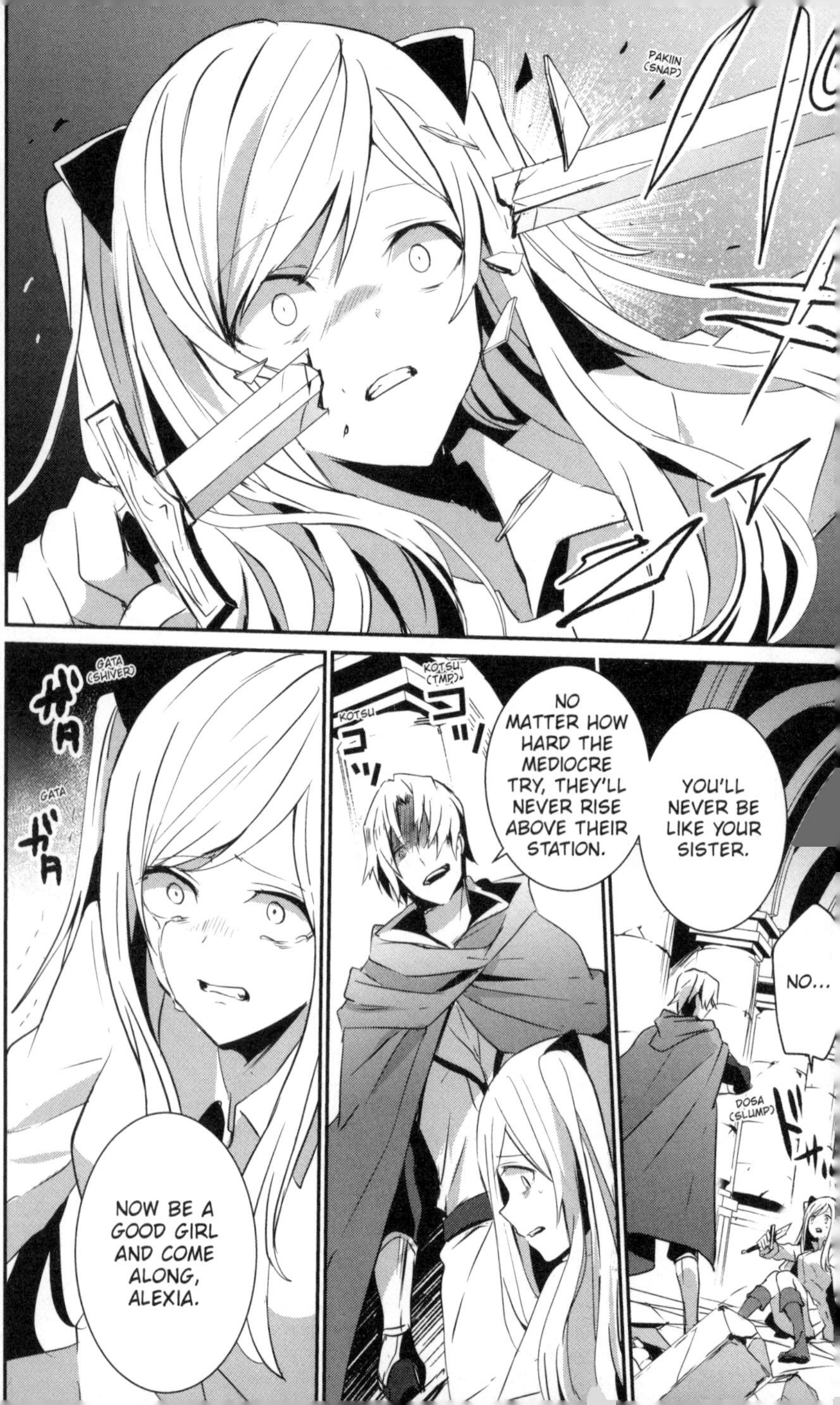
PAKIIN (SNAP)
YOU'LL NEVER BE LIKE YOUR SISTER.
NO...
DOSA (SLUMP)
KOTSU (TMP)
KOTSU
NO MATTER HOW HARD THE MEDIOCRE TRY, THEY'LL NEVER RISE ABOVE THEIR STATION.
GATA (SHIVER)
GATA
NOW BE A GOOD GIRL AND COME ALONG, ALEXIA.

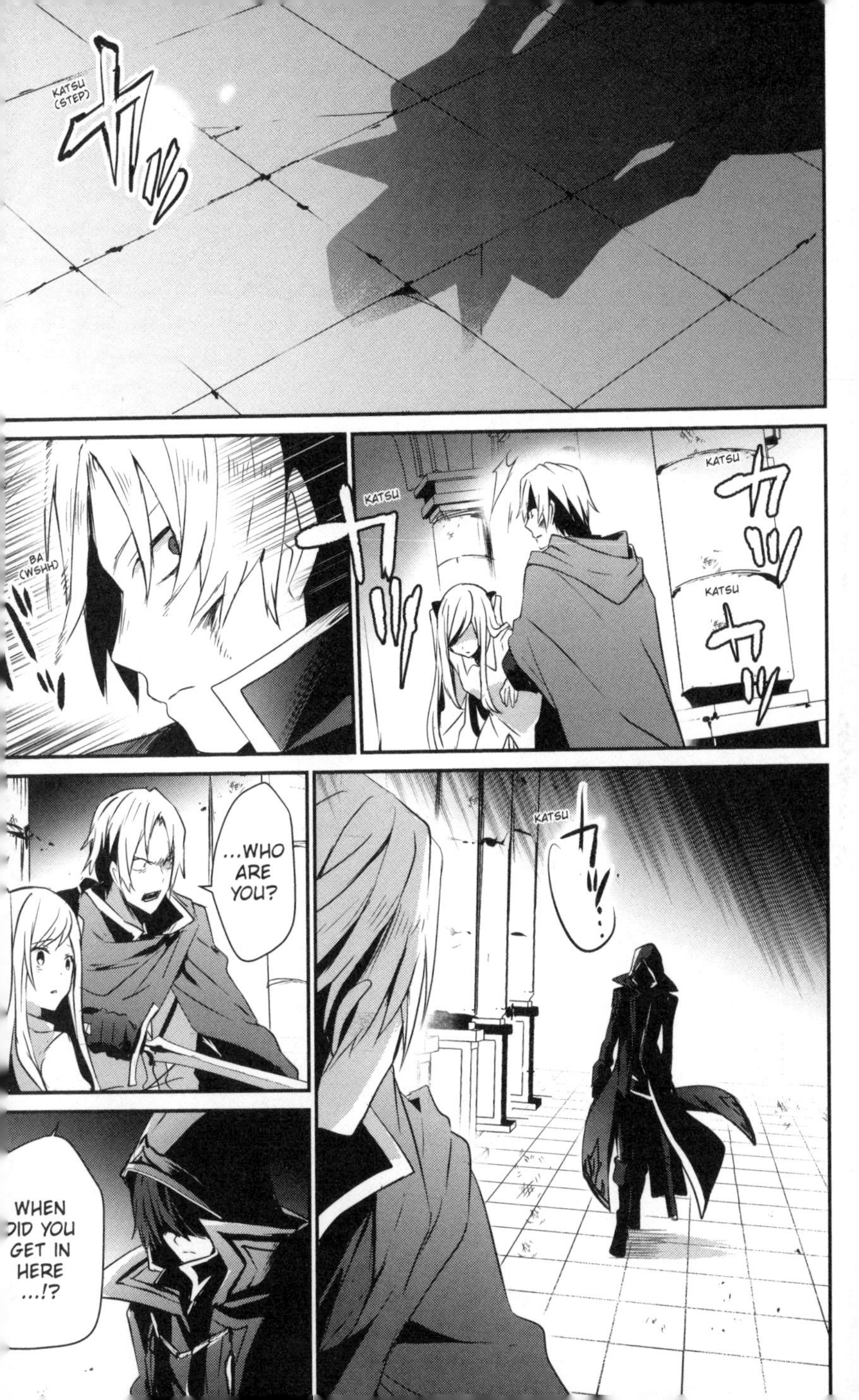

KATSU (STEP)
KATSU
KATSU
KATSU
BA (WSHH)
KATSU
...WHO ARE YOU?
WHEN DID YOU GET IN HERE ...!?

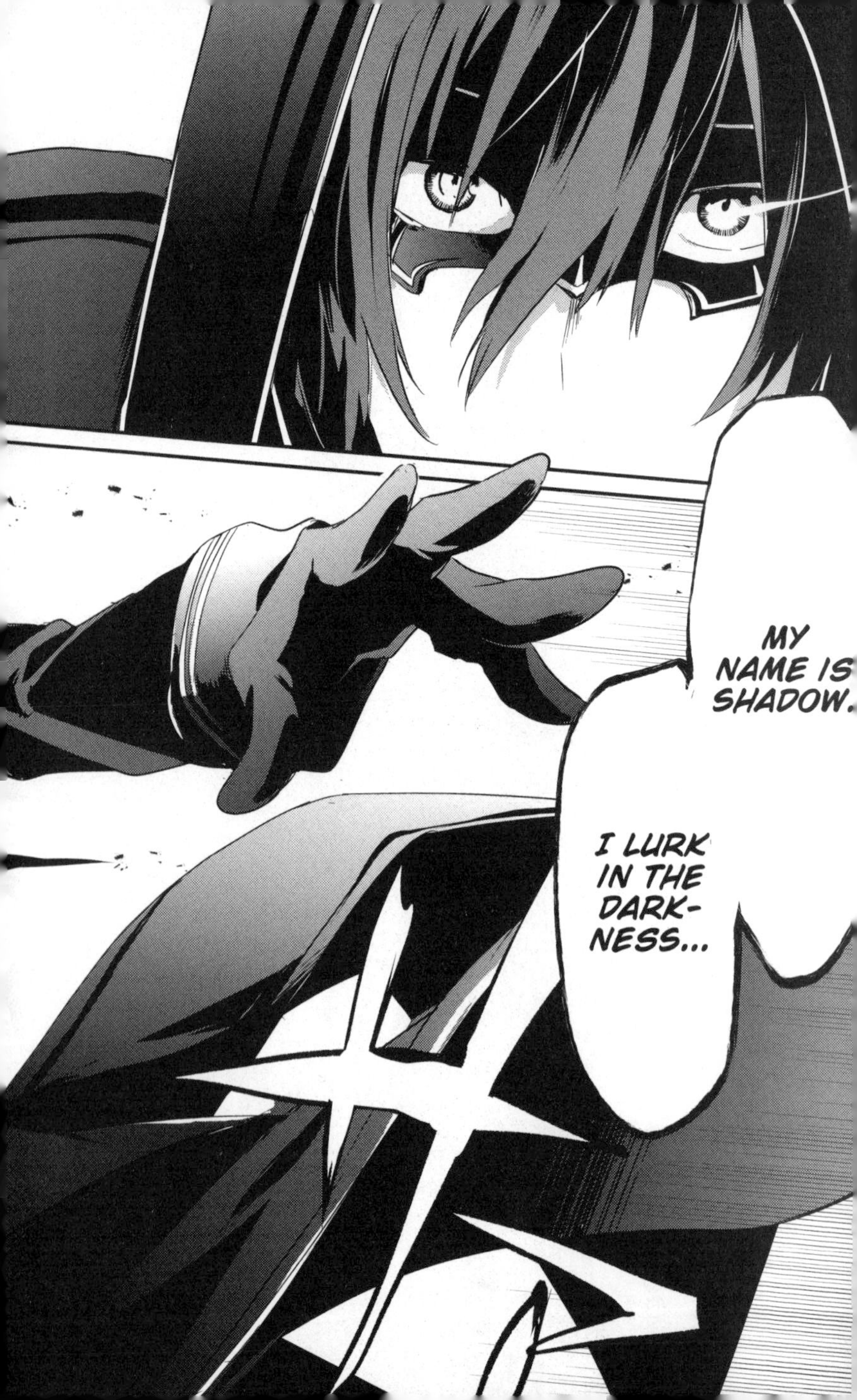
MY NAME IS SHADOW.
I LURK IN THE DARK-NESS...

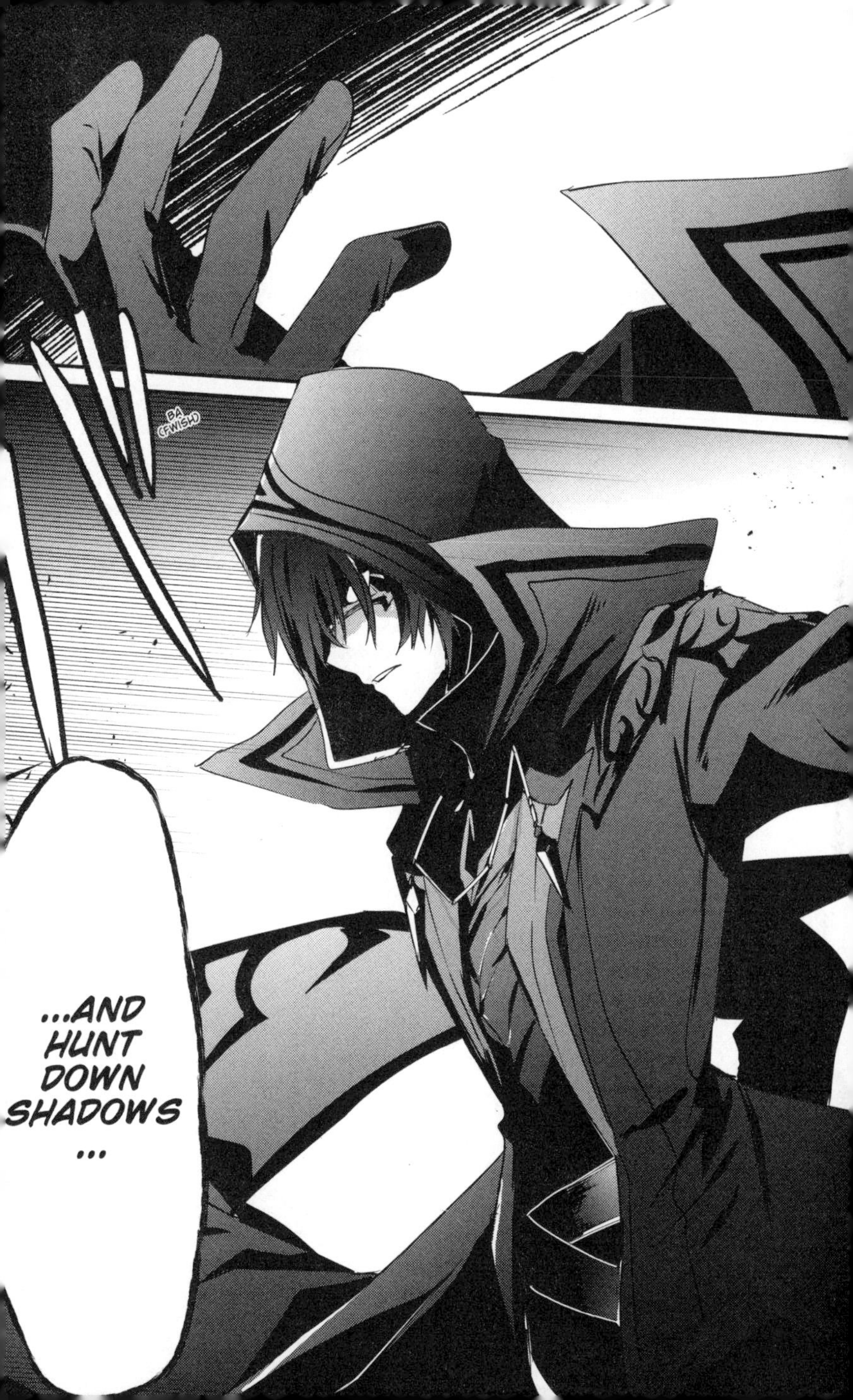
BA (FWISH)
...AND HUNT DOWN SHADOWS ...

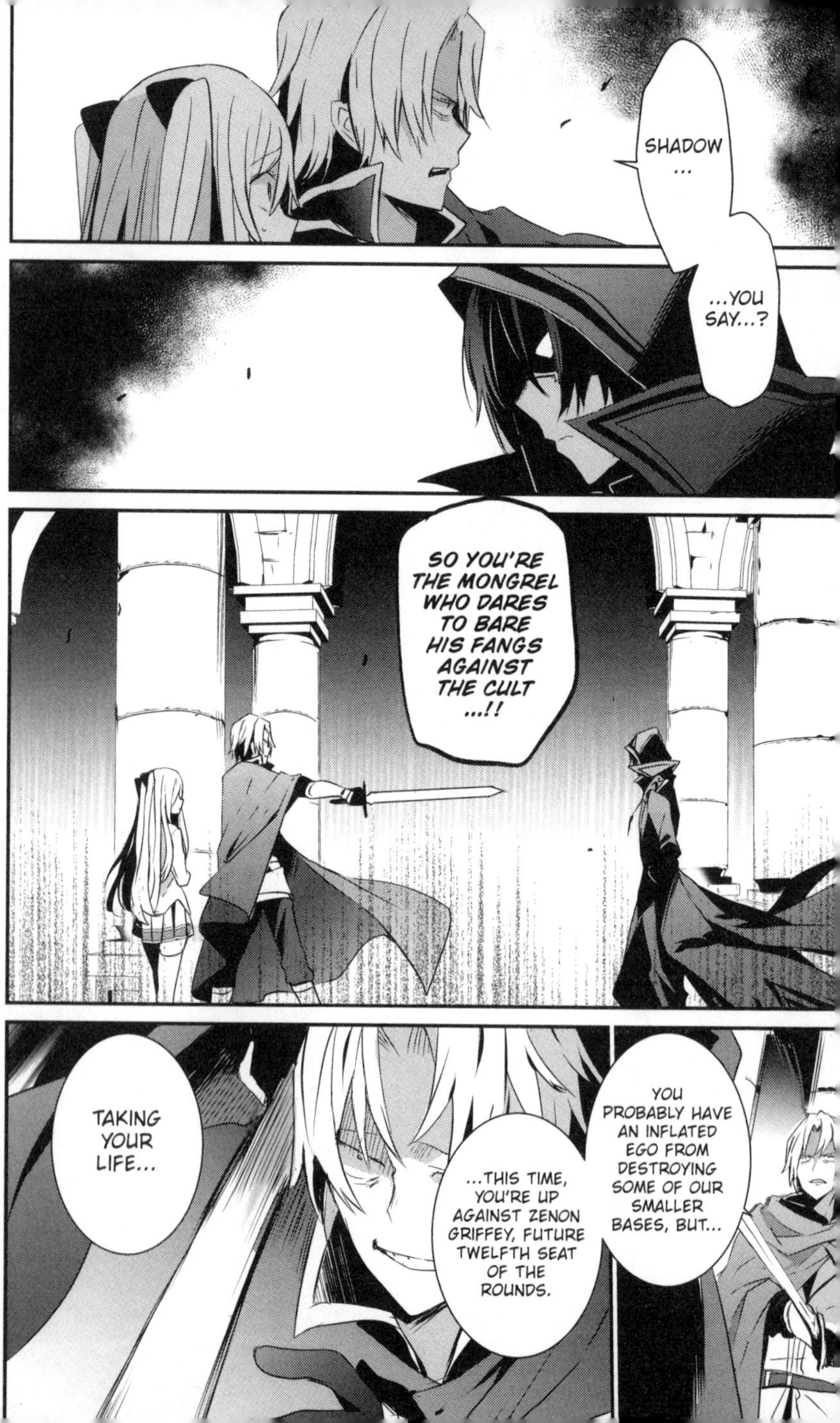
SHADOW …
…YOU SAY…?
SO YOU'RE THE MONGREL WHO DARES TO BARE HIS FANGS AGAINST THE CULT …!!
YOU PROBABLY HAVE AN INFLATED EGO FROM DESTROYING SOME OF OUR SMALLER BASES, BUT…
…THIS TIME, YOU'RE UP AGAINST ZENON GRIFFEY, FUTURE TWELFTH SEAT OF THE ROUNDS.
TAKING YOUR LIFE…

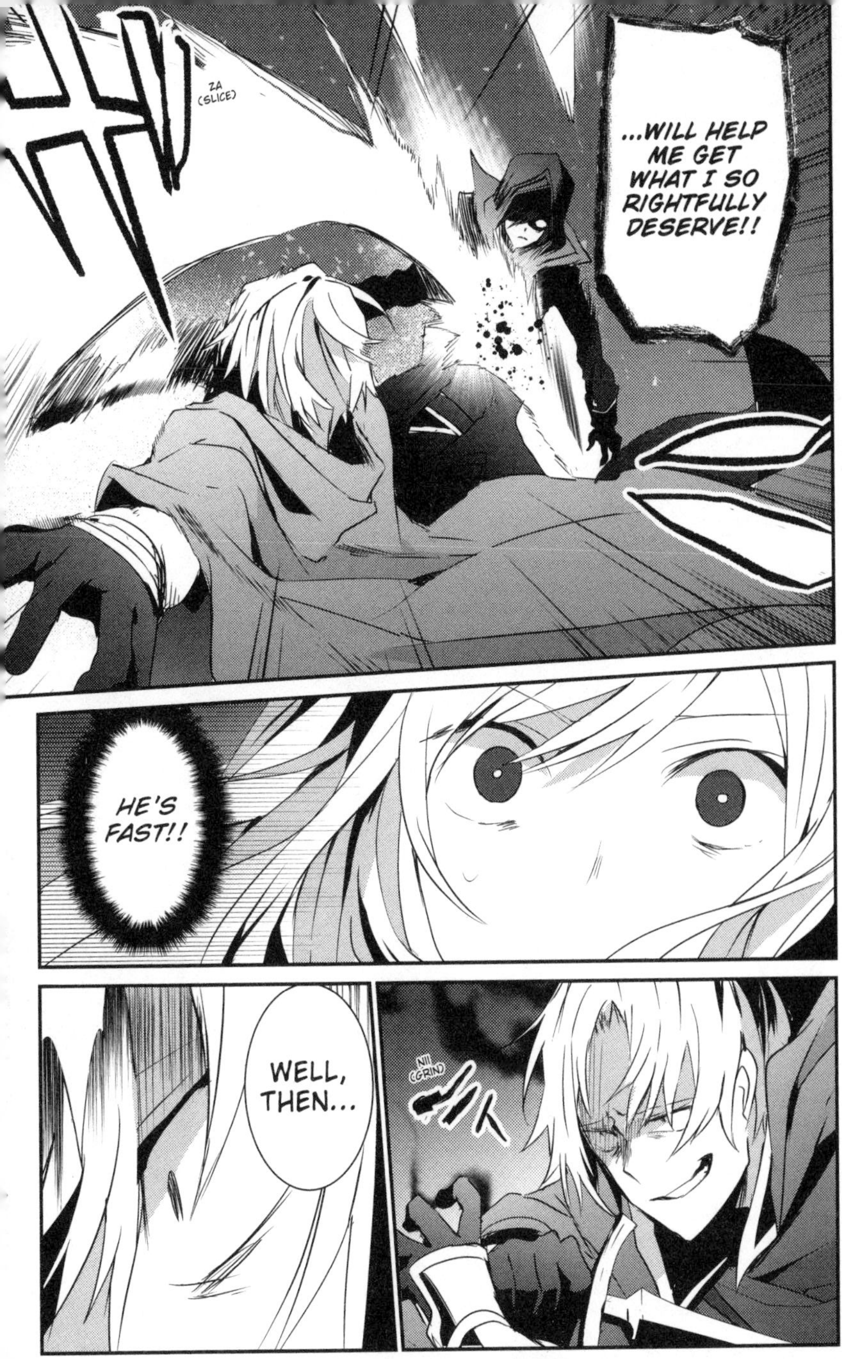
...WILL HELP ME GET WHAT I SO RIGHTFULLY DESERVE!!
ZA (SLICE)
HE'S FAST!!
NII (GRIN)
WELL, THEN...

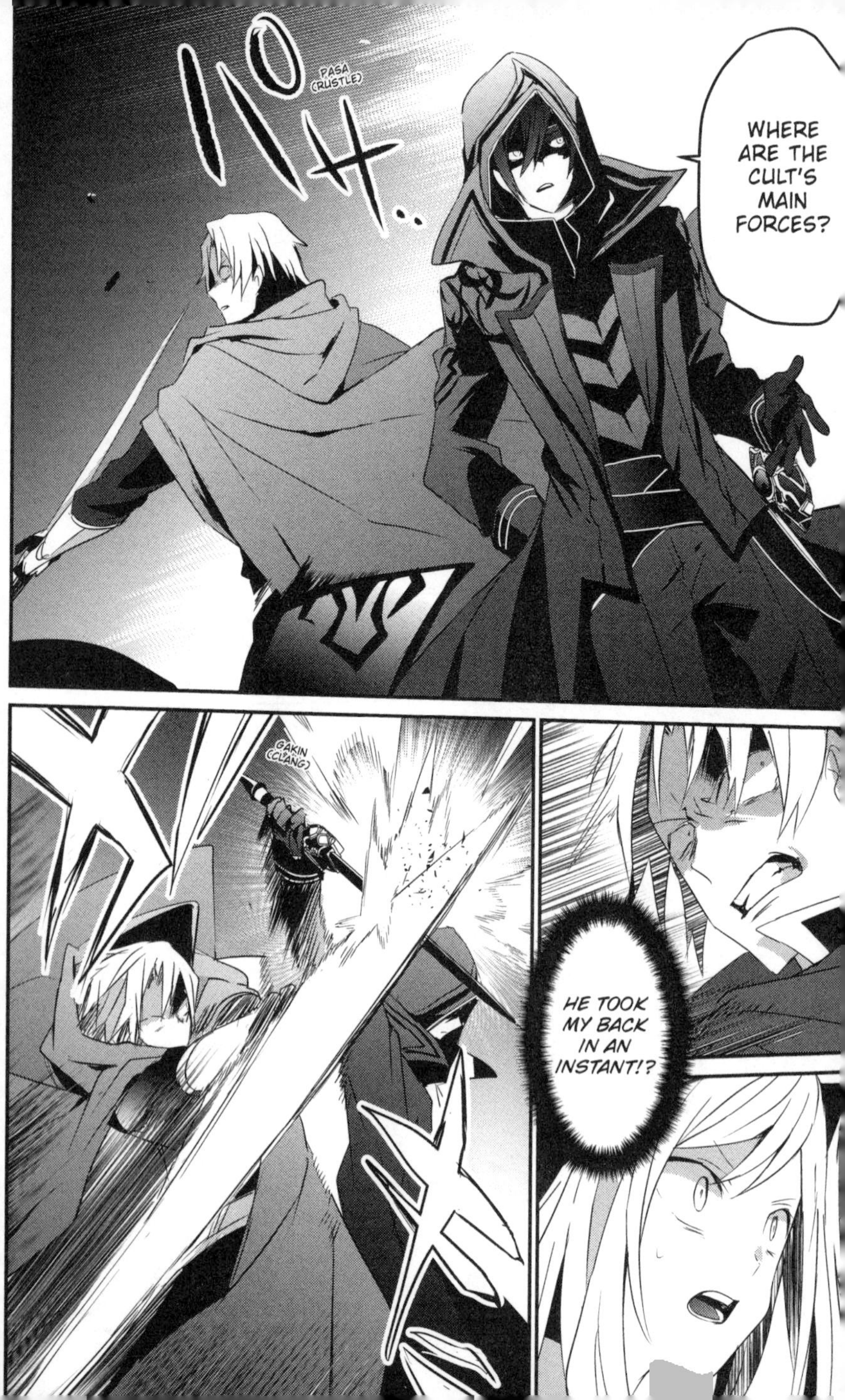
WHERE ARE THE CULT'S MAIN FORCES?
PASA (RUSTLE)
GAKIN (CLANG)
HE TOOK MY BACK IN AN INSTANT!?

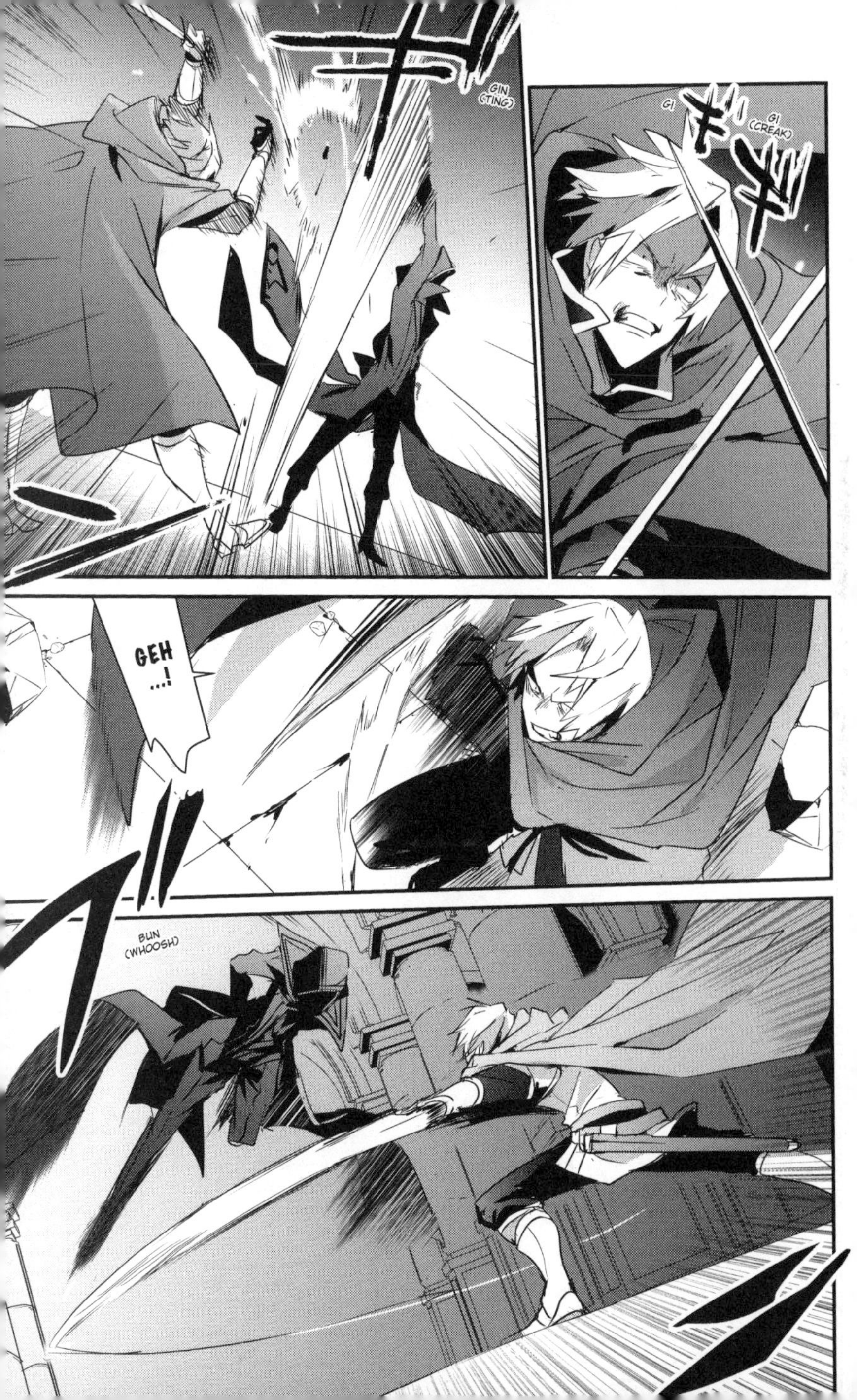
GI!
GI (CREAK)
GIN (TING)
GEH ...!
BUN (WHOOSH)

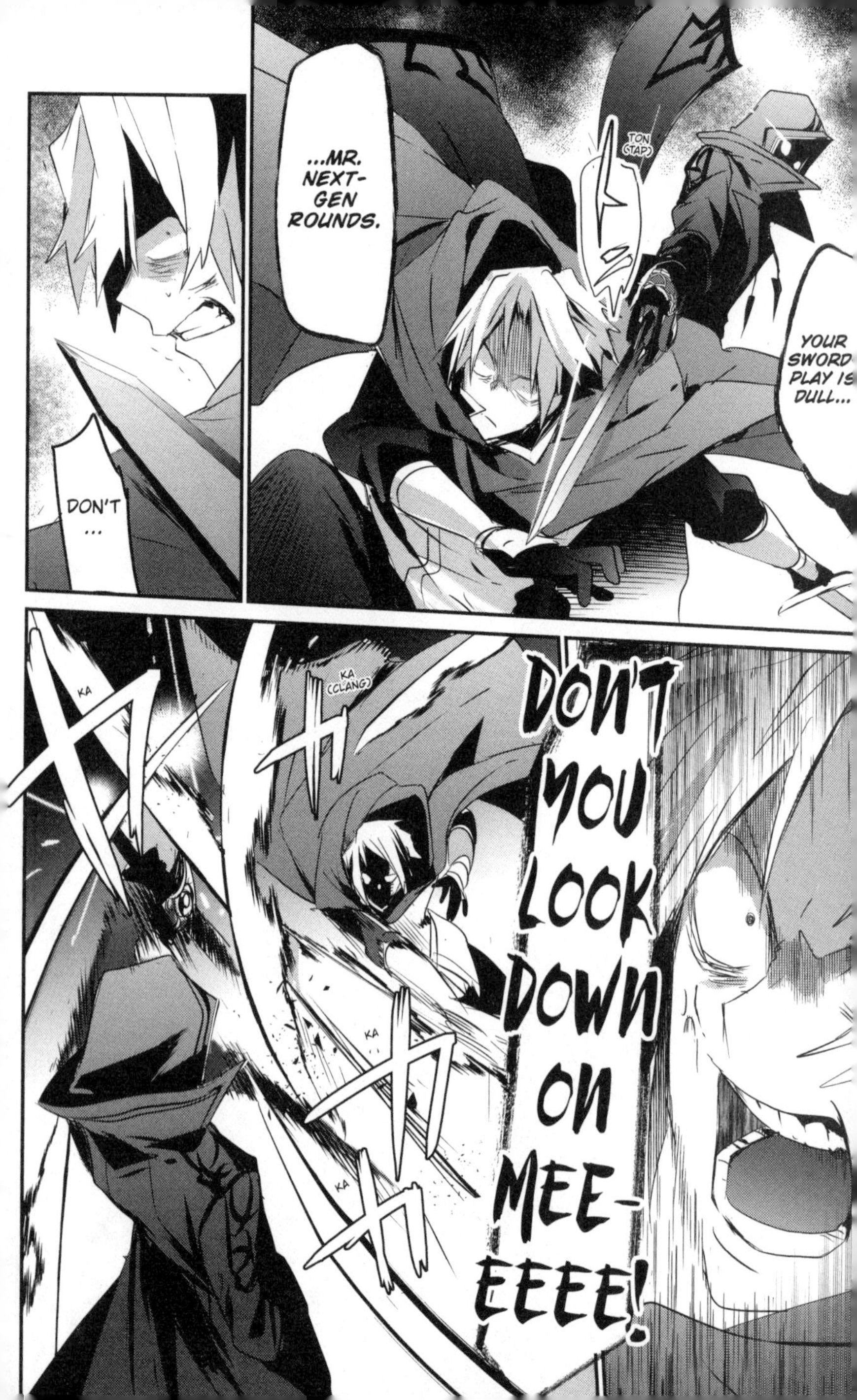
YOUR SWORD-PLAY IS DULL...
TON (TAP)
...MR. NEXT-GEN ROUNDS.
DON'T ...
KA (CLANG)
KA
DON'T YOU LOOK DOWN ON MEE-EEEE!
KA
KA

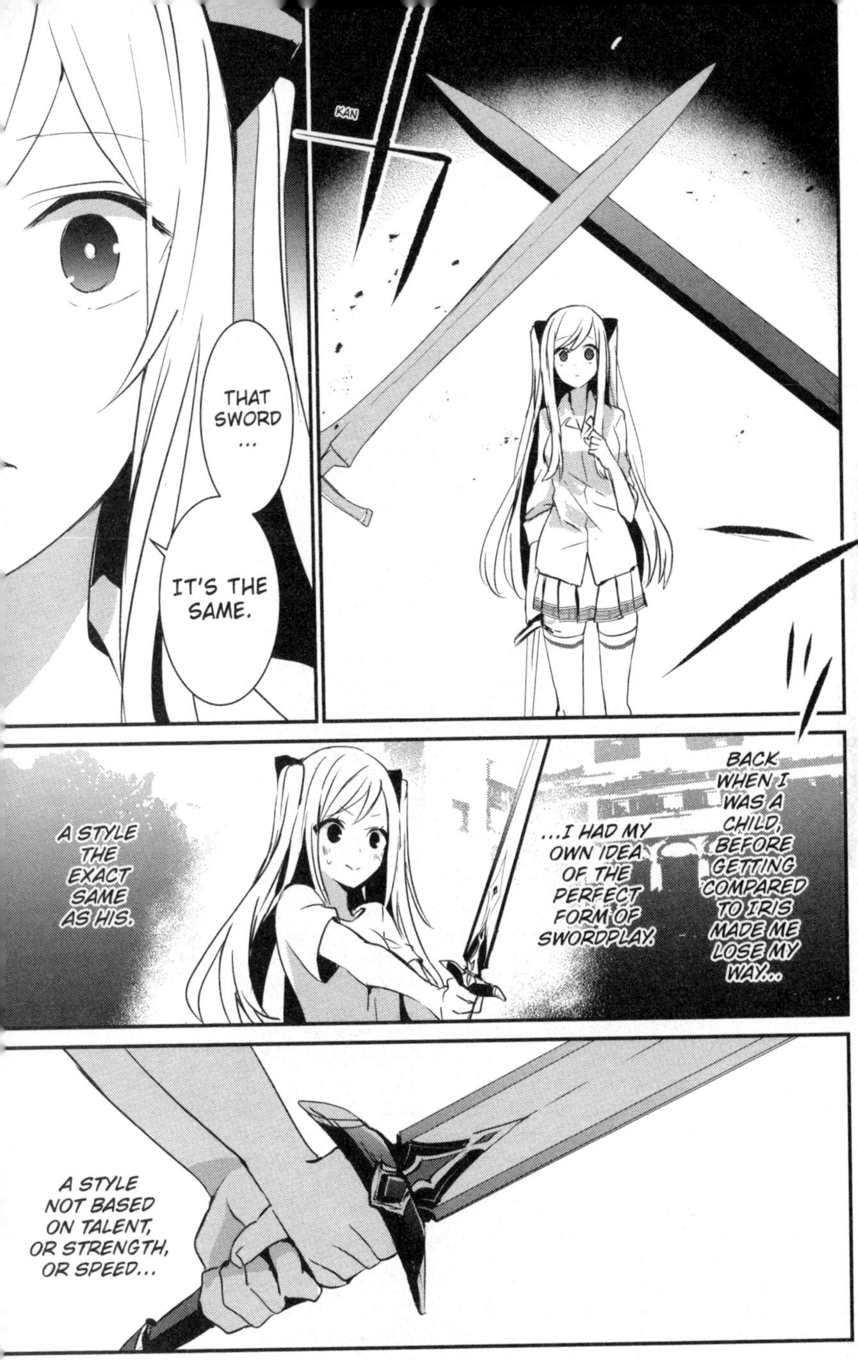
KAN
THAT SWORD...
IT'S THE SAME.
BACK WHEN I WAS A CHILD, BEFORE GETTING COMPARED TO IRIS MADE ME LOSE MY WAY...
...I HAD MY OWN IDEA OF THE PERFECT FORM OF SWORDPLAY.
A STYLE THE EXACT SAME AS HIS.
A STYLE NOT BASED ON TALENT, OR STRENGTH, OR SPEED...

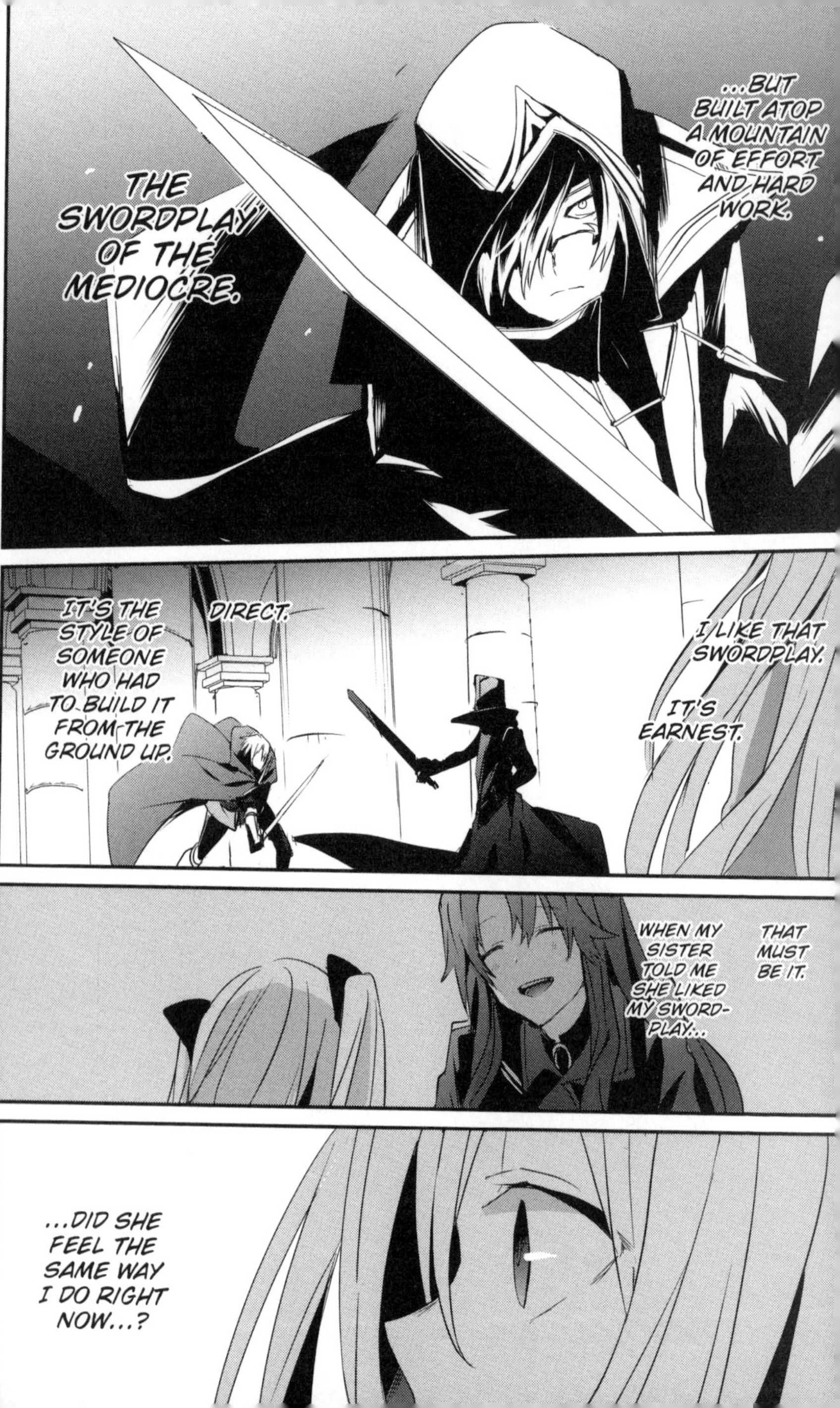
THE SWORDPLAY OF THE MEDIOCRE.
...BUT BUILT ATOP A MOUNTAIN OF EFFORT AND HARD WORK.
I LIKE THAT SWORDPLAY.
IT'S EARNEST.
DIRECT.
IT'S THE STYLE OF SOMEONE WHO HAD TO BUILD IT FROM THE GROUND UP.
THAT MUST BE IT.
WHEN MY SISTER TOLD ME SHE LIKED MY SWORD-PLAY...
...DID SHE FEEL THE SAME WAY I DO RIGHT NOW...?

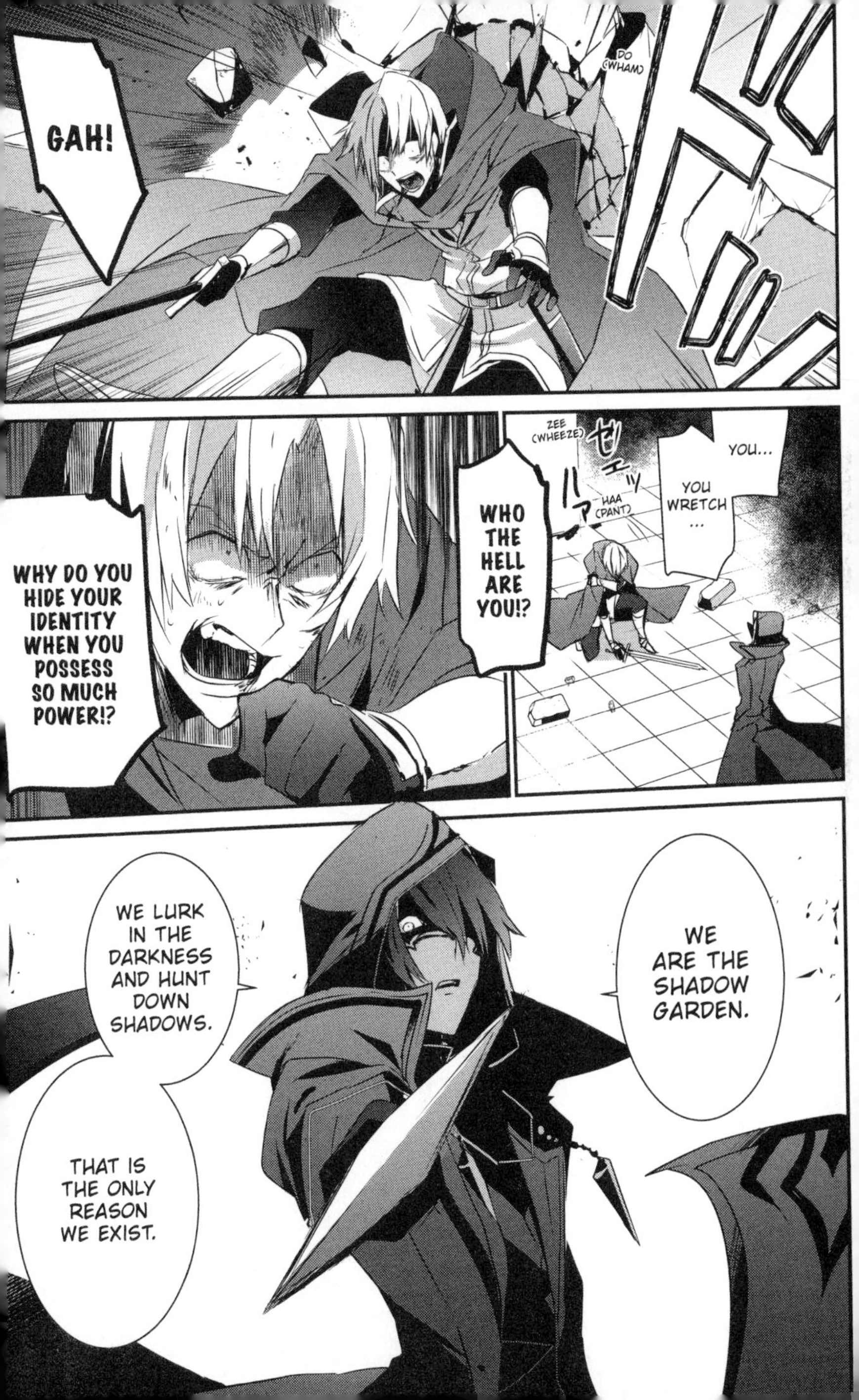
DO (WHAM)
GAH!
ZEE (WHEEZE)
ゼェッ
ハァ
HAA (PANT)
YOU...
YOU WRETCH...
WHO THE HELL ARE YOU!?
WHY DO YOU HIDE YOUR IDENTITY WHEN YOU POSSESS SO MUCH POWER!?
WE ARE THE SHADOW GARDEN.
WE LURK IN THE DARKNESS AND HUNT DOWN SHADOWS.
THAT IS THE ONLY REASON WE EXIST.

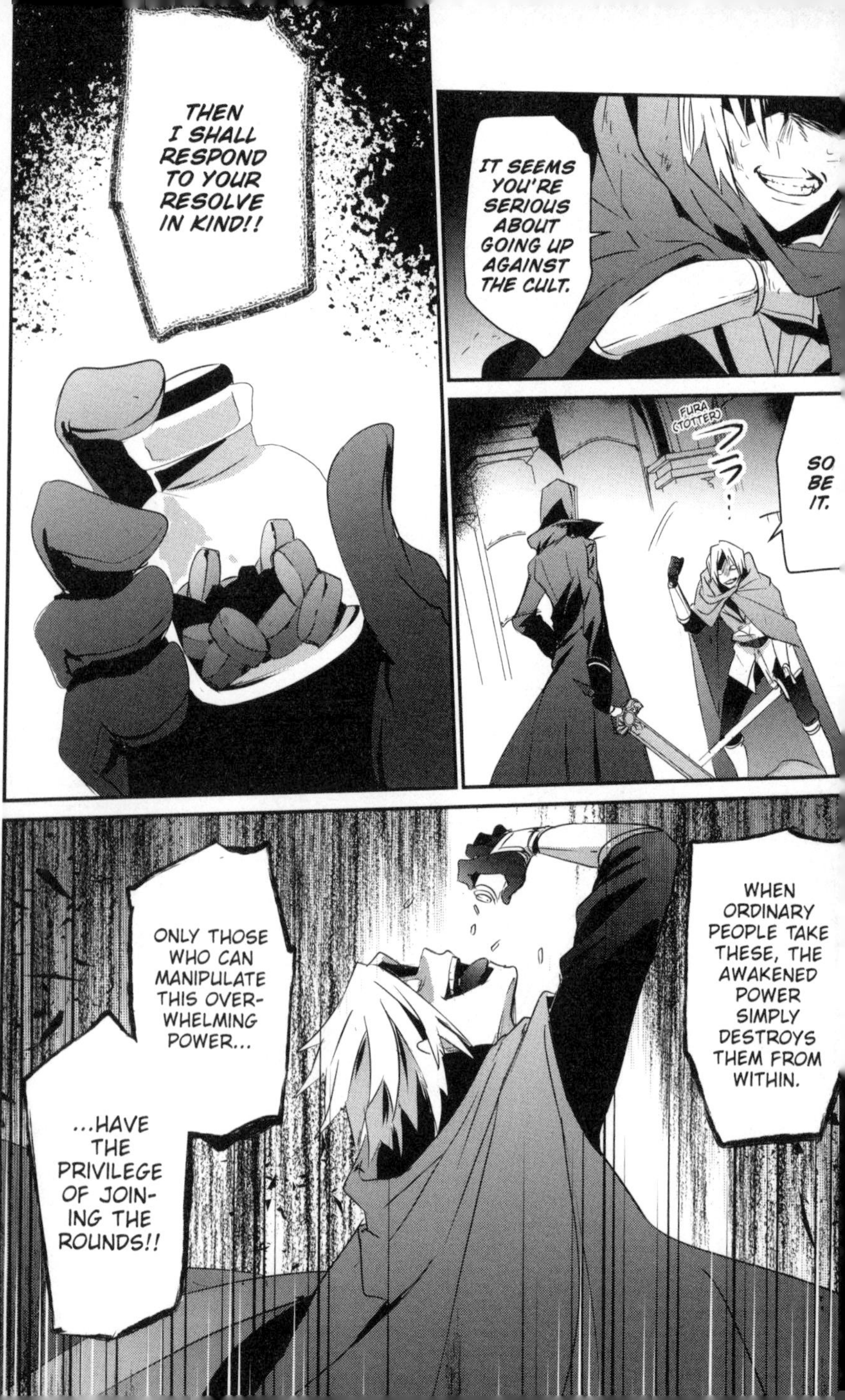
IT SEEMS YOU'RE SERIOUS ABOUT GOING UP AGAINST THE CULT.
FURA (TOTTER)
SO BE IT.
THEN I SHALL RESPOND TO YOUR RESOLVE IN KIND!!
WHEN ORDINARY PEOPLE TAKE THESE, THE AWAKENED POWER SIMPLY DESTROYS THEM FROM WITHIN.
ONLY THOSE WHO CAN MANIPULATE THIS OVER-WHELMING POWER...
...HAVE THE PRIVILEGE OF JOIN-ING THE ROUNDS!!

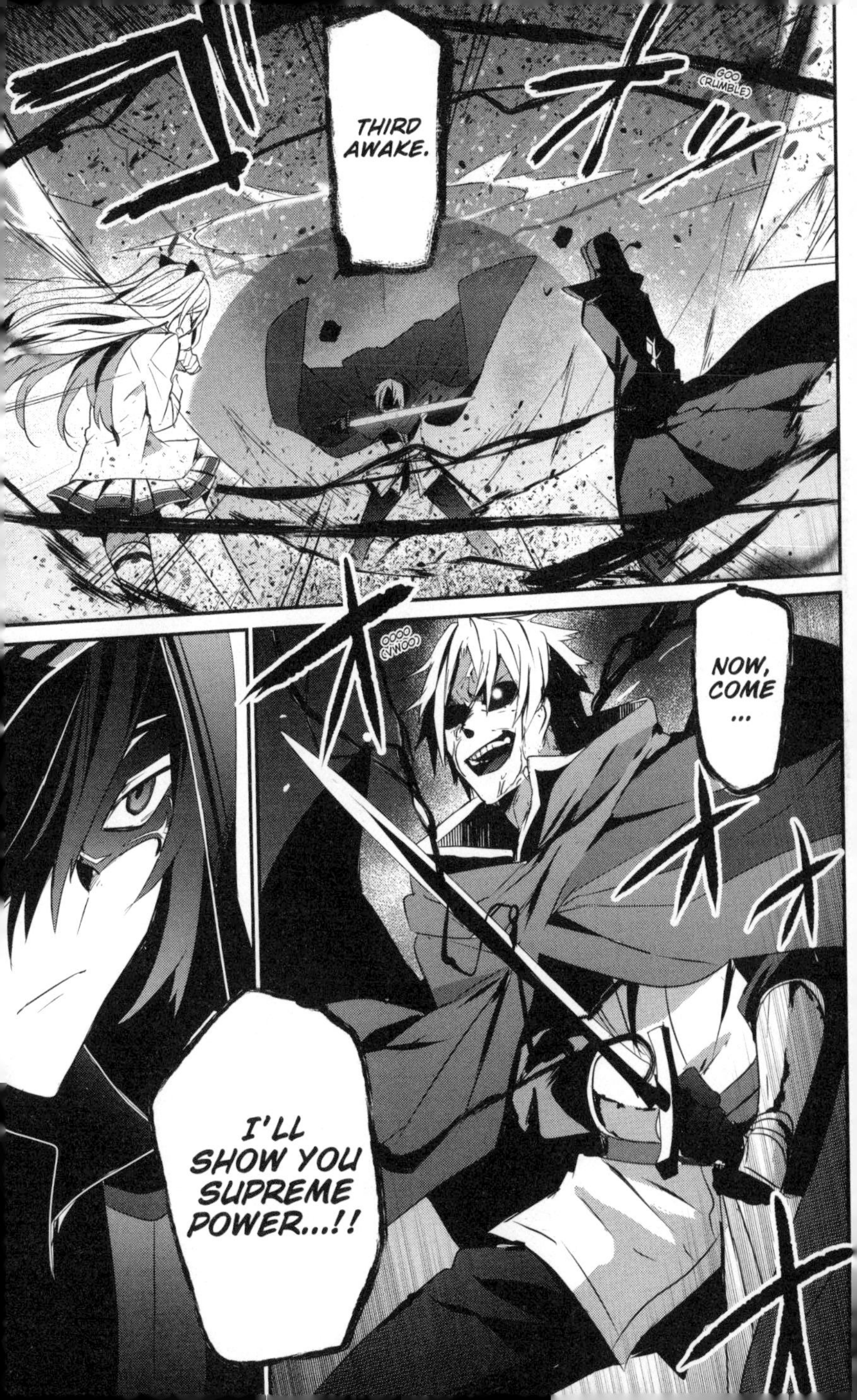
GOO (RUMBLE)
THIRD AWAKE.
NOW, COME ...
OOOO (VWOO)
I'LL SHOW YOU SUPREME POWER...!!

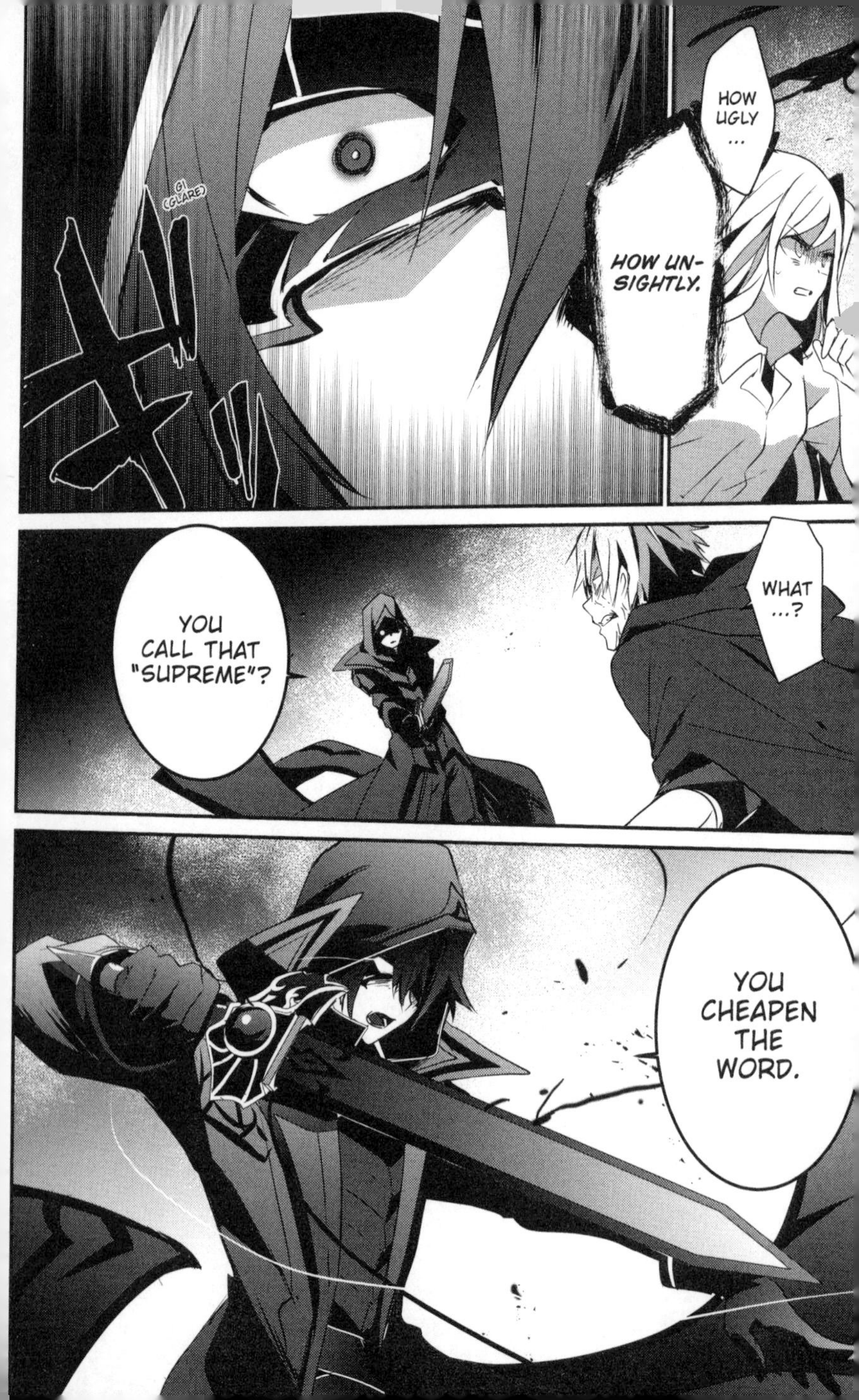
HOW UGLY ...
HOW UN-SIGHTLY.
GI (GLARE)
WHAT ...?
YOU CALL THAT "SUPREME"?
YOU CHEAPEN THE WORD.

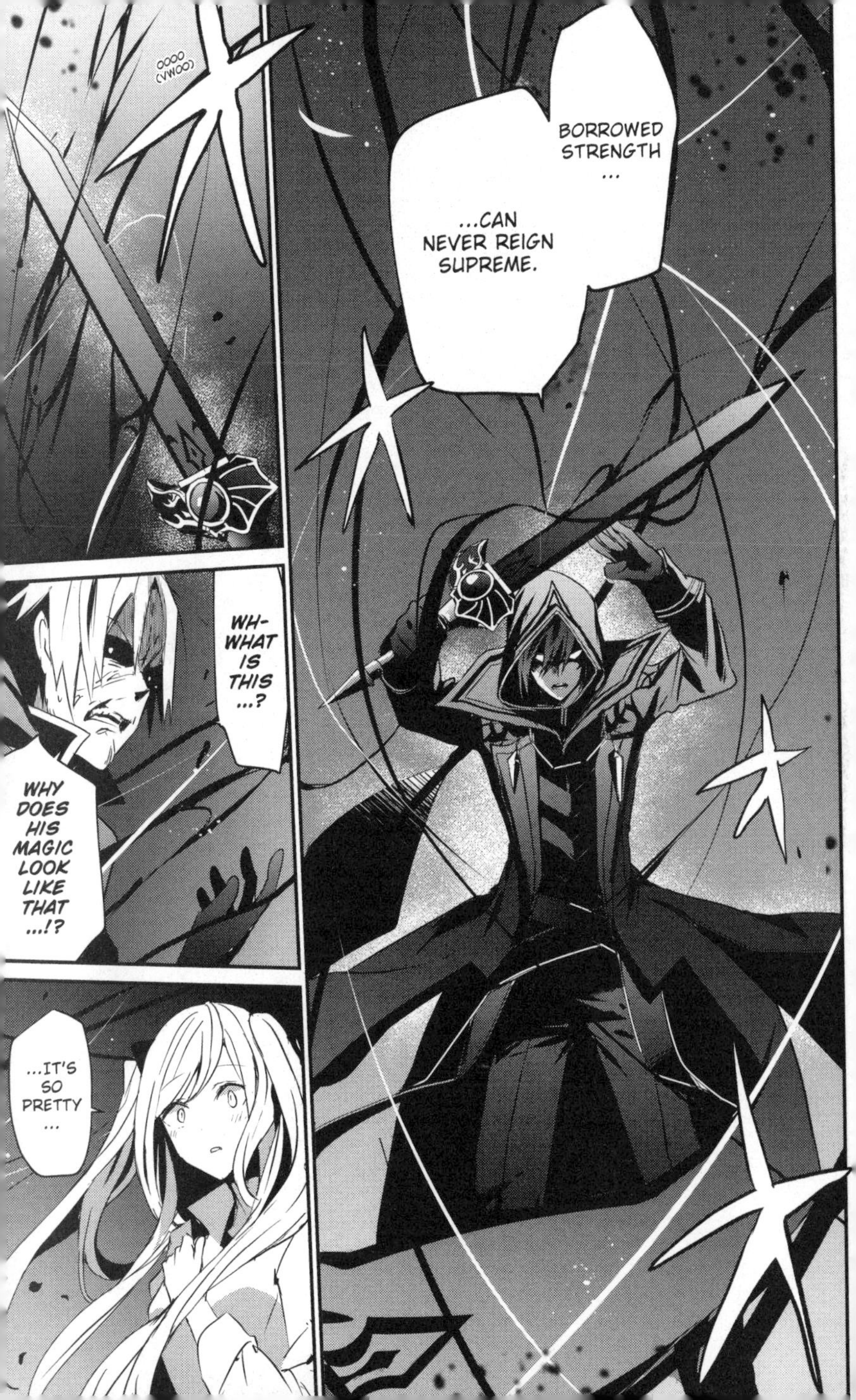
BORROWED STRENGTH ...
...CAN NEVER REIGN SUPREME.
OOOO (VWOO)
WH-WHAT IS THIS ...?
WHY DOES HIS MAGIC LOOK LIKE THAT ...!?
...IT'S SO PRETTY ...

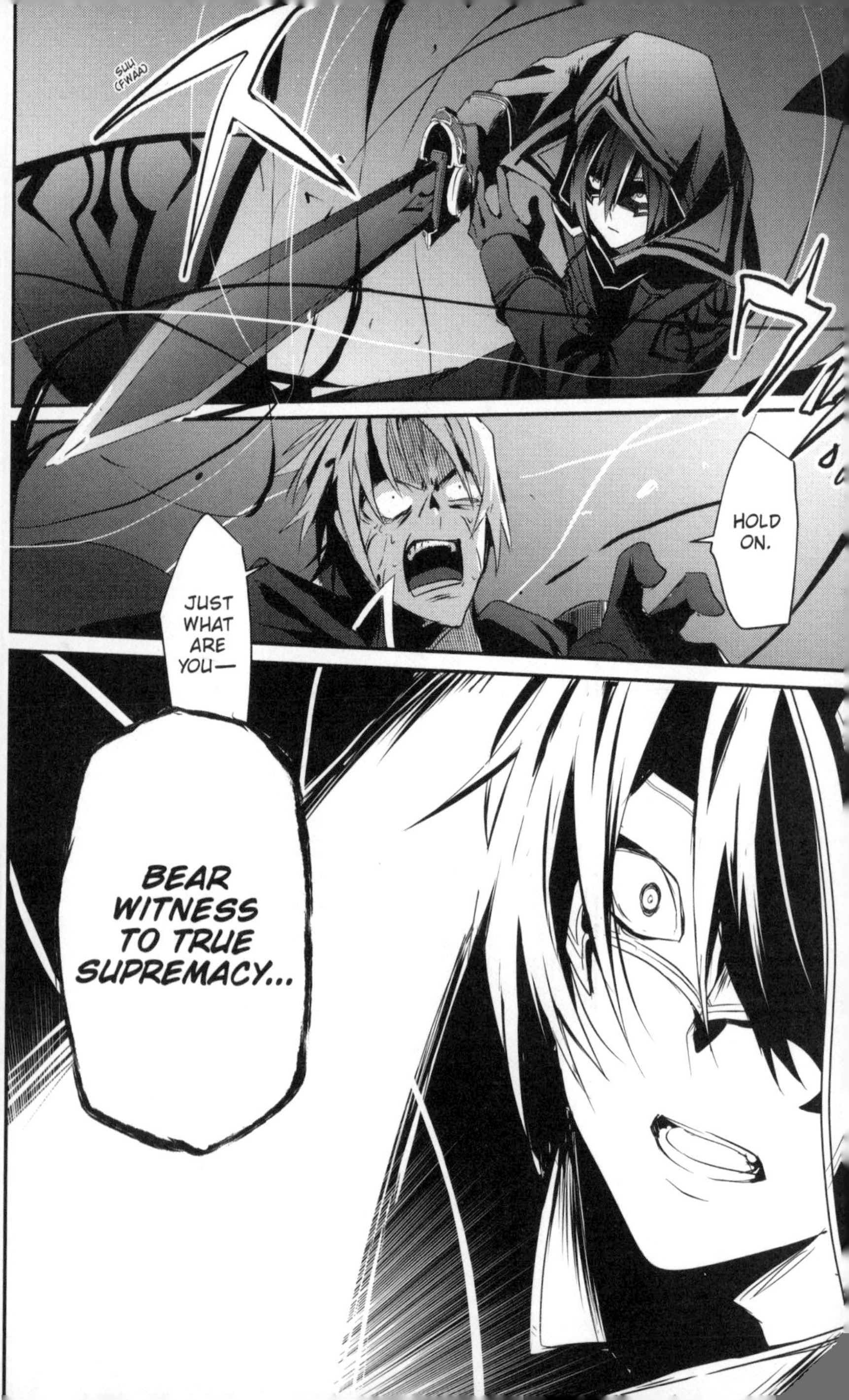
SUU (FWAA)
HOLD ON.
JUST WHAT ARE YOU—
BEAR WITNESS TO TRUE SUPREMACY...

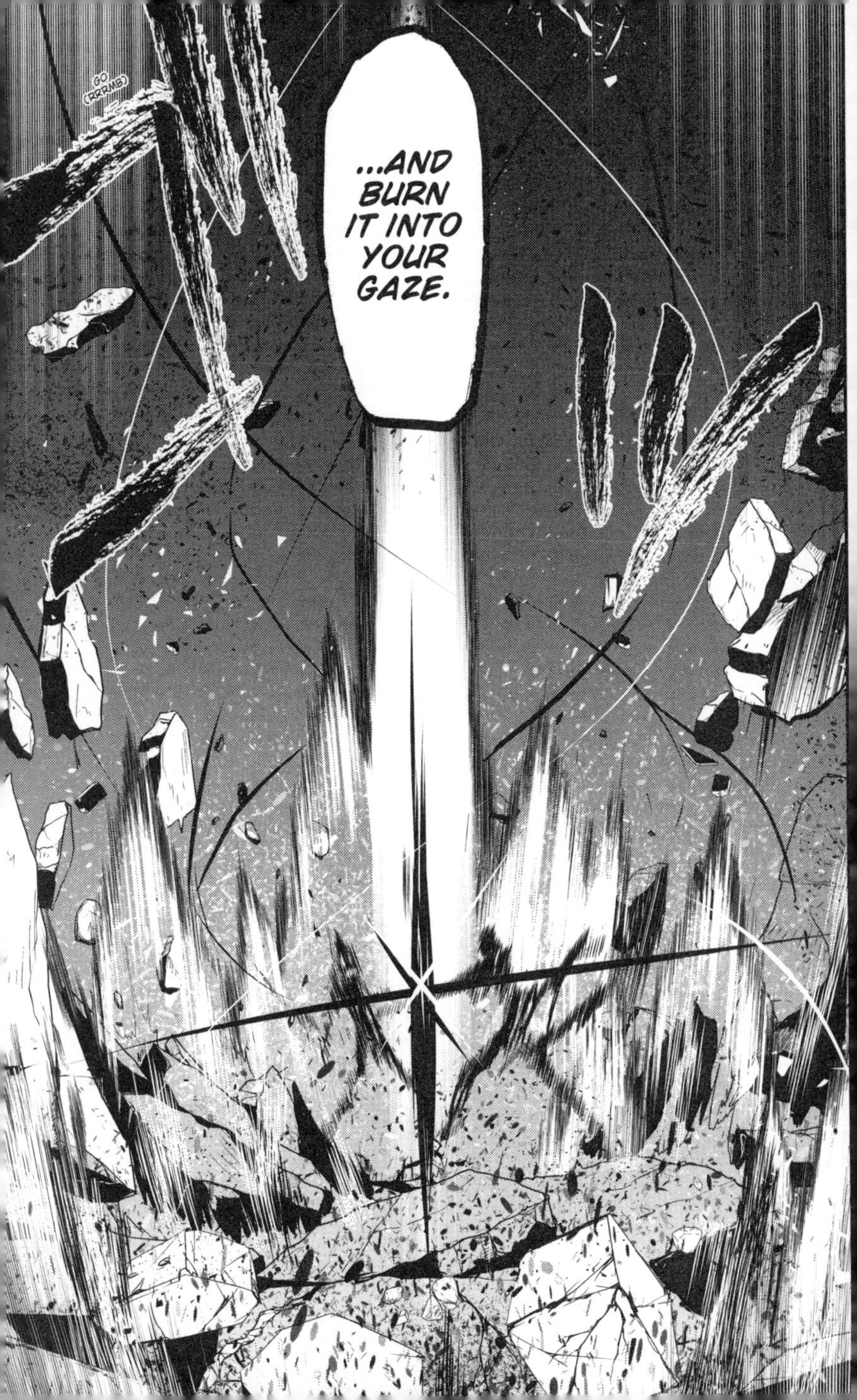
...AND BURN IT INTO YOUR GAZE.
GO (RRRMB)

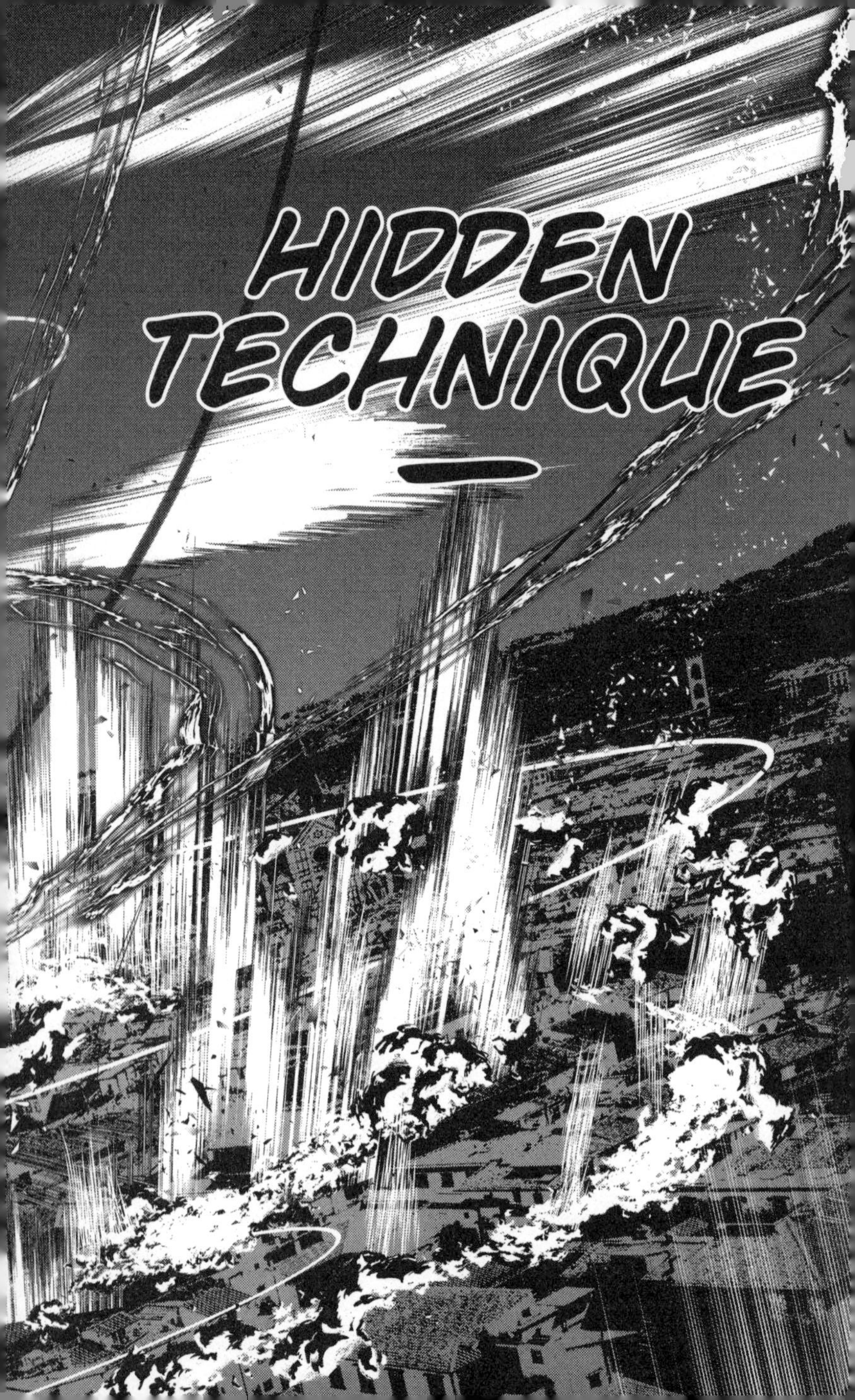
HIDDEN TECHNIQUE—

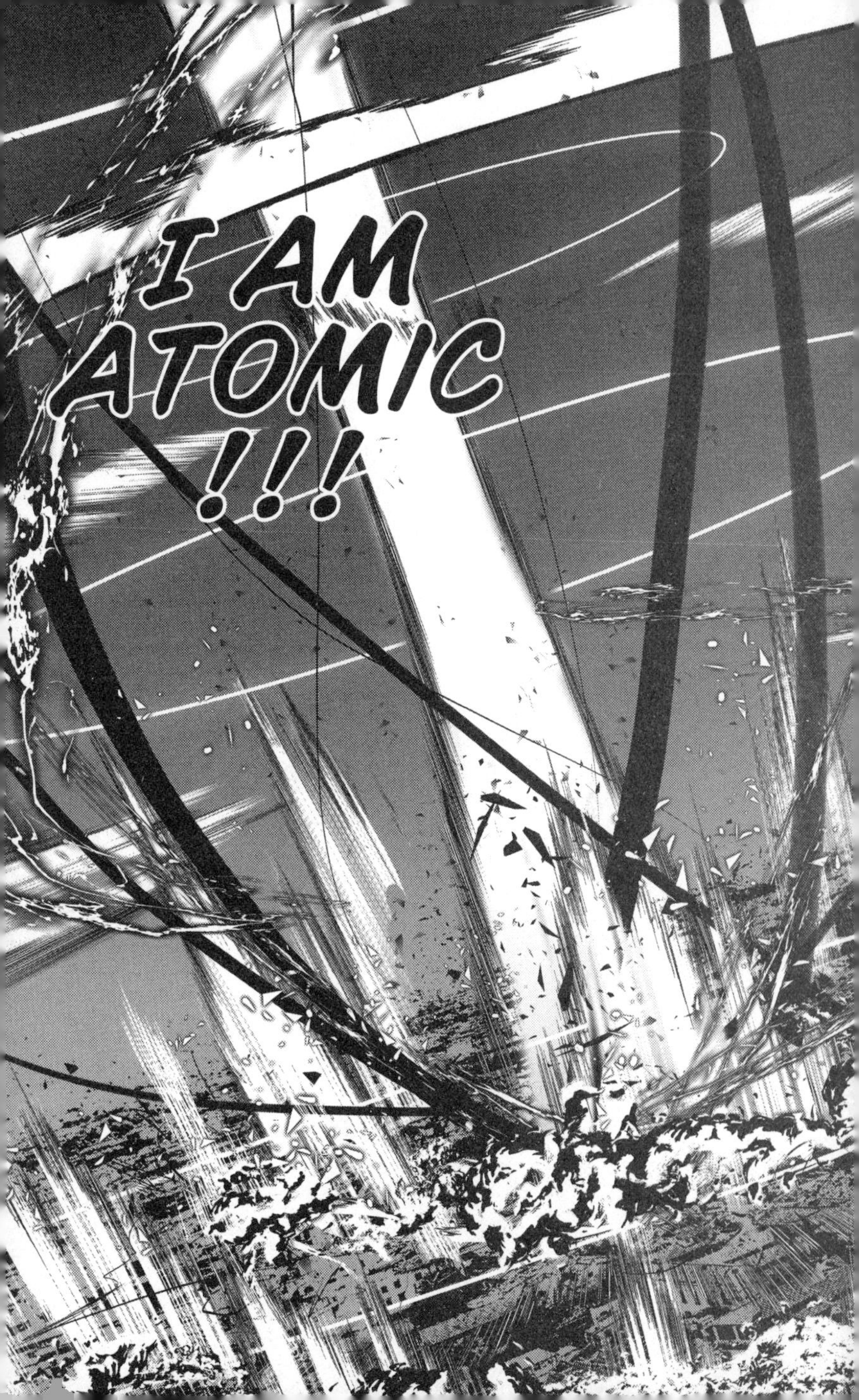
I AM ATOMIC !!!

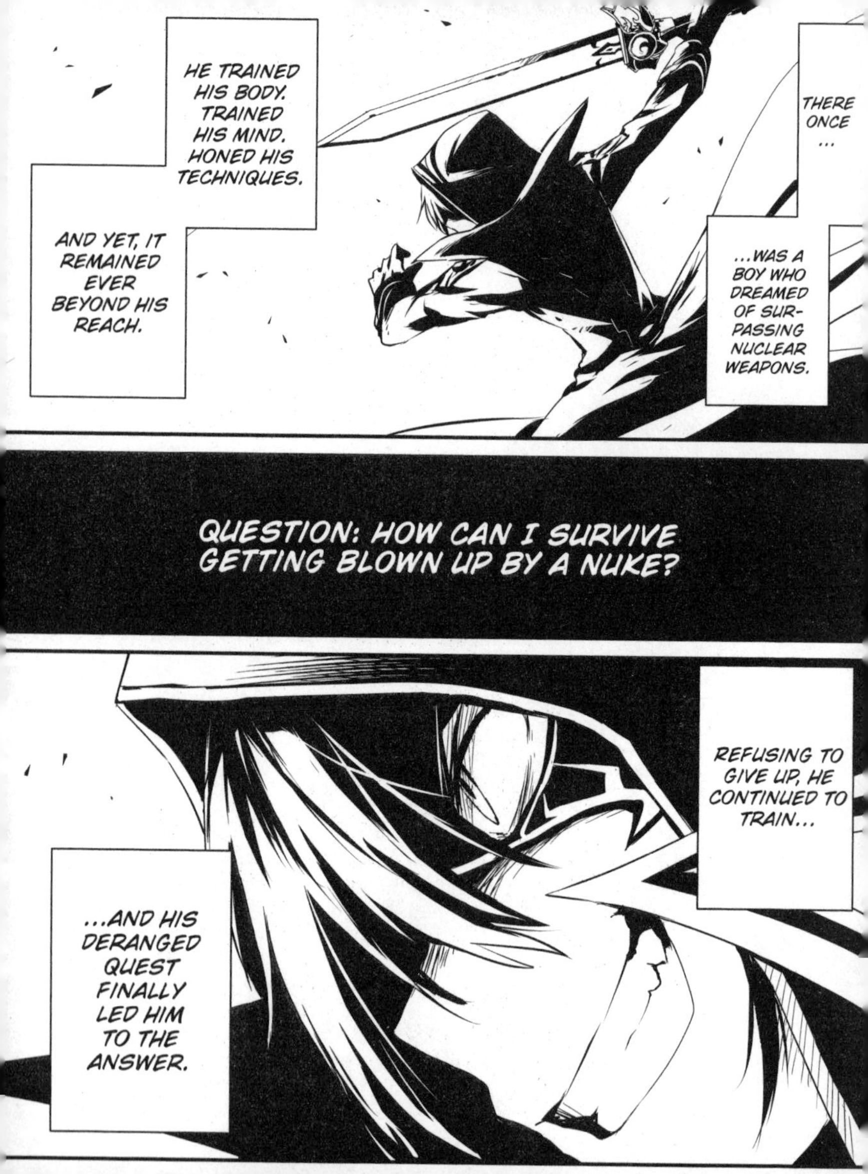
THERE ONCE...
...WAS A BOY WHO DREAMED OF SUR-PASSING NUCLEAR WEAPONS.
HE TRAINED HIS BODY. TRAINED HIS MIND. HONED HIS TECHNIQUES.
AND YET, IT REMAINED EVER BEYOND HIS REACH.
QUESTION: HOW CAN I SURVIVE GETTING BLOWN UP BY A NUKE?
REFUSING TO GIVE UP, HE CONTINUED TO TRAIN...
...AND HIS DERANGED QUEST FINALLY LED HIM TO THE ANSWER.

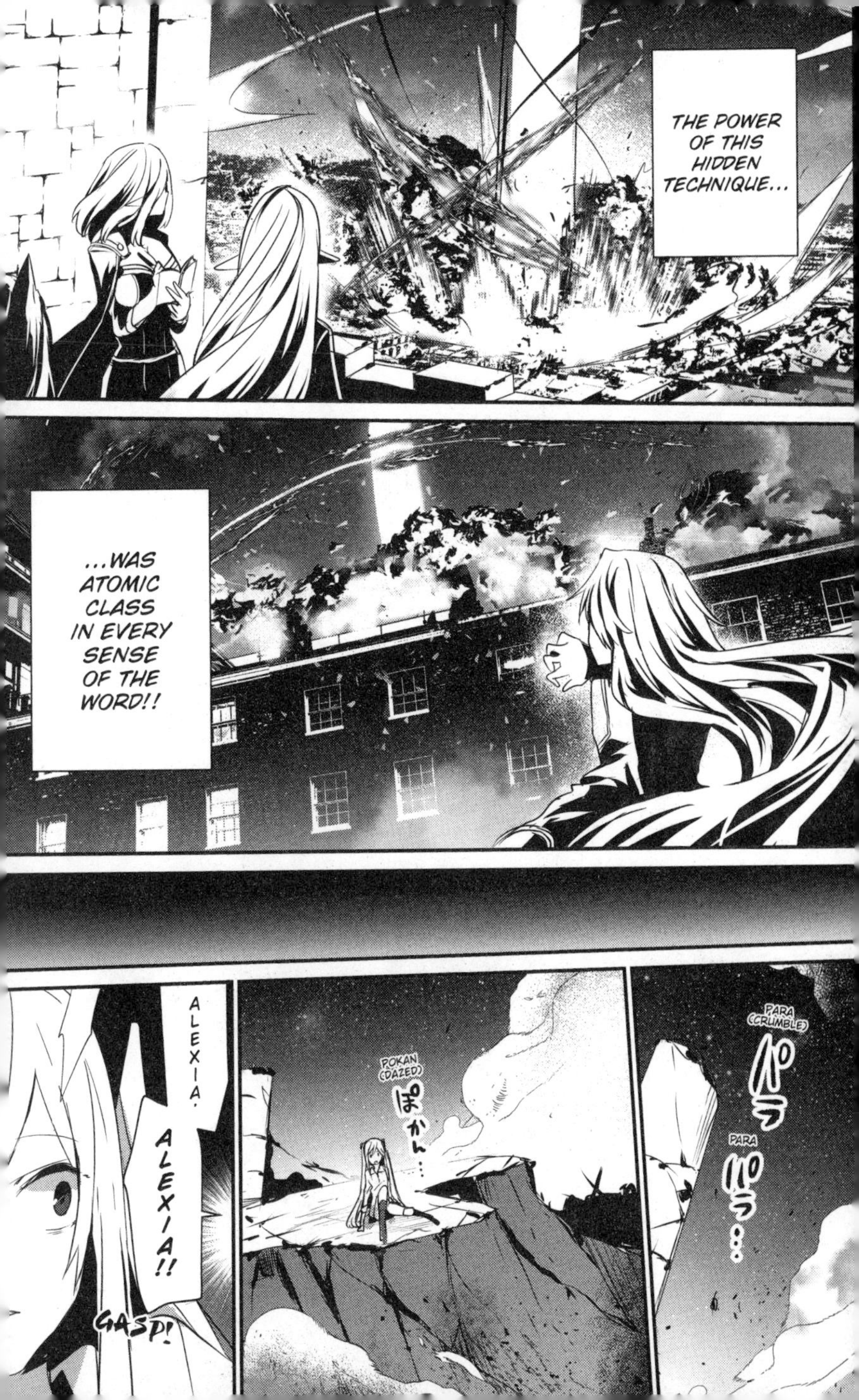
THE POWER OF THIS HIDDEN TECHNIQUE...
...WAS ATOMIC CLASS IN EVERY SENSE OF THE WORD!!
PARA (CRUMBLE)
パラ
PARA
パラ…
POKAN (DAZED)
ぽかん…
ALEXIA.
ALEXIA!!
GASP!

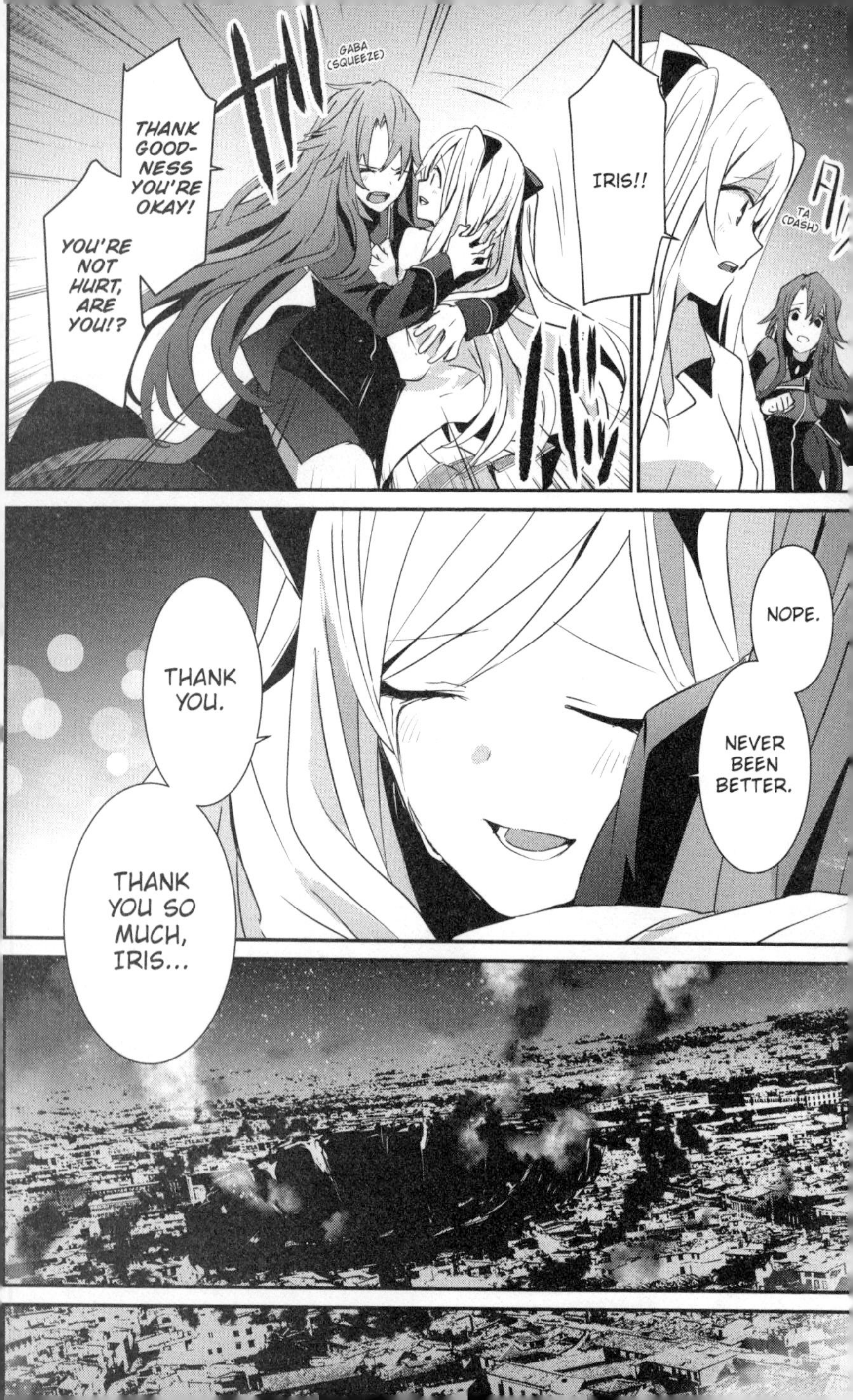
IRIS!!
TA (DASH)
GABA (SQUEEZE)
THANK GOODNESS YOU'RE OKAY!
YOU'RE NOT HURT, ARE YOU!?
NOPE.
NEVER BEEN BETTER.
THANK YOU.
THANK YOU SO MUCH, IRIS...

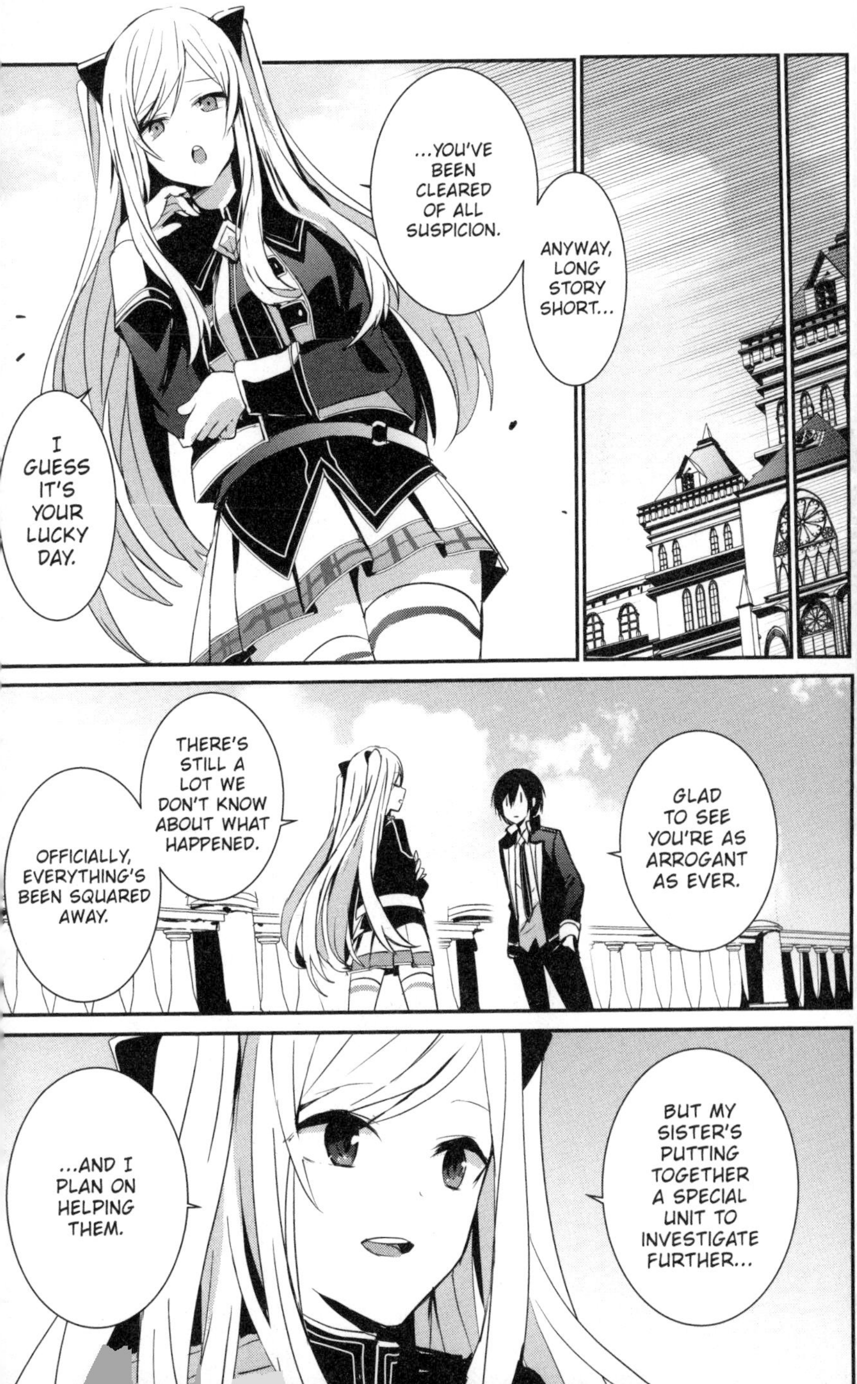
ANYWAY, LONG STORY SHORT...
...YOU'VE BEEN CLEARED OF ALL SUSPICION.
I GUESS IT'S YOUR LUCKY DAY.
GLAD TO SEE YOU'RE AS ARROGANT AS EVER.
THERE'S STILL A LOT WE DON'T KNOW ABOUT WHAT HAPPENED.
OFFICIALLY, EVERYTHING'S BEEN SQUARED AWAY.
BUT MY SISTER'S PUTTING TOGETHER A SPECIAL UNIT TO INVESTIGATE FURTHER...
...AND I PLAN ON HELPING THEM.

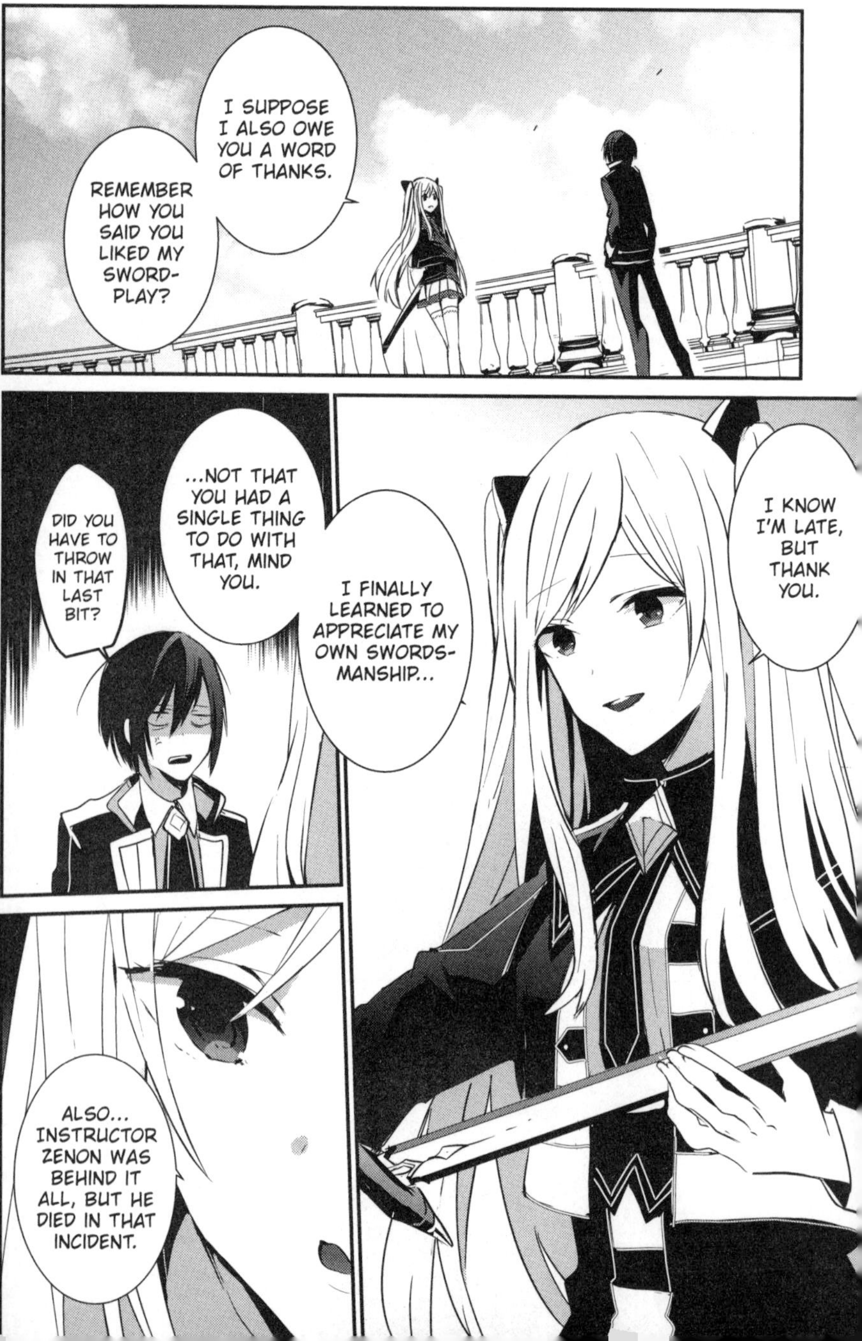
I SUPPOSE I ALSO OWE YOU A WORD OF THANKS.
REMEMBER HOW YOU SAID YOU LIKED MY SWORD-PLAY?
I KNOW I'M LATE, BUT THANK YOU.
I FINALLY LEARNED TO APPRECIATE MY OWN SWORDS-MANSHIP...
...NOT THAT YOU HAD A SINGLE THING TO DO WITH THAT, MIND YOU.
DID YOU HAVE TO THROW IN THAT LAST BIT?
ALSO... INSTRUCTOR ZENON WAS BEHIND IT ALL, BUT HE DIED IN THAT INCIDENT.

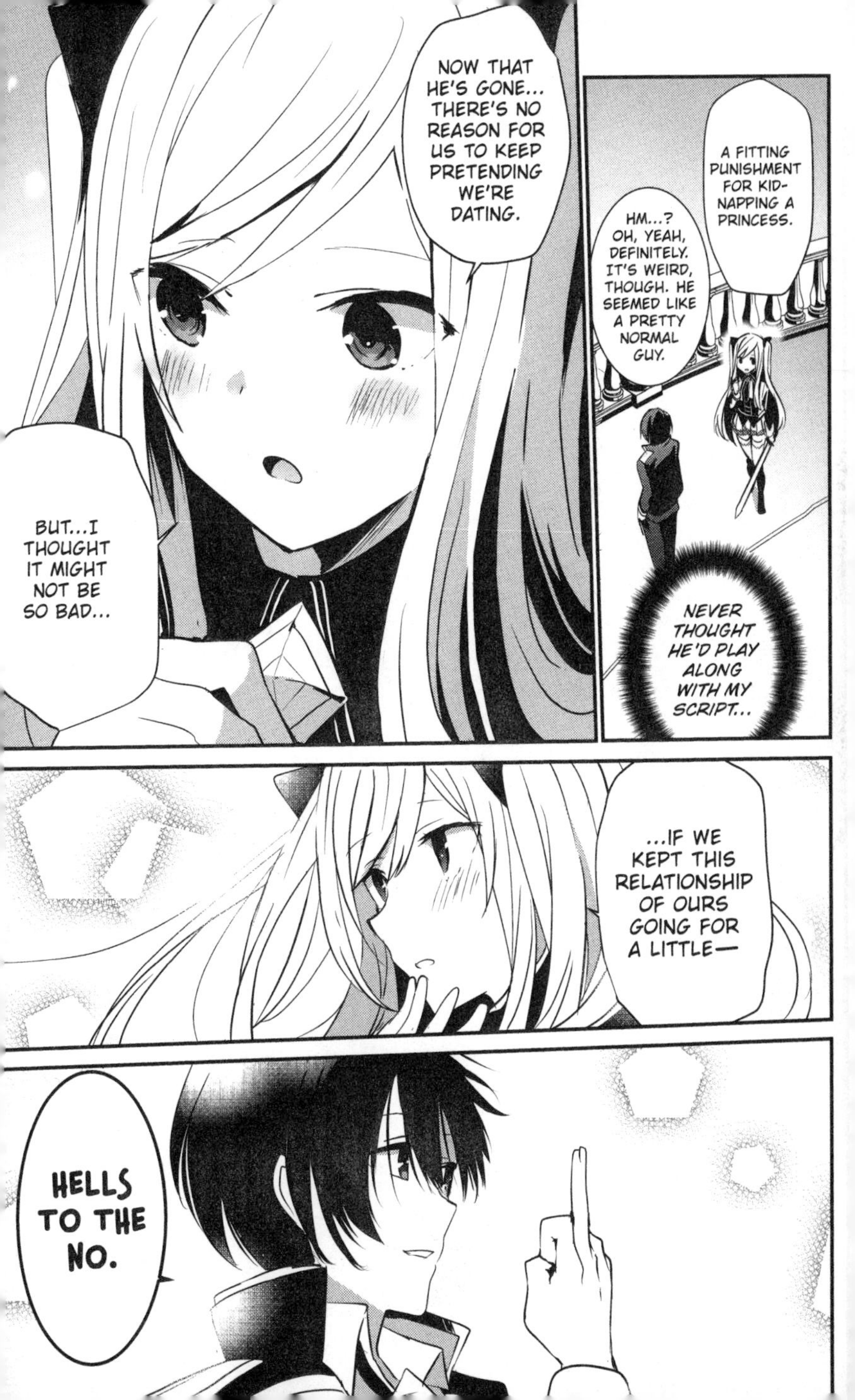
A FITTING PUNISHMENT FOR KID-NAPPING A PRINCESS.
HM...? OH, YEAH, DEFINITELY. IT'S WEIRD, THOUGH. HE SEEMED LIKE A PRETTY NORMAL GUY.
NEVER THOUGHT HE'D PLAY ALONG WITH MY SCRIPT...
NOW THAT HE'S GONE... THERE'S NO REASON FOR US TO KEEP PRETENDING WE'RE DATING.
BUT...I THOUGHT IT MIGHT NOT BE SO BAD...
...IF WE KEPT THIS RELATIONSHIP OF OURS GOING FOR A LITTLE—
HELLS TO THE NO.

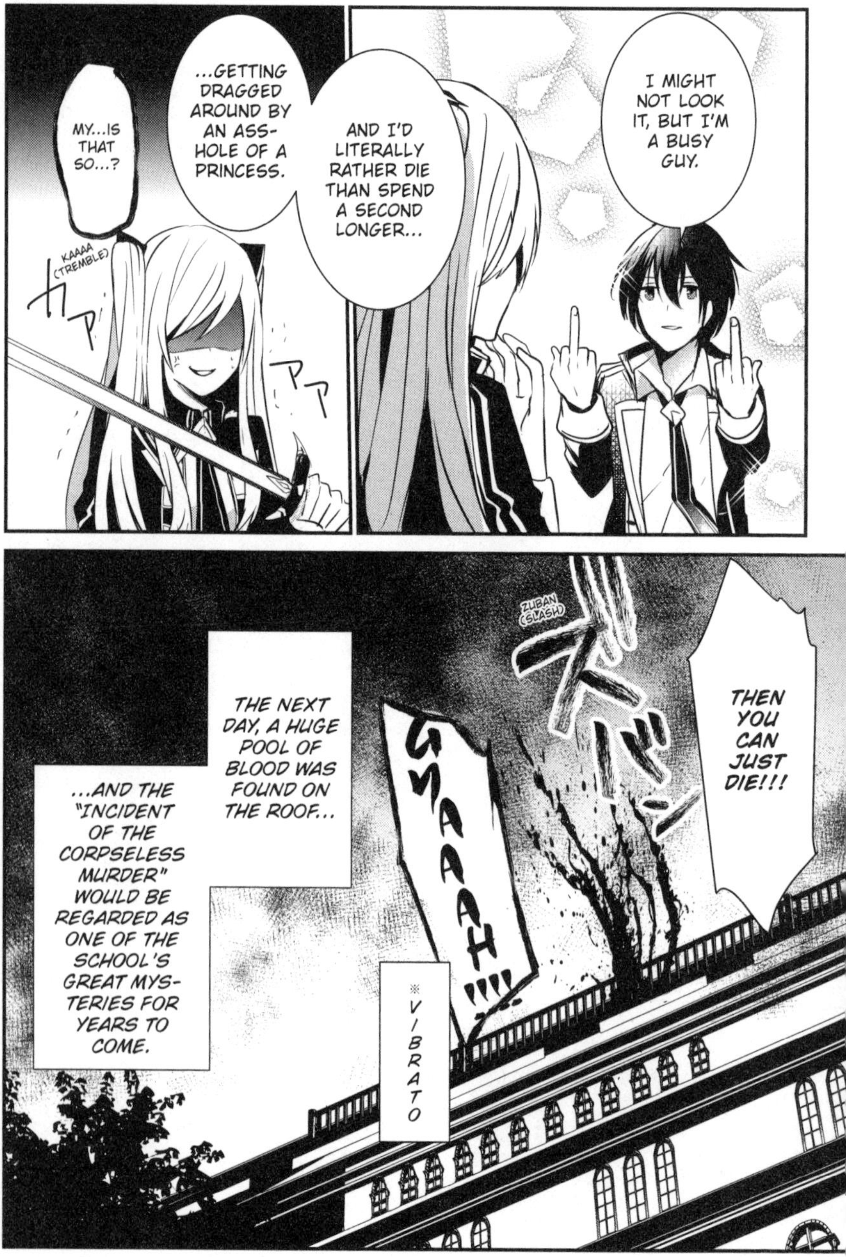
I MIGHT NOT LOOK IT, BUT I'M A BUSY GUY.
AND I'D LITERALLY RATHER DIE THAN SPEND A SECOND LONGER...
...GETTING DRAGGED AROUND BY AN ASS-HOLE OF A PRINCESS.
MY...IS THAT SO...?
KAAAA (TREMBLE)
THEN YOU CAN JUST DIE!!!
ZUBAN (SLASH)
GYAAAAH!!!!
※VIBRATO
THE NEXT DAY, A HUGE POOL OF BLOOD WAS FOUND ON THE ROOF...
...AND THE "INCIDENT OF THE CORPSELESS MURDER" WOULD BE REGARDED AS ONE OF THE SCHOOL'S GREAT MYS-TERIES FOR YEARS TO COME.

end

Episode.7

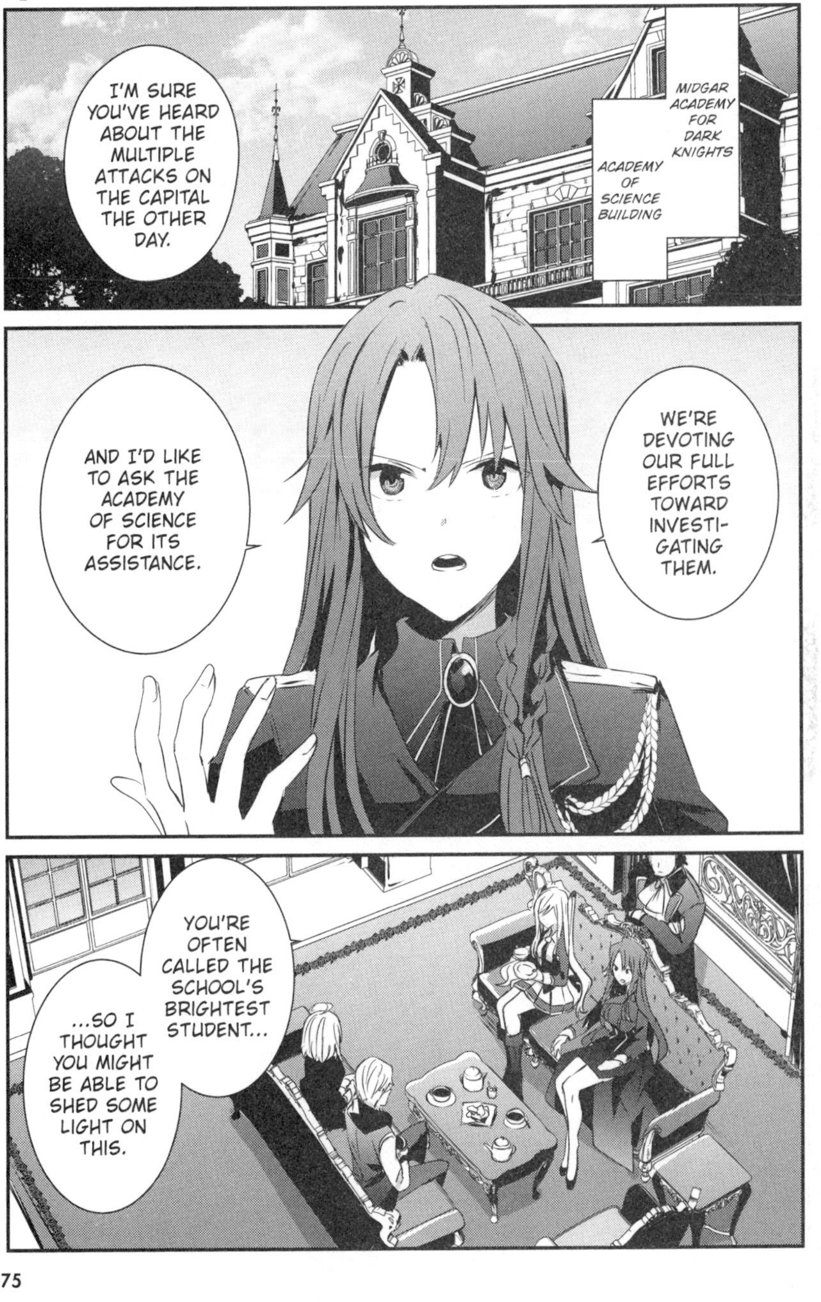
MIDGAR ACADEMY FOR DARK KNIGHTS
ACADEMY OF SCIENCE BUILDING
I'M SURE YOU'VE HEARD ABOUT THE MULTIPLE ATTACKS ON THE CAPITAL THE OTHER DAY.
WE'RE DEVOTING OUR FULL EFFORTS TOWARD INVESTI-GATING THEM.
AND I'D LIKE TO ASK THE ACADEMY OF SCIENCE FOR ITS ASSISTANCE.
YOU'RE OFTEN CALLED THE SCHOOL'S BRIGHTEST STUDENT...
...SO I THOUGHT YOU MIGHT BE ABLE TO SHED SOME LIGHT ON THIS.

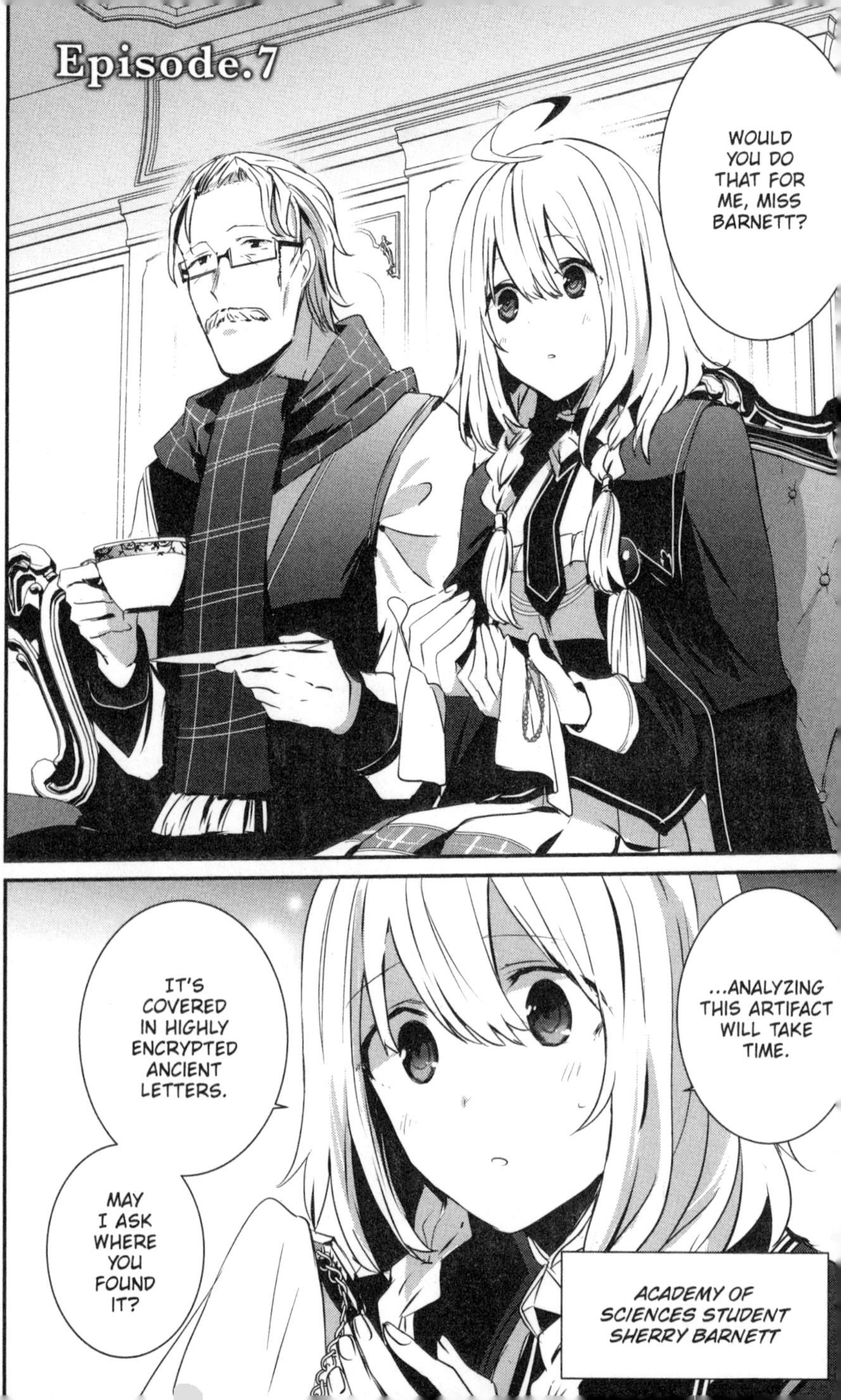
Episode.7
WOULD YOU DO THAT FOR ME, MISS BARNETT?
...ANALYZING THIS ARTIFACT WILL TAKE TIME.
IT'S COVERED IN HIGHLY ENCRYPTED ANCIENT LETTERS.
MAY I ASK WHERE YOU FOUND IT?
ACADEMY OF SCIENCES STUDENT SHERRY BARNETT

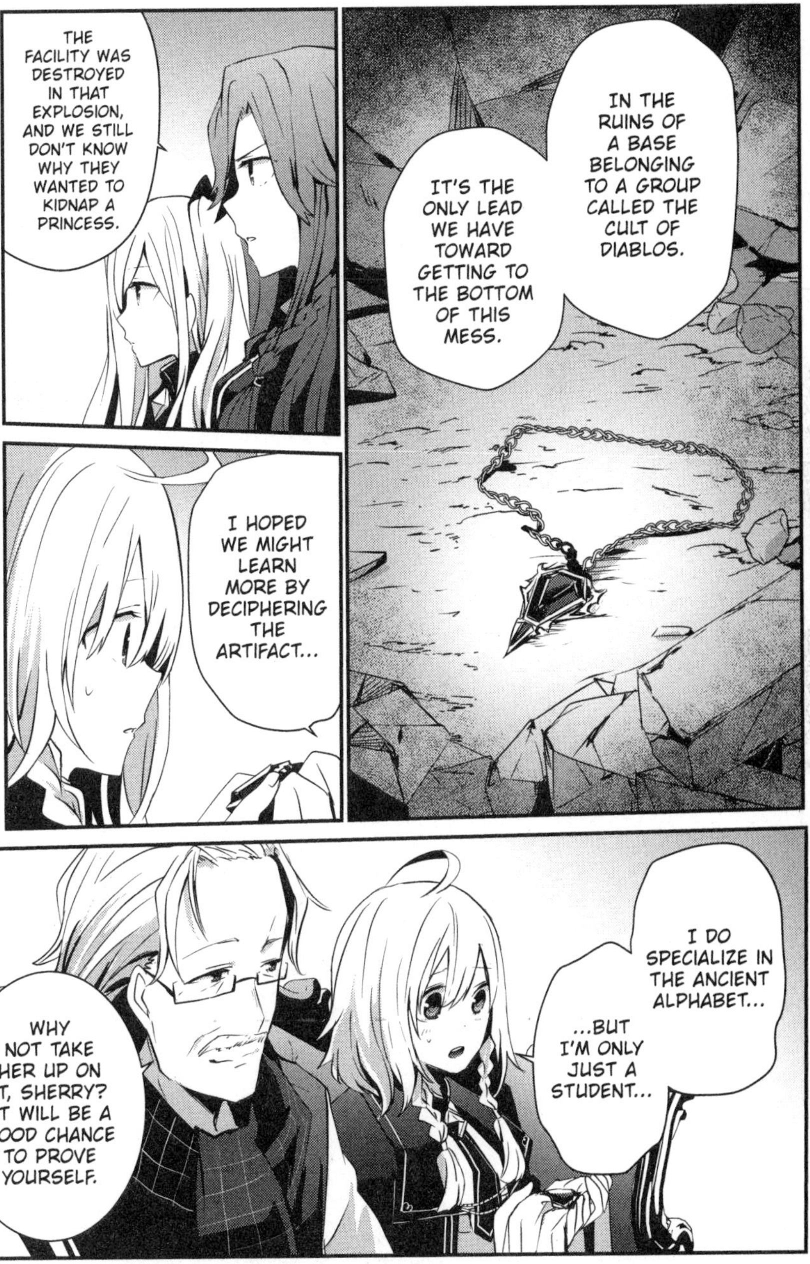
IN THE RUINS OF A BASE BELONGING TO A GROUP CALLED THE CULT OF DIABLOS.
IT'S THE ONLY LEAD WE HAVE TOWARD GETTING TO THE BOTTOM OF THIS MESS.
THE FACILITY WAS DESTROYED IN THAT EXPLOSION, AND WE STILL DON'T KNOW WHY THEY WANTED TO KIDNAP A PRINCESS.
I HOPED WE MIGHT LEARN MORE BY DECIPHERING THE ARTIFACT...
I DO SPECIALIZE IN THE ANCIENT ALPHABET...
...BUT I'M ONLY JUST A STUDENT...
WHY NOT TAKE HER UP ON IT, SHERRY? IT WILL BE A GOOD CHANCE TO PROVE YOURSELF.

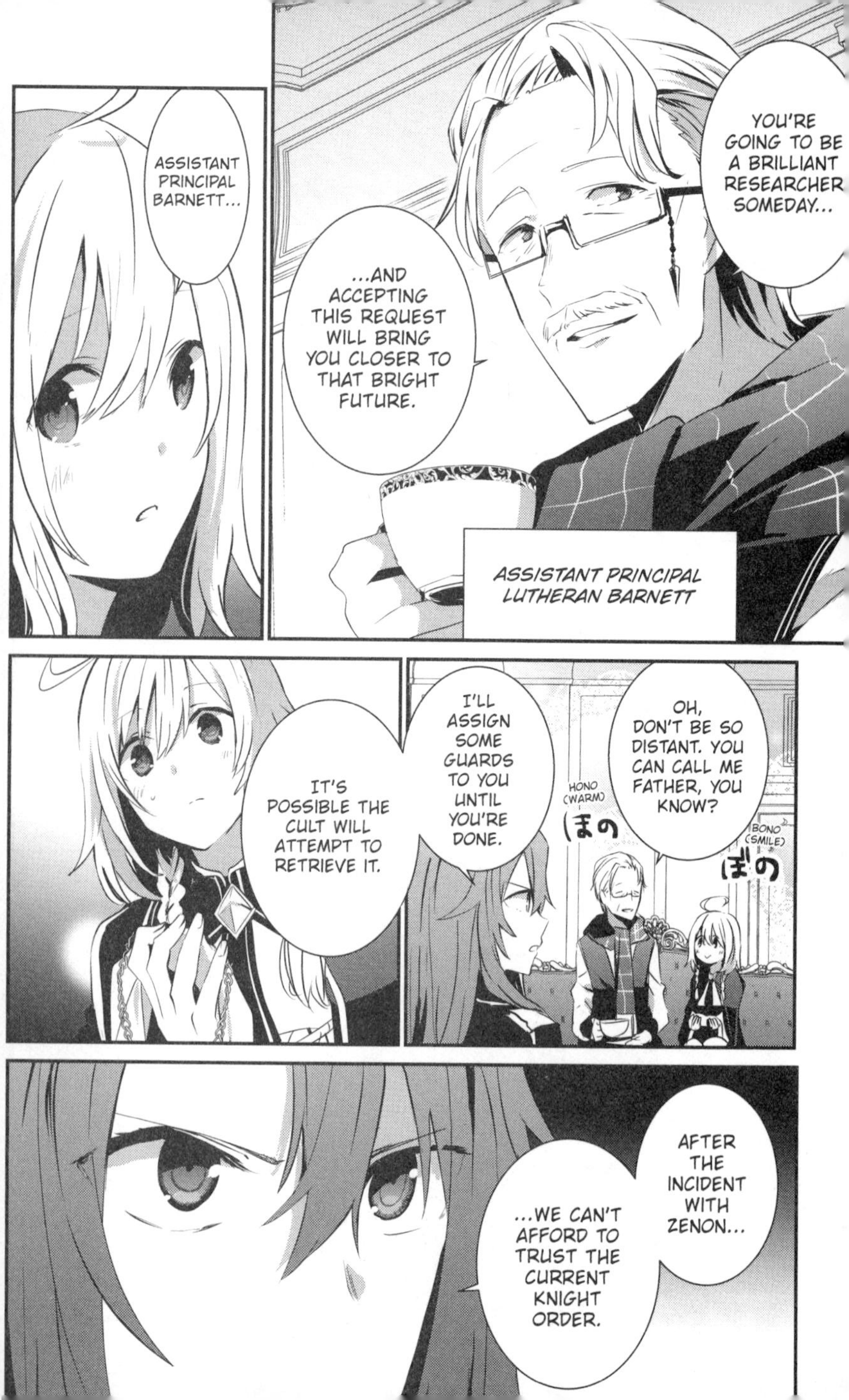
YOU'RE GOING TO BE A BRILLIANT RESEARCHER SOMEDAY...
...AND ACCEPTING THIS REQUEST WILL BRING YOU CLOSER TO THAT BRIGHT FUTURE.
ASSISTANT PRINCIPAL LUTHERAN BARNETT
ASSISTANT PRINCIPAL BARNETT...
OH, DON'T BE SO DISTANT. YOU CAN CALL ME FATHER, YOU KNOW?
ほの HONO (WARM)
ぼの BONO (SMILE)
I'LL ASSIGN SOME GUARDS TO YOU UNTIL YOU'RE DONE.
IT'S POSSIBLE THE CULT WILL ATTEMPT TO RETRIEVE IT.
AFTER THE INCIDENT WITH ZENON...
...WE CAN'T AFFORD TO TRUST THE CURRENT KNIGHT ORDER.

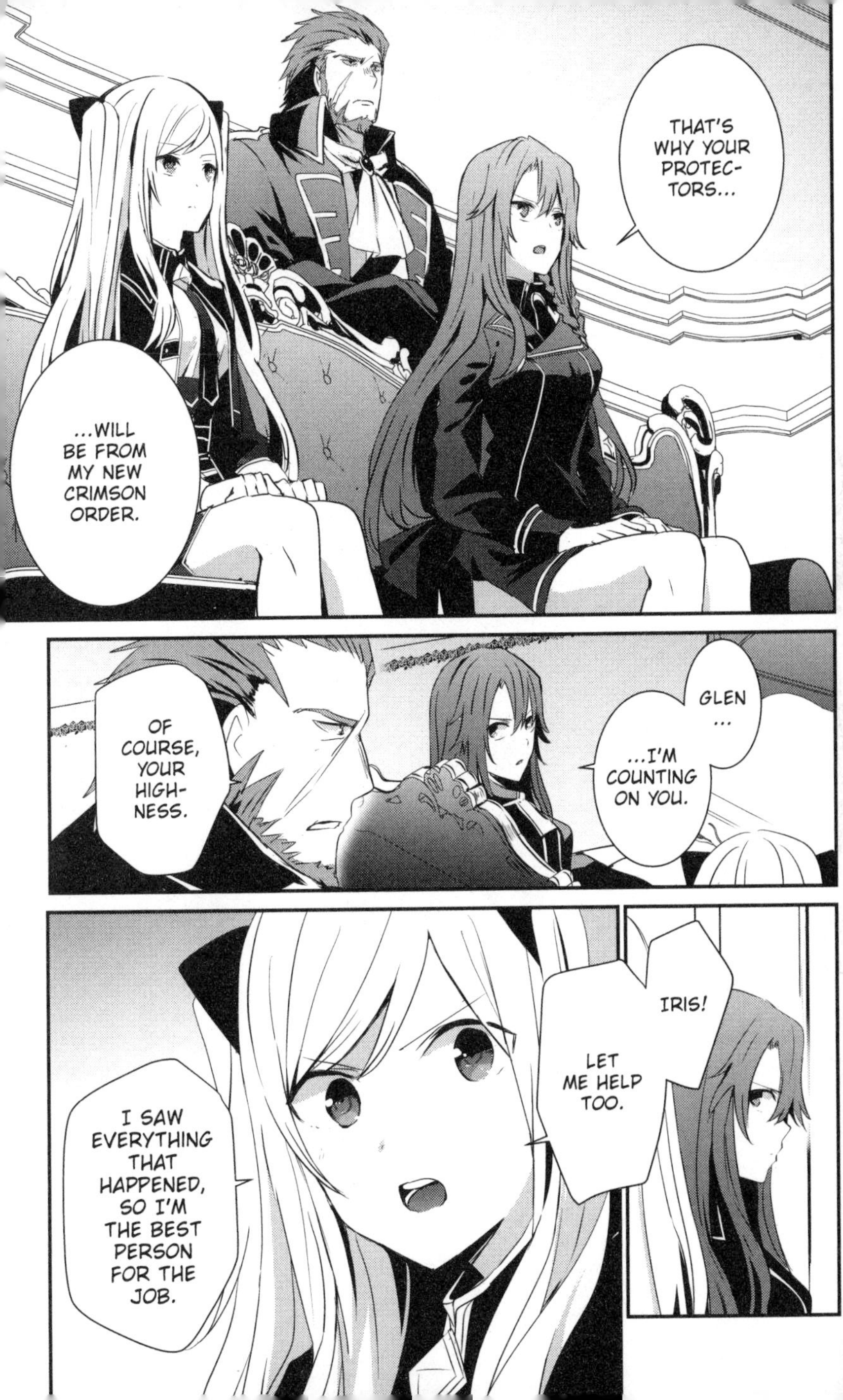
THAT'S WHY YOUR PROTECTORS...
...WILL BE FROM MY NEW CRIMSON ORDER.
GLEN...
...I'M COUNTING ON YOU.
OF COURSE, YOUR HIGHNESS.
IRIS!
LET ME HELP TOO.
I SAW EVERYTHING THAT HAPPENED, SO I'M THE BEST PERSON FOR THE JOB.

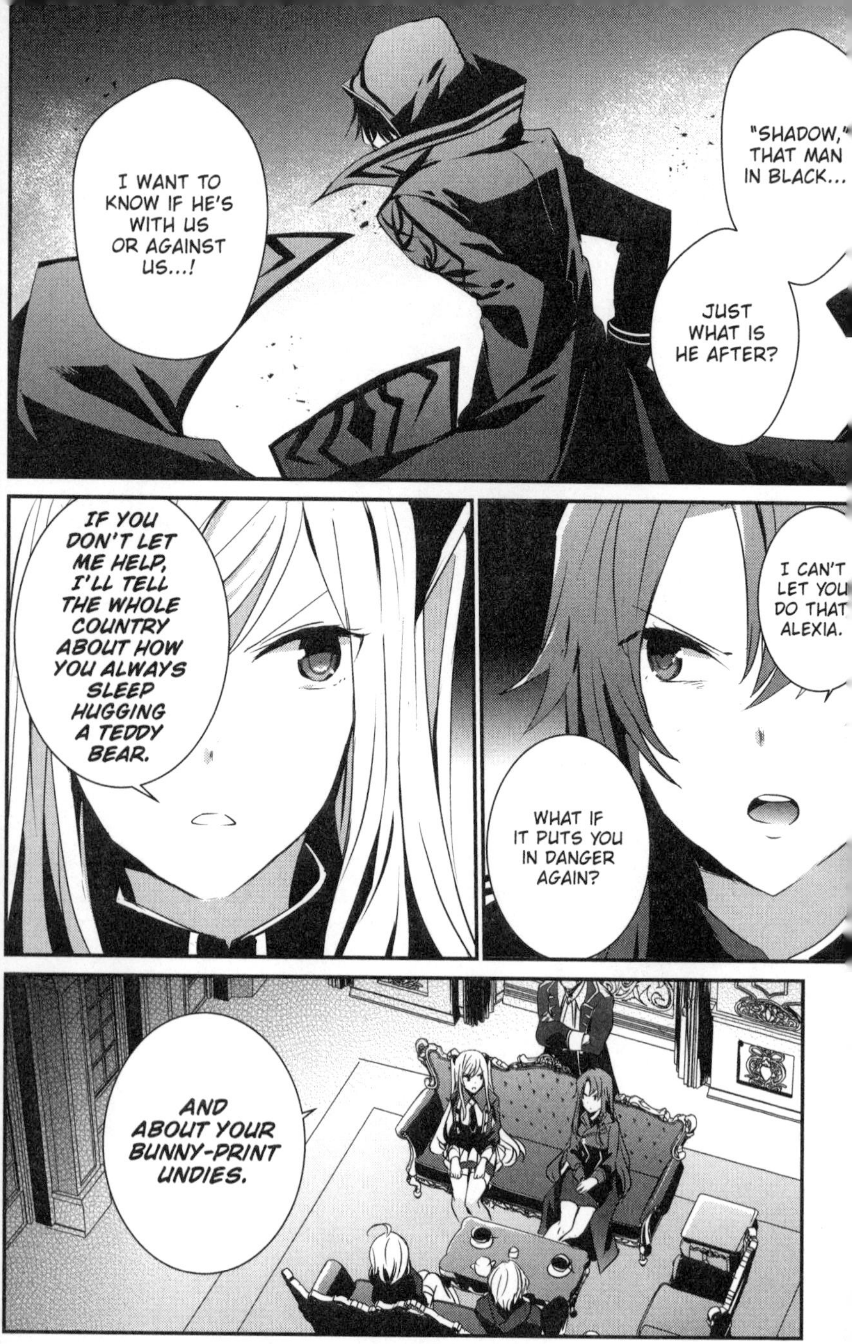
"SHADOW," THAT MAN IN BLACK...
JUST WHAT IS HE AFTER?
I WANT TO KNOW IF HE'S WITH US OR AGAINST US...!
I CAN'T LET YOU DO THAT ALEXIA.
WHAT IF IT PUTS YOU IN DANGER AGAIN?
IF YOU DON'T LET ME HELP, I'LL TELL THE WHOLE COUNTRY ABOUT HOW YOU ALWAYS SLEEP HUGGING A TEDDY BEAR.
AND ABOUT YOUR BUNNY-PRINT UNDIES.

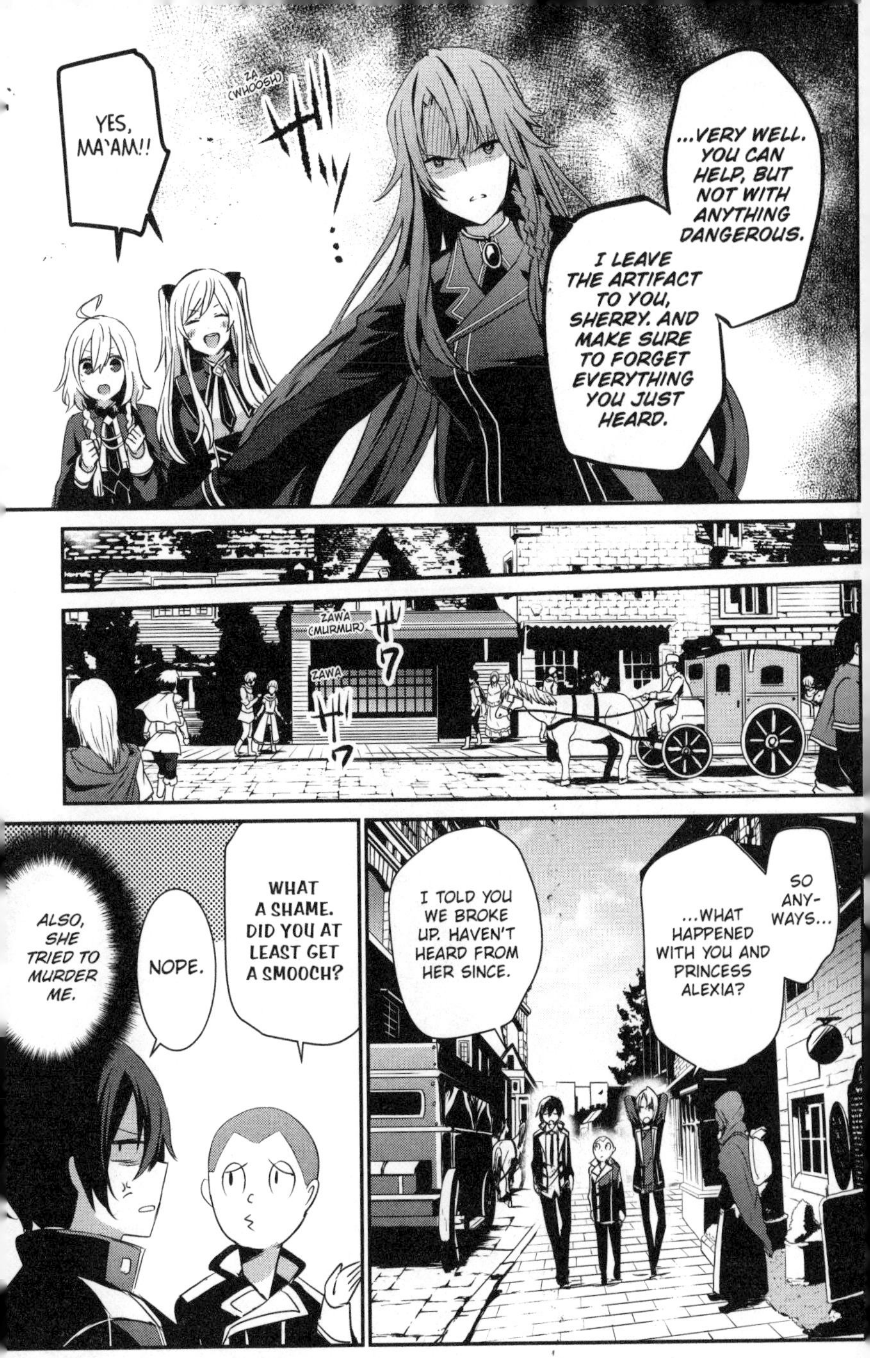
...VERY WELL. YOU CAN HELP, BUT NOT WITH ANYTHING DANGEROUS.
I LEAVE THE ARTIFACT TO YOU, SHERRY. AND MAKE SURE TO FORGET EVERYTHING YOU JUST HEARD.
ZA (WHOOSH)
YES, MA'AM!!
ZAWA (MURMUR)
ZAWA
SO ANYWAYS...
...WHAT HAPPENED WITH YOU AND PRINCESS ALEXIA?
I TOLD YOU WE BROKE UP. HAVEN'T HEARD FROM HER SINCE.
WHAT A SHAME. DID YOU AT LEAST GET A SMOOCH?
NOPE.
ALSO, SHE TRIED TO MURDER ME.

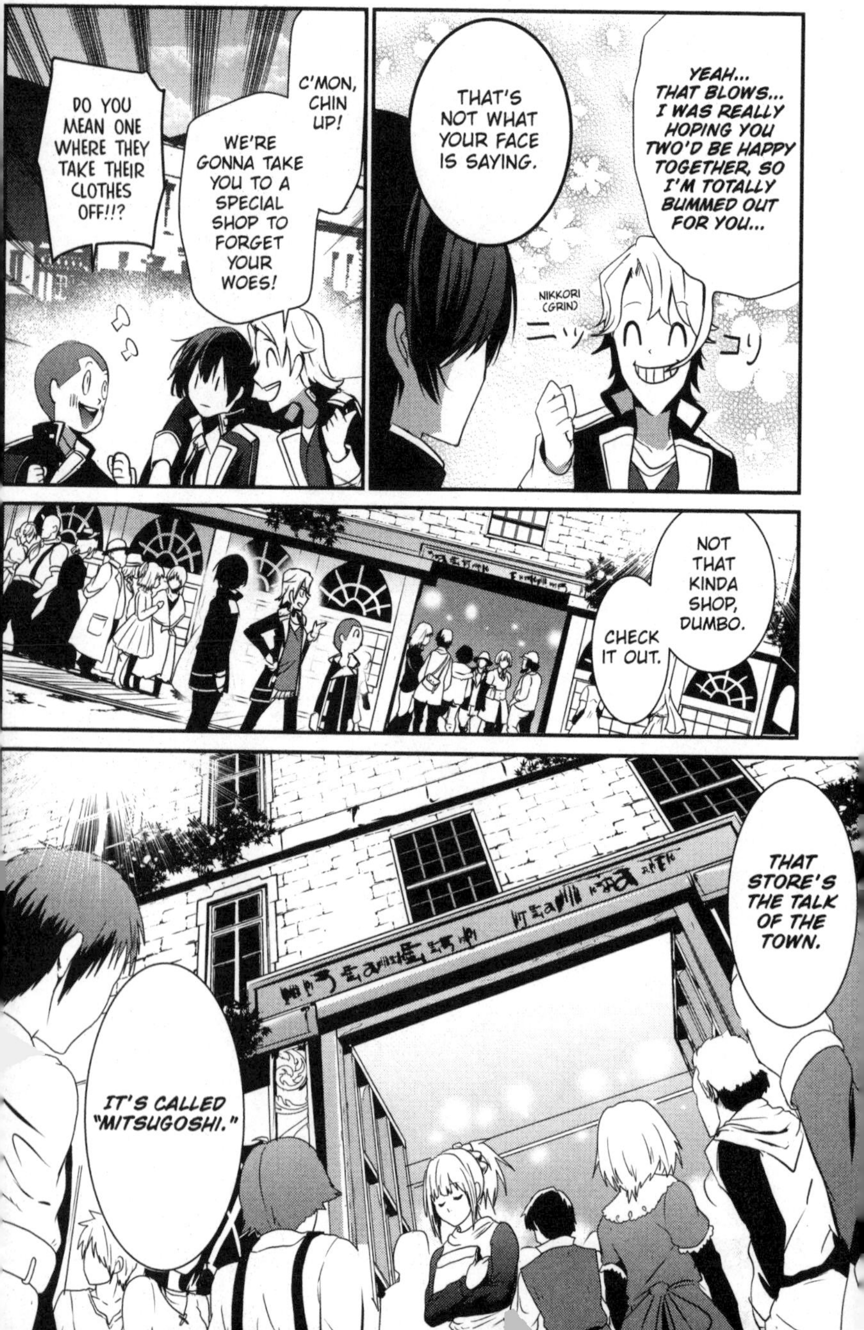
YEAH... THAT BLOWS... I WAS REALLY HOPING YOU TWO'D BE HAPPY TOGETHER, SO I'M TOTALLY BUMMED OUT FOR YOU...
THAT'S NOT WHAT YOUR FACE IS SAYING.
NIKKORI (GRIN)
C'MON, CHIN UP!
WE'RE GONNA TAKE YOU TO A SPECIAL SHOP TO FORGET YOUR WOES!
DO YOU MEAN ONE WHERE THEY TAKE THEIR CLOTHES OFF!!?
NOT THAT KINDA SHOP, DUMBO.
CHECK IT OUT.
THAT STORE'S THE TALK OF THE TOWN.
IT'S CALLED "MITSUGOSHI."

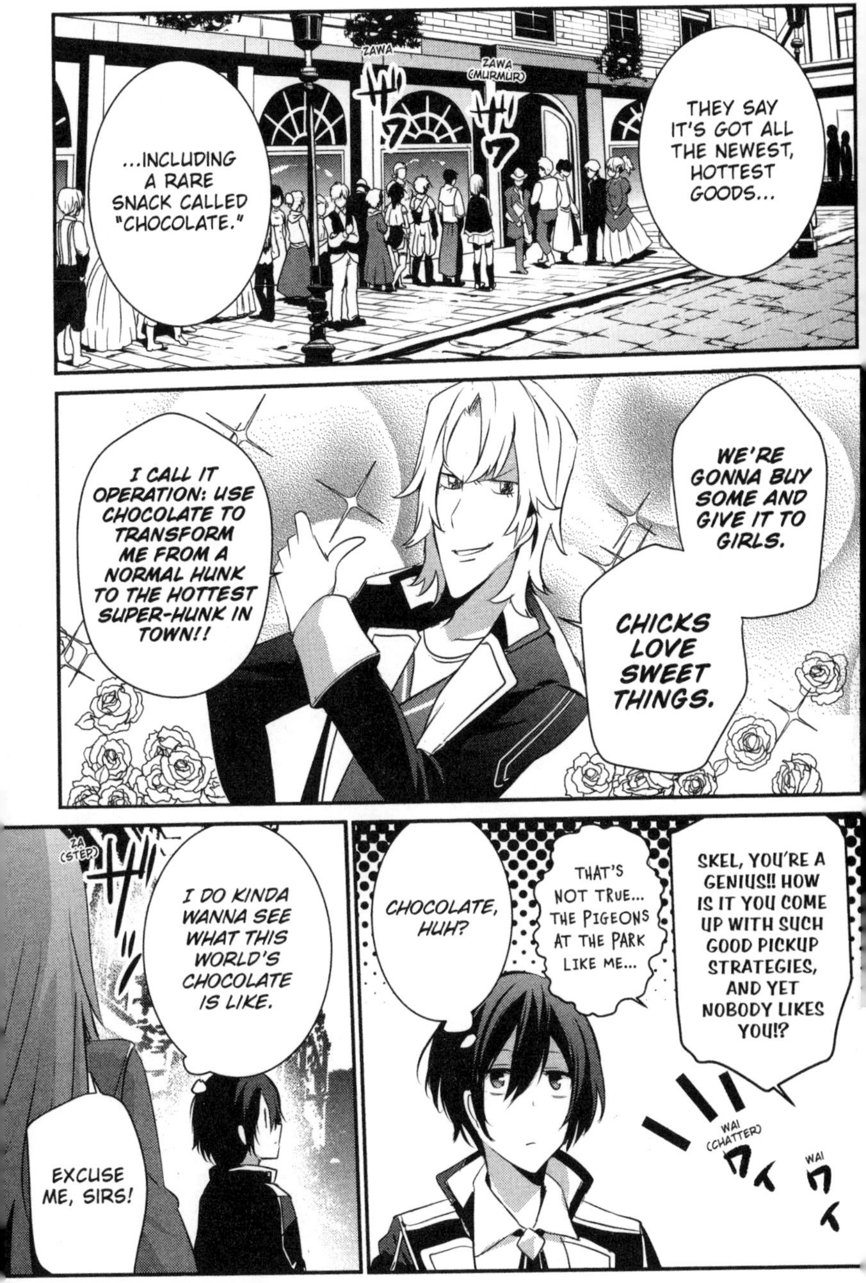
THEY SAY IT'S GOT ALL THE NEWEST, HOTTEST GOODS...
ZAWA (MURMUR)
ZAWA
...INCLUDING A RARE SNACK CALLED "CHOCOLATE."
WE'RE GONNA BUY SOME AND GIVE IT TO GIRLS.
CHICKS LOVE SWEET THINGS.
I CALL IT OPERATION: USE CHOCOLATE TO TRANSFORM ME FROM A NORMAL HUNK TO THE HOTTEST SUPER-HUNK IN TOWN!!
SKEL, YOU'RE A GENIUS!! HOW IS IT YOU COME UP WITH SUCH GOOD PICKUP STRATEGIES, AND YET NOBODY LIKES YOU!?
THAT'S NOT TRUE... THE PIGEONS AT THE PARK LIKE ME...
CHOCOLATE, HUH?
WAI (CHATTER)
WAI
ZA (STEP)
I DO KINDA WANNA SEE WHAT THIS WORLD'S CHOCOLATE IS LIKE.
EXCUSE ME, SIRS!

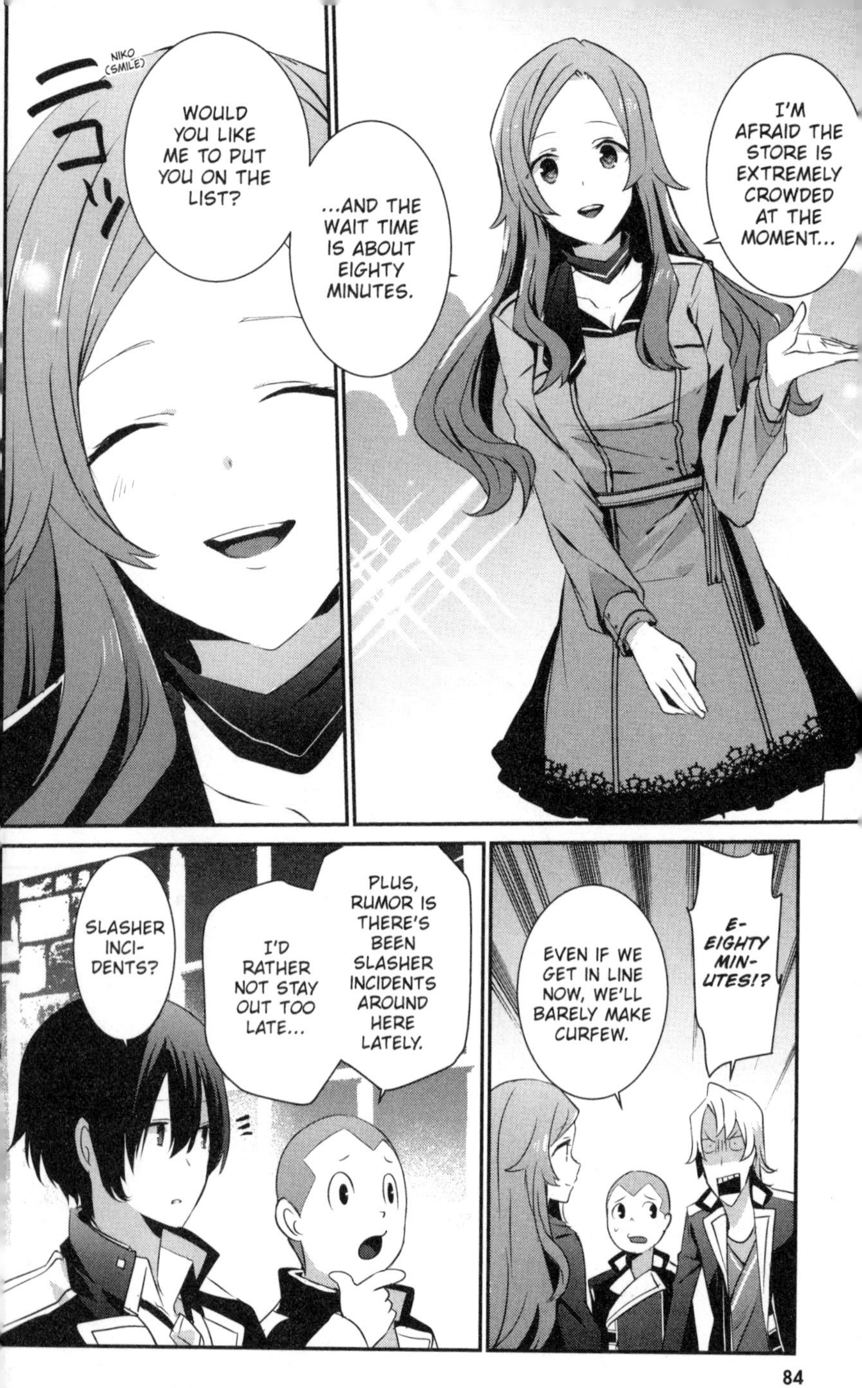
I'M AFRAID THE STORE IS EXTREMELY CROWDED AT THE MOMENT...
...AND THE WAIT TIME IS ABOUT EIGHTY MINUTES.
NIKO (SMILE)
WOULD YOU LIKE ME TO PUT YOU ON THE LIST?
E-EIGHTY MIN-UTES!?
EVEN IF WE GET IN LINE NOW, WE'LL BARELY MAKE CURFEW.
I'D RATHER NOT STAY OUT TOO LATE...
PLUS, RUMOR IS THERE'S BEEN SLASHER INCIDENTS AROUND HERE LATELY.
SLASHER INCI-DENTS?

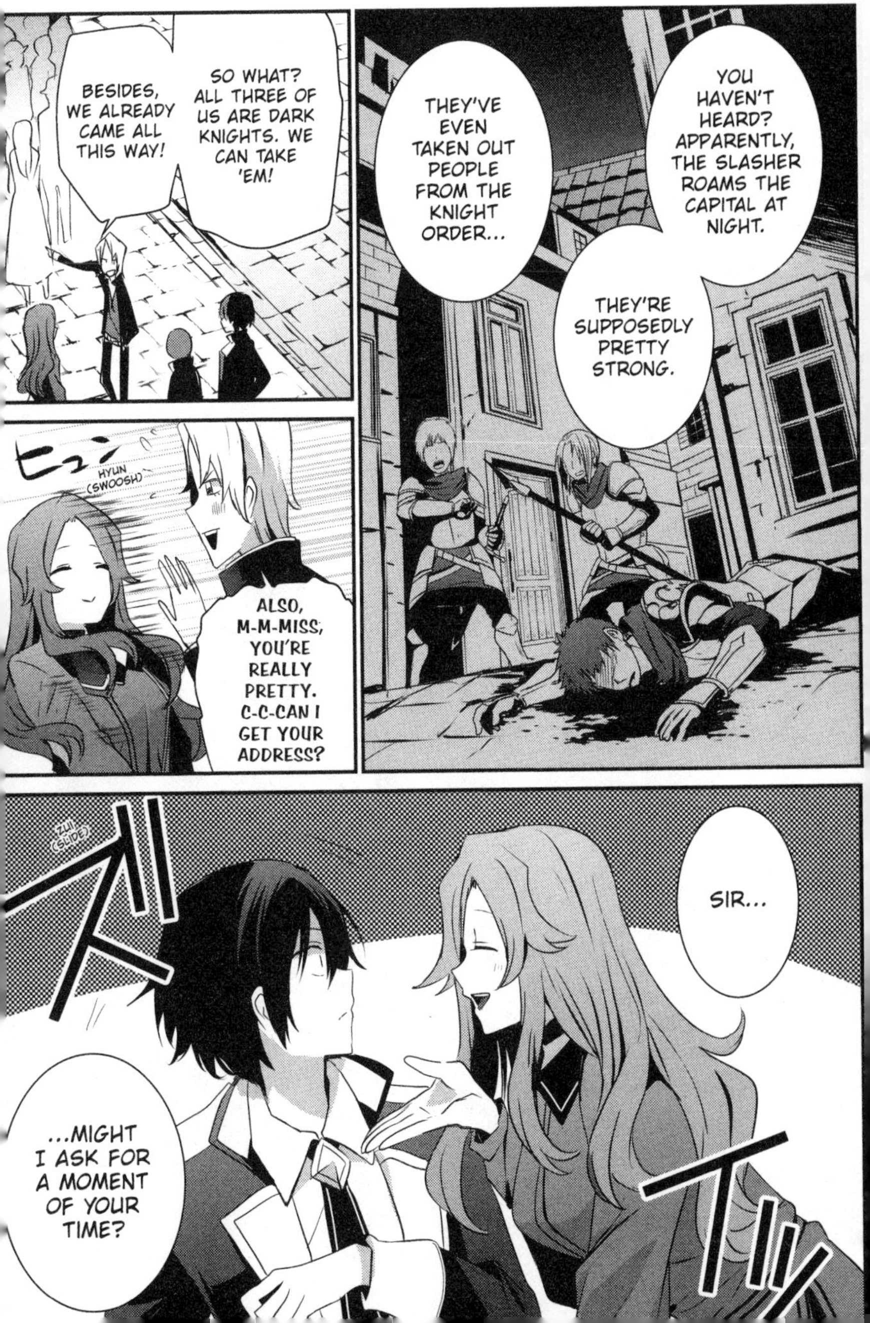
YOU HAVEN'T HEARD? APPARENTLY, THE SLASHER ROAMS THE CAPITAL AT NIGHT.
THEY'VE EVEN TAKEN OUT PEOPLE FROM THE KNIGHT ORDER...
THEY'RE SUPPOSEDLY PRETTY STRONG.
SO WHAT? ALL THREE OF US ARE DARK KNIGHTS. WE CAN TAKE 'EM!
BESIDES, WE ALREADY CAME ALL THIS WAY!
ヒュン
HYUN (SWOOSH)
ALSO, M-M-MISS, YOU'RE REALLY PRETTY. C-C-CAN I GET YOUR ADDRESS?
ZUI (SLIDE)
SIR...
...MIGHT I ASK FOR A MOMENT OF YOUR TIME?

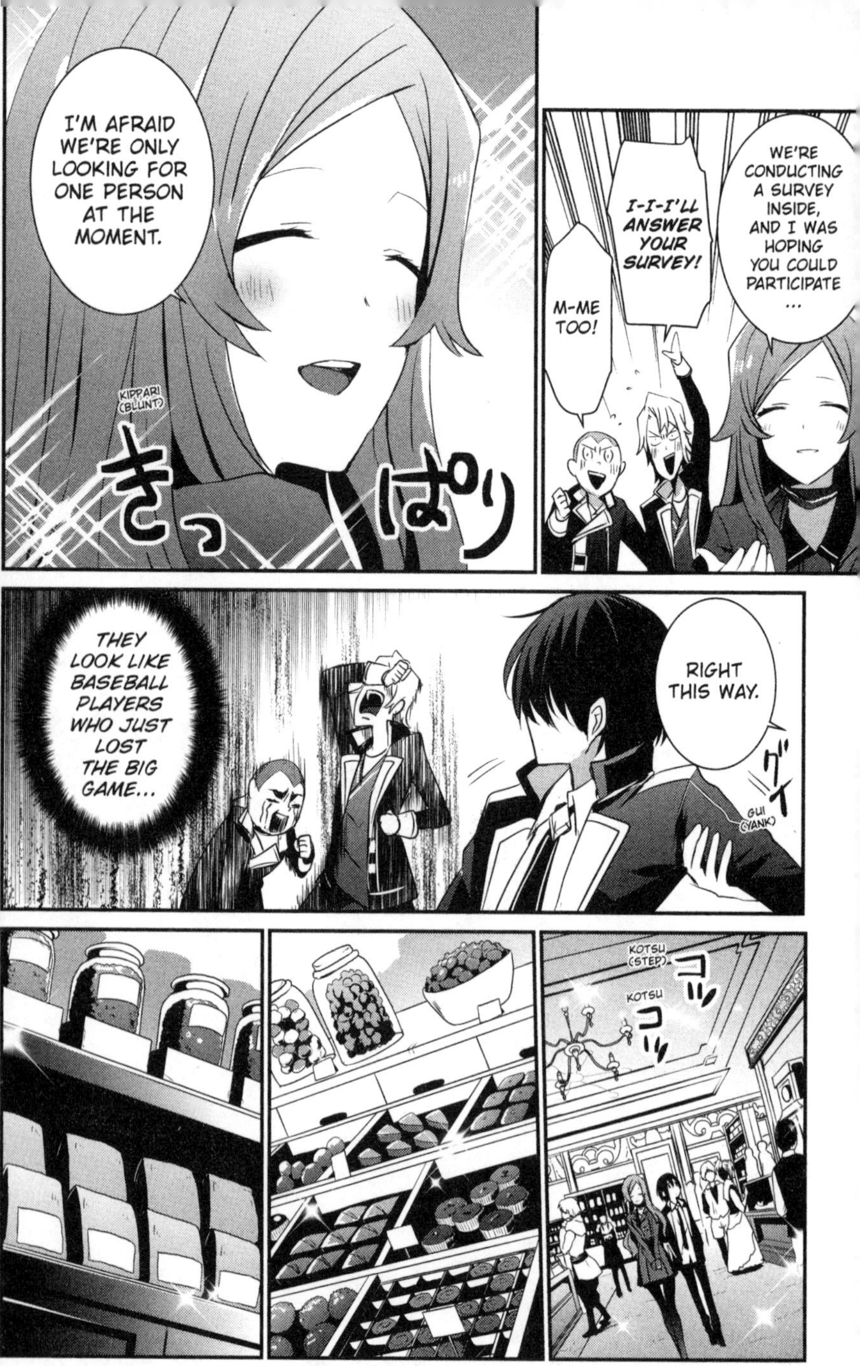
WE'RE CONDUCTING A SURVEY INSIDE, AND I WAS HOPING YOU COULD PARTICIPATE ...
I-I-I'LL ANSWER YOUR SURVEY!
M-ME TOO!
I'M AFRAID WE'RE ONLY LOOKING FOR ONE PERSON AT THE MOMENT.
KIPPARI (BLUNT)
きっぱり
RIGHT THIS WAY.
グイ
GUI (YANK)
THEY LOOK LIKE BASEBALL PLAYERS WHO JUST LOST THE BIG GAME...
KOTSU (STEP)
コツ
KOTSU
コツ

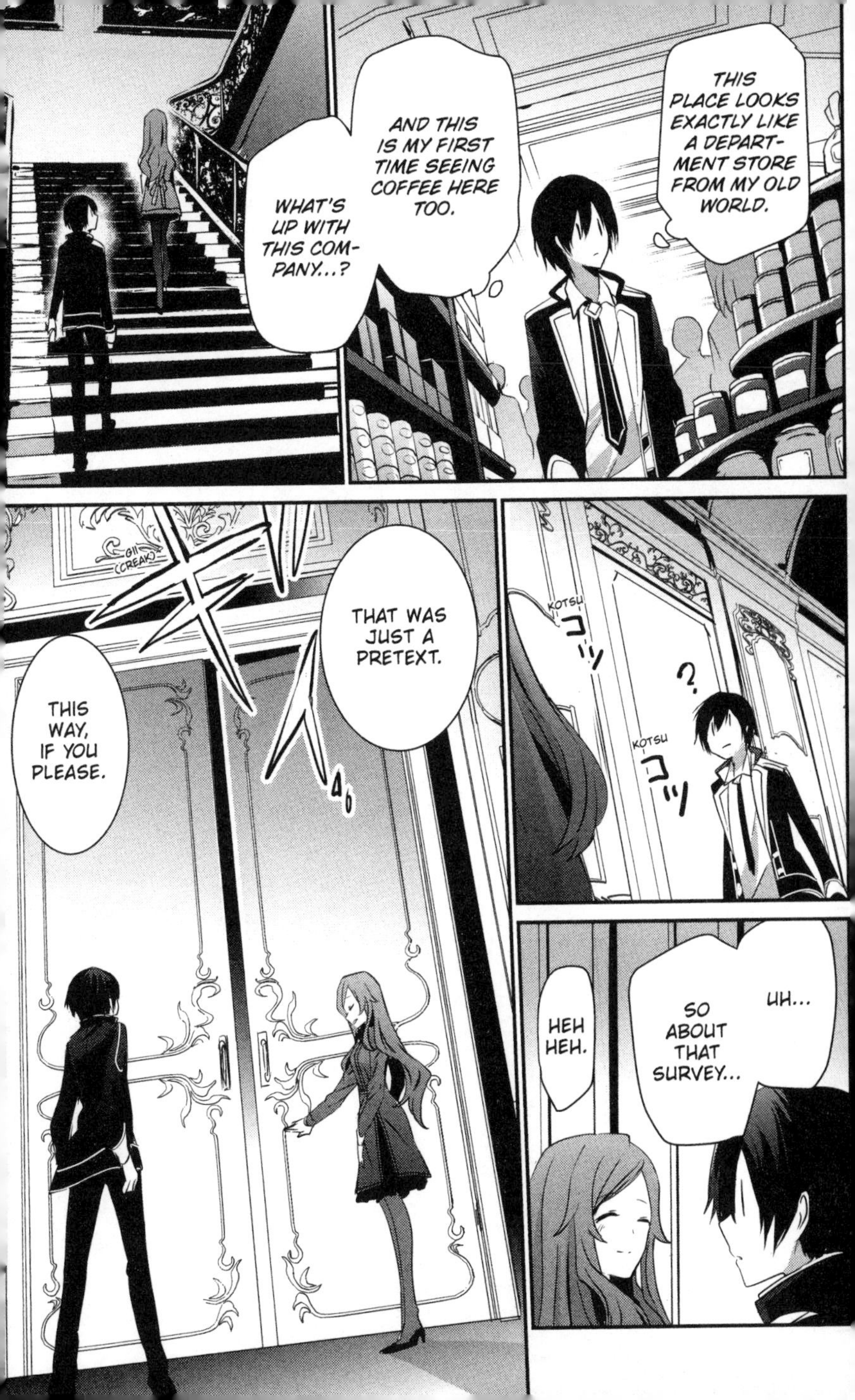
THIS PLACE LOOKS EXACTLY LIKE A DEPARTMENT STORE FROM MY OLD WORLD.
AND THIS IS MY FIRST TIME SEEING COFFEE HERE TOO.
WHAT'S UP WITH THIS COMPANY...?
KOTSU コッ
?
KOTSU コッ
UH...
SO ABOUT THAT SURVEY...
HEH HEH.
GII (CREAK)
THAT WAS JUST A PRETEXT.
THIS WAY, IF YOU PLEASE.

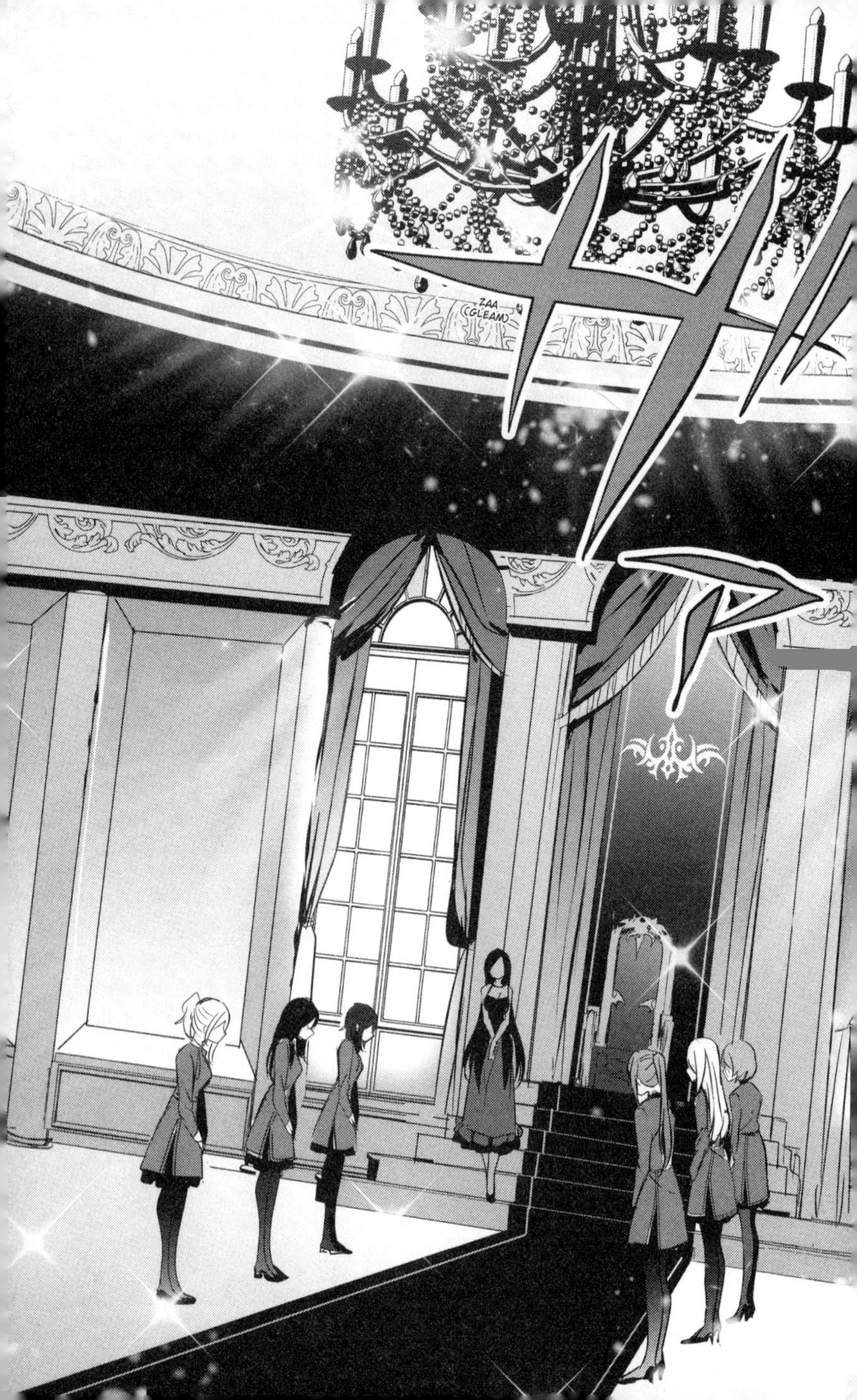
ZAA
(GLEAM)

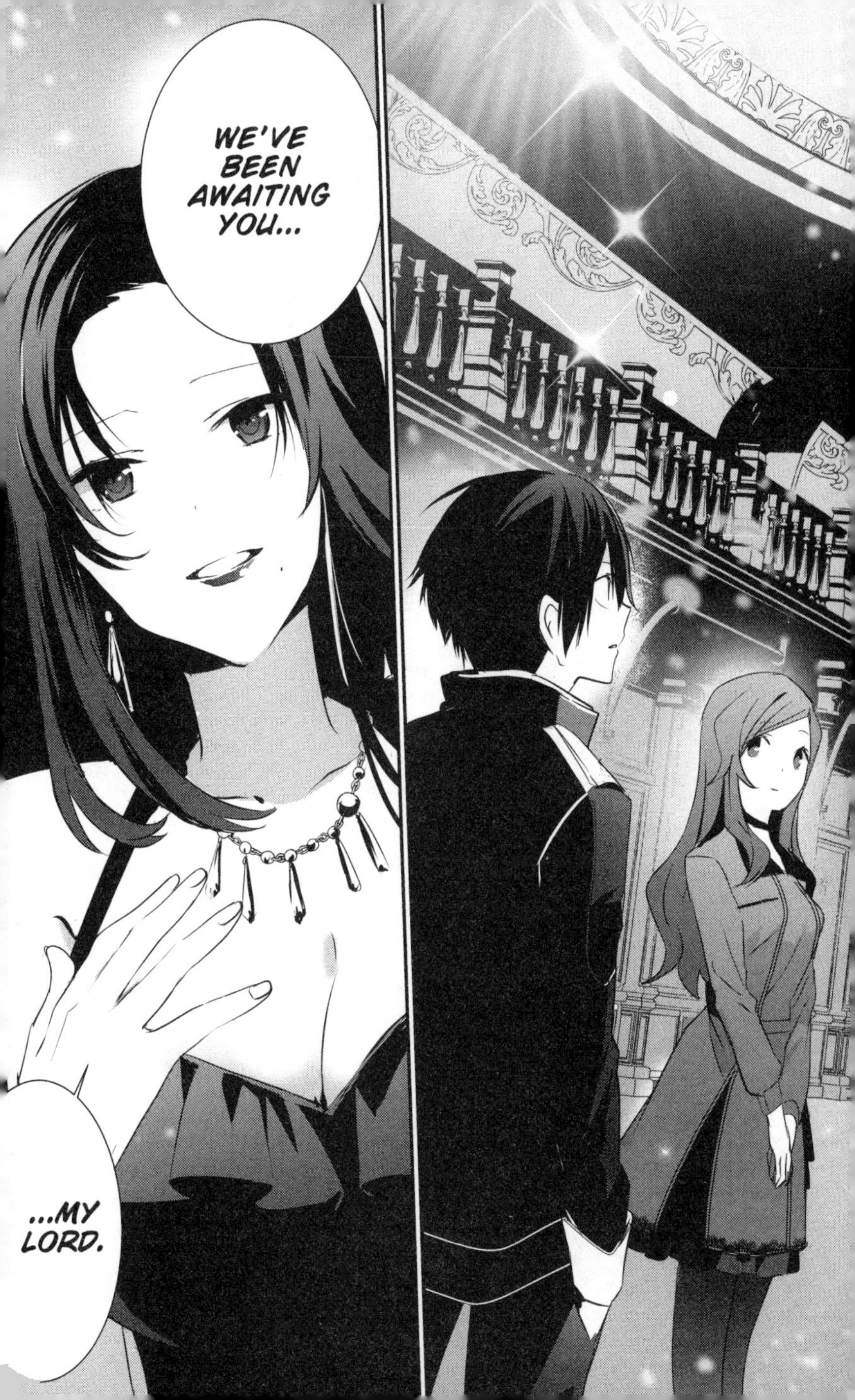
WE'VE BEEN AWAITING YOU...
...MY LORD.

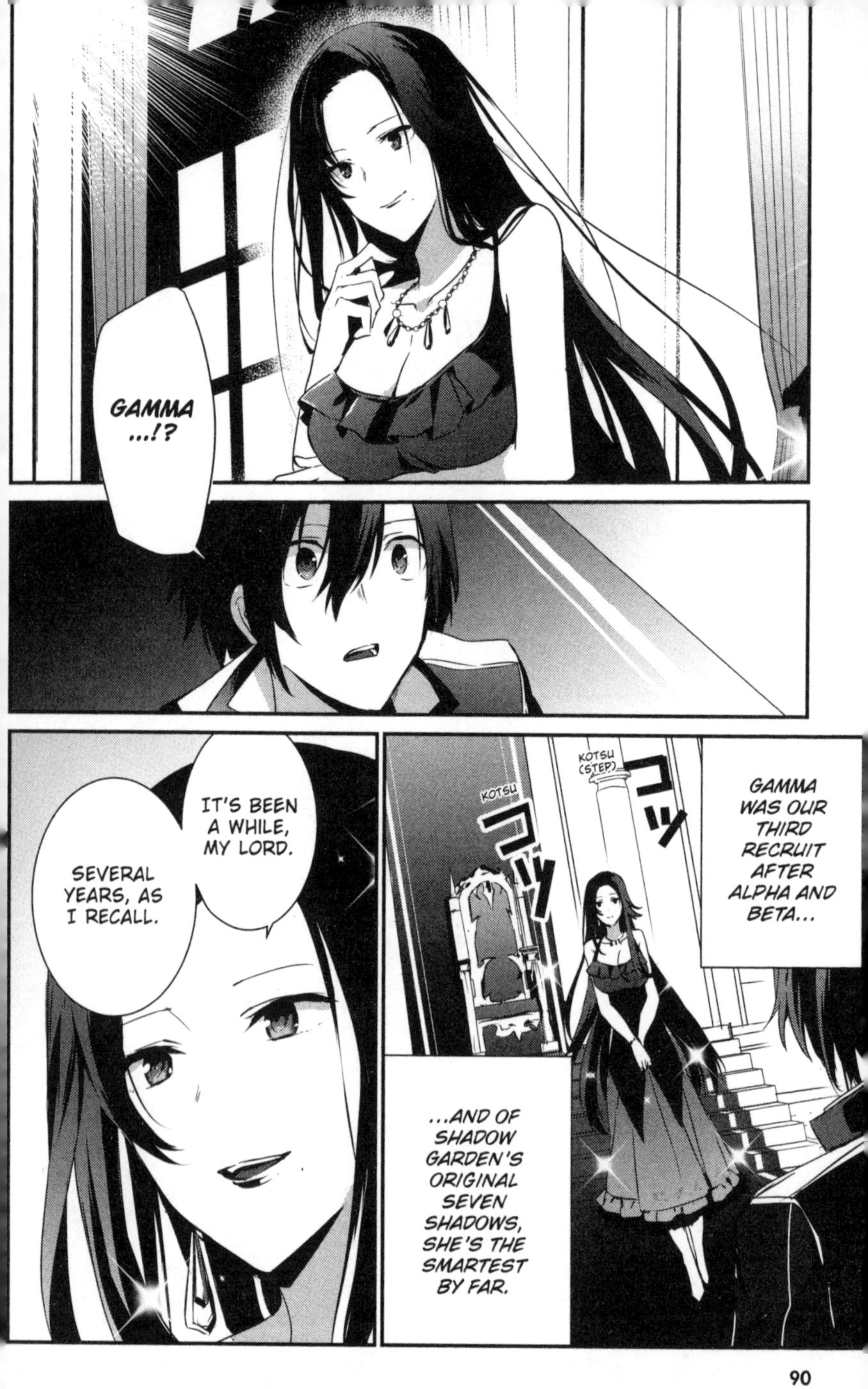
GAMMA ...!?
KOTSU (STEP)
KOTSU
GAMMA WAS OUR THIRD RECRUIT AFTER ALPHA AND BETA...
...AND OF SHADOW GARDEN'S ORIGINAL SEVEN SHADOWS, SHE'S THE SMARTEST BY FAR.
IT'S BEEN A WHILE, MY LORD.
SEVERAL YEARS, AS I RECALL.

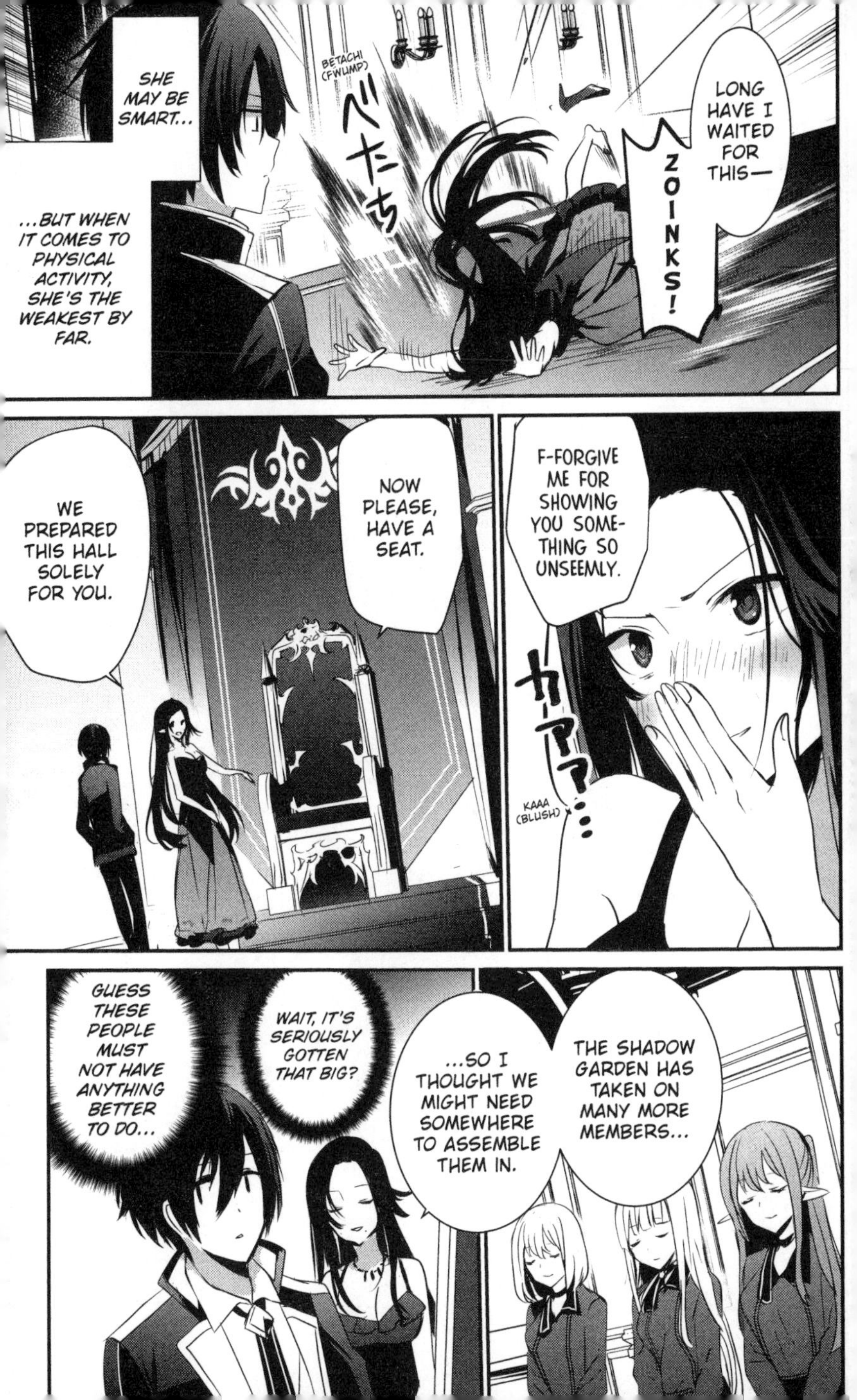
LONG HAVE I WAITED FOR THIS—
ZOINKS!
BETACHI (FWUMP)
SHE MAY BE SMART...
...BUT WHEN IT COMES TO PHYSICAL ACTIVITY, SHE'S THE WEAKEST BY FAR.
F-FORGIVE ME FOR SHOWING YOU SOME-THING SO UNSEEMLY.
KAAA (BLUSH)
NOW PLEASE, HAVE A SEAT.
WE PREPARED THIS HALL SOLELY FOR YOU.
THE SHADOW GARDEN HAS TAKEN ON MANY MORE MEMBERS...
...SO I THOUGHT WE MIGHT NEED SOMEWHERE TO ASSEMBLE THEM IN.
WAIT, IT'S SERIOUSLY GOTTEN THAT BIG?
GUESS THESE PEOPLE MUST NOT HAVE ANYTHING BETTER TO DO...

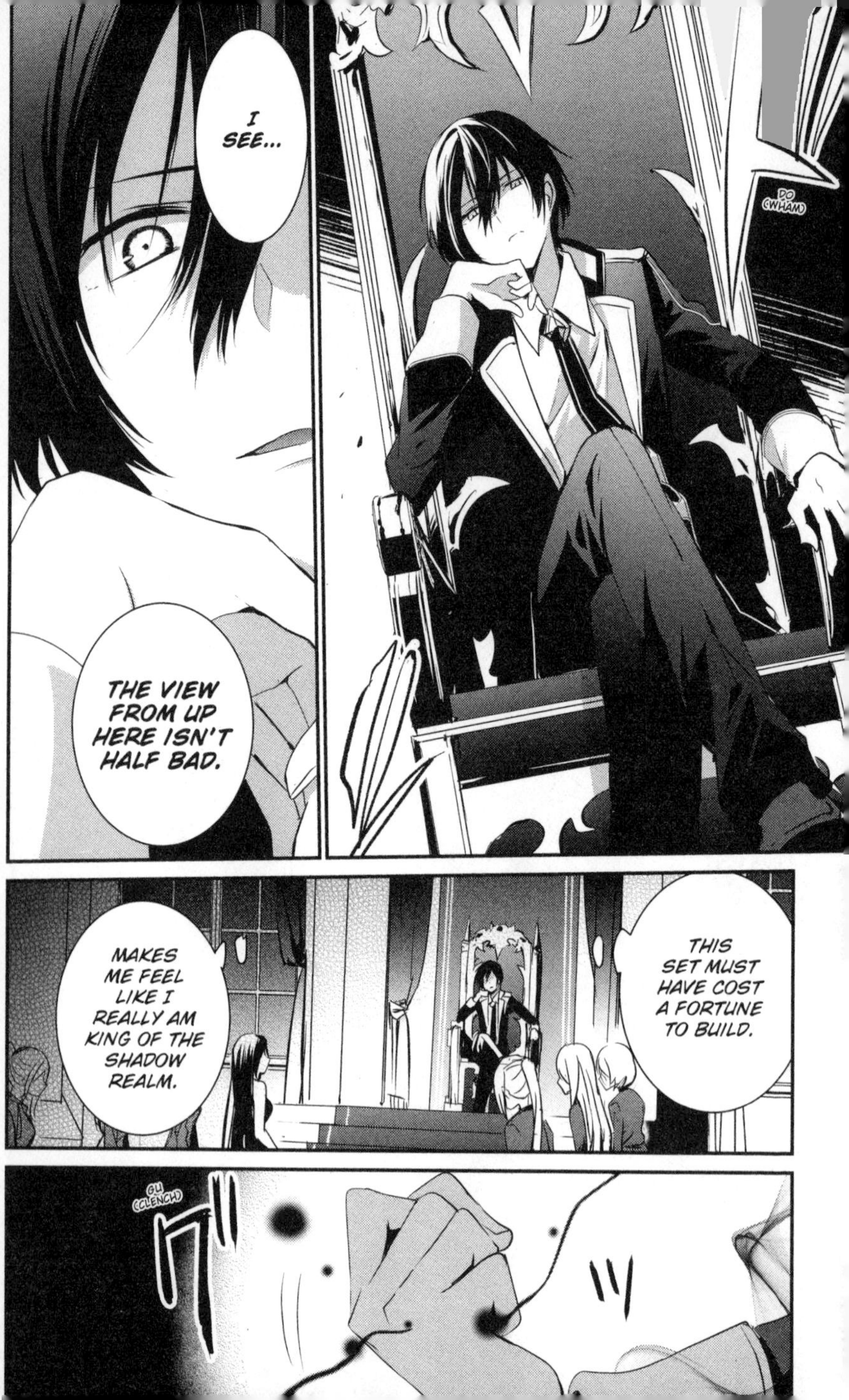
DO (WHAM)
I SEE...
THE VIEW FROM UP HERE ISN'T HALF BAD.
THIS SET MUST HAVE COST A FORTUNE TO BUILD.
MAKES ME FEEL LIKE I REALLY AM KING OF THE SHADOW REALM.
GU (CLENCH)

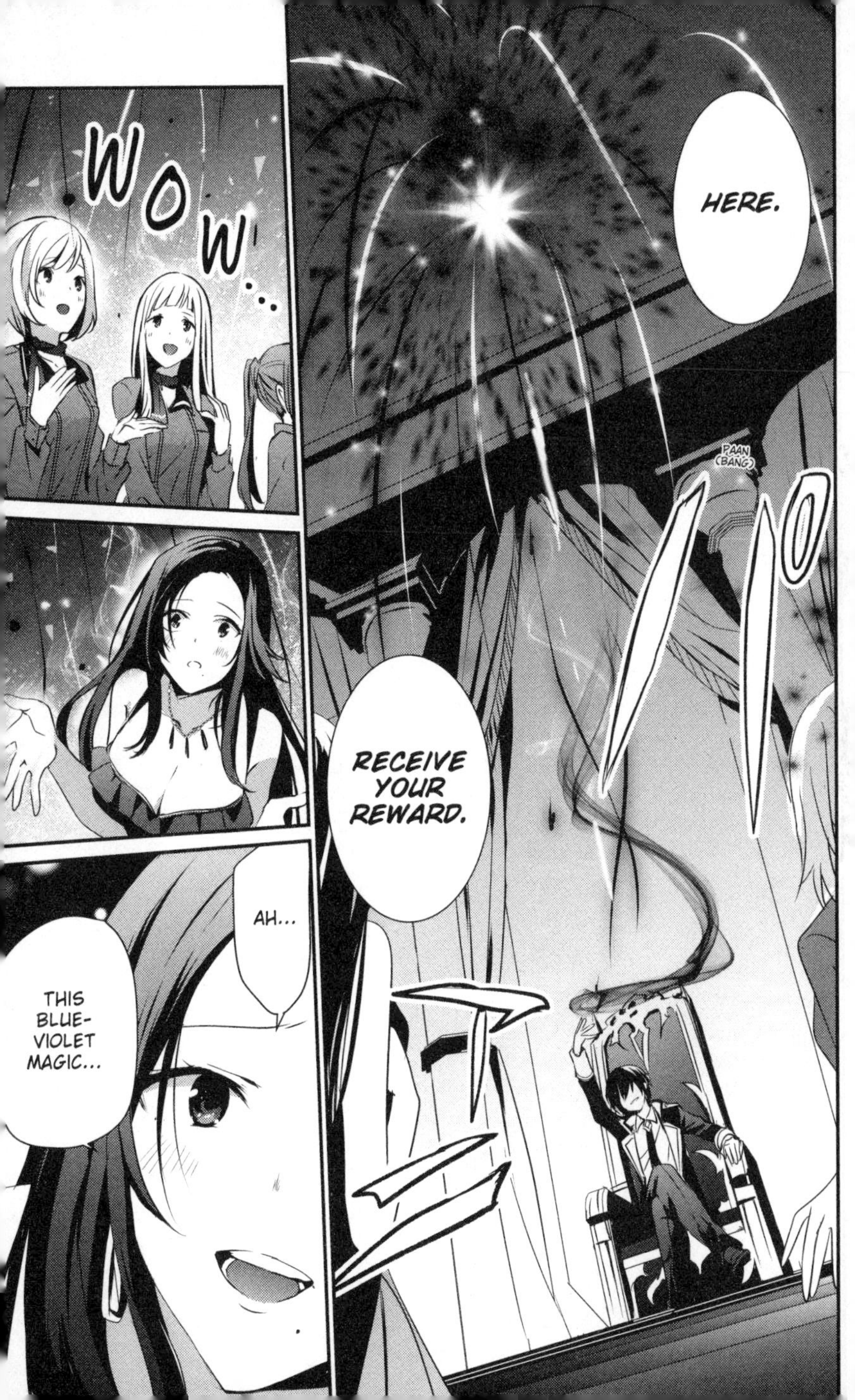
HERE.
PAAN (BANG)
RECEIVE YOUR REWARD.
WOW...
AH...
THIS BLUE-VIOLET MAGIC...

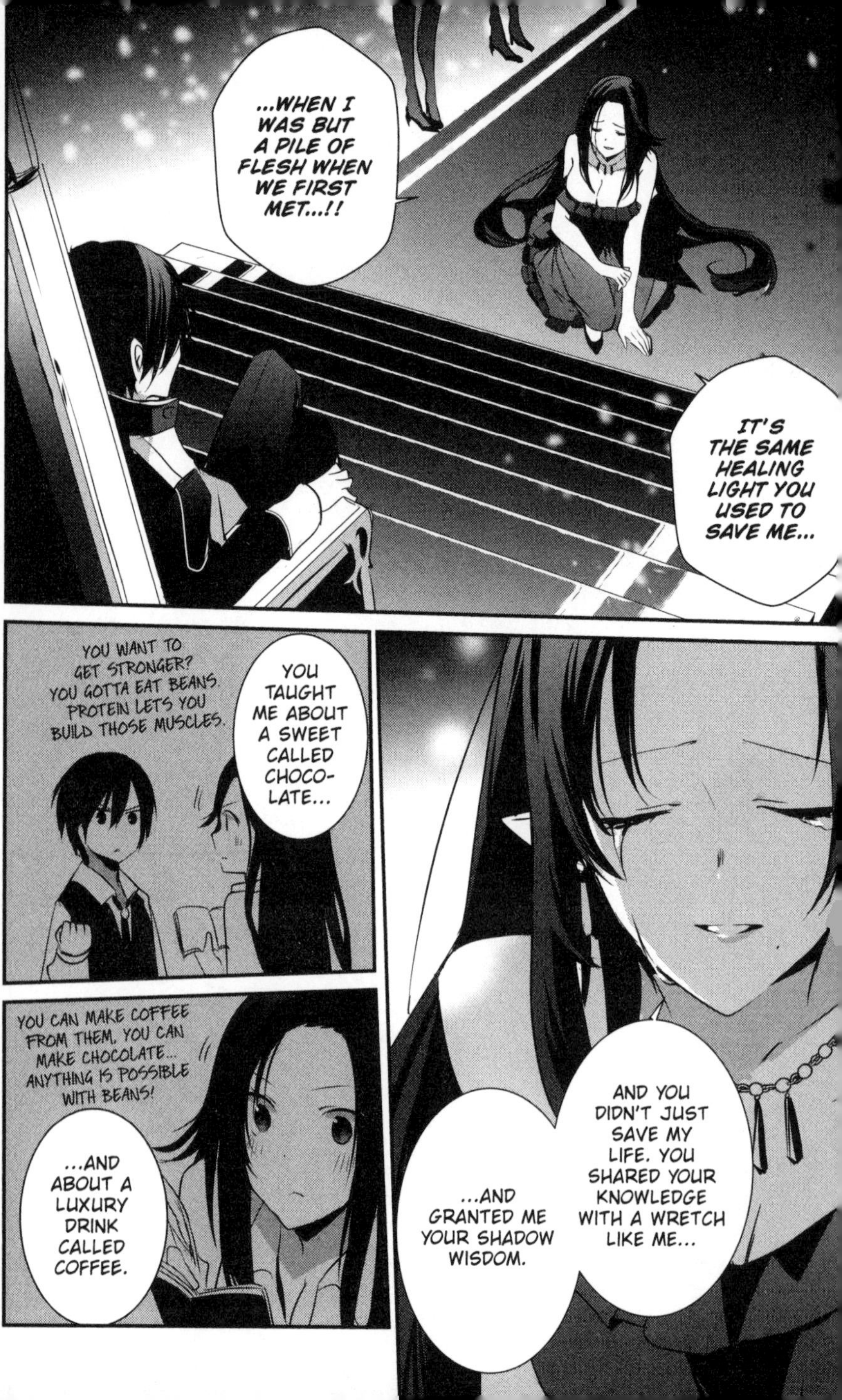
IT'S THE SAME HEALING LIGHT YOU USED TO SAVE ME...
...WHEN I WAS BUT A PILE OF FLESH WHEN WE FIRST MET...!!
AND YOU DIDN'T JUST SAVE MY LIFE. YOU SHARED YOUR KNOWLEDGE WITH A WRETCH LIKE ME...
...AND GRANTED ME YOUR SHADOW WISDOM.
YOU TAUGHT ME ABOUT A SWEET CALLED CHOCO-LATE...
YOU WANT TO GET STRONGER? YOU GOTTA EAT BEANS PROTEIN LETS YOU BUILD THOSE MUSCLES.
YOU CAN MAKE COFFEE FROM THEM, YOU CAN MAKE CHOCOLATE... ANYTHING IS POSSIBLE WITH BEANS!
...AND ABOUT A LUXURY DRINK CALLED COFFEE.

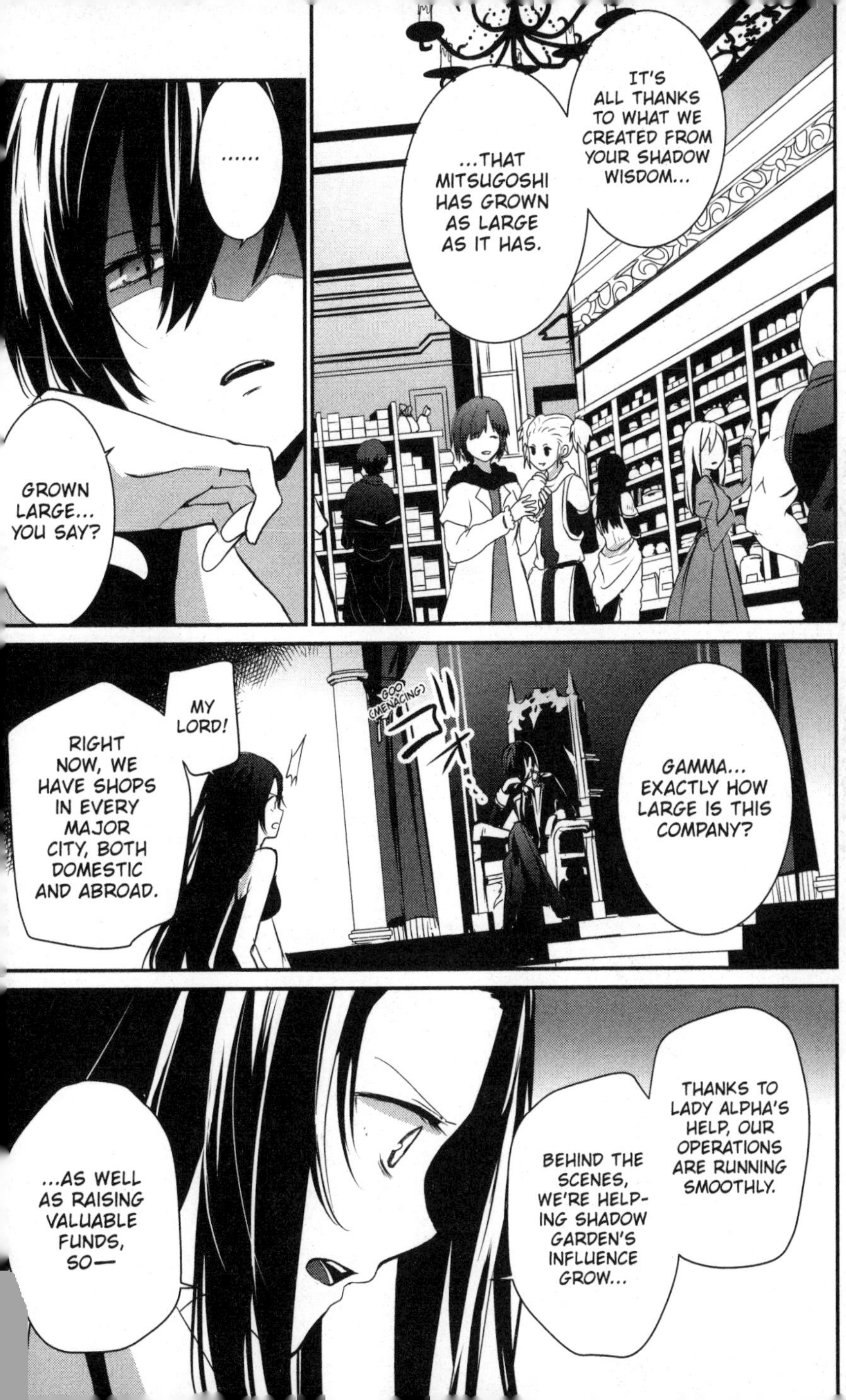
IT'S ALL THANKS TO WHAT WE CREATED FROM YOUR SHADOW WISDOM...
...THAT MITSUGOSHI HAS GROWN AS LARGE AS IT HAS.
......
GROWN LARGE... YOU SAY?
GAMMA... EXACTLY HOW LARGE IS THIS COMPANY?
GOO (MENACING)
MY LORD!
RIGHT NOW, WE HAVE SHOPS IN EVERY MAJOR CITY, BOTH DOMESTIC AND ABROAD.
THANKS TO LADY ALPHA'S HELP, OUR OPERATIONS ARE RUNNING SMOOTHLY.
BEHIND THE SCENES, WE'RE HELPING SHADOW GARDEN'S INFLUENCE GROW...
...AS WELL AS RAISING VALUABLE FUNDS, SO—

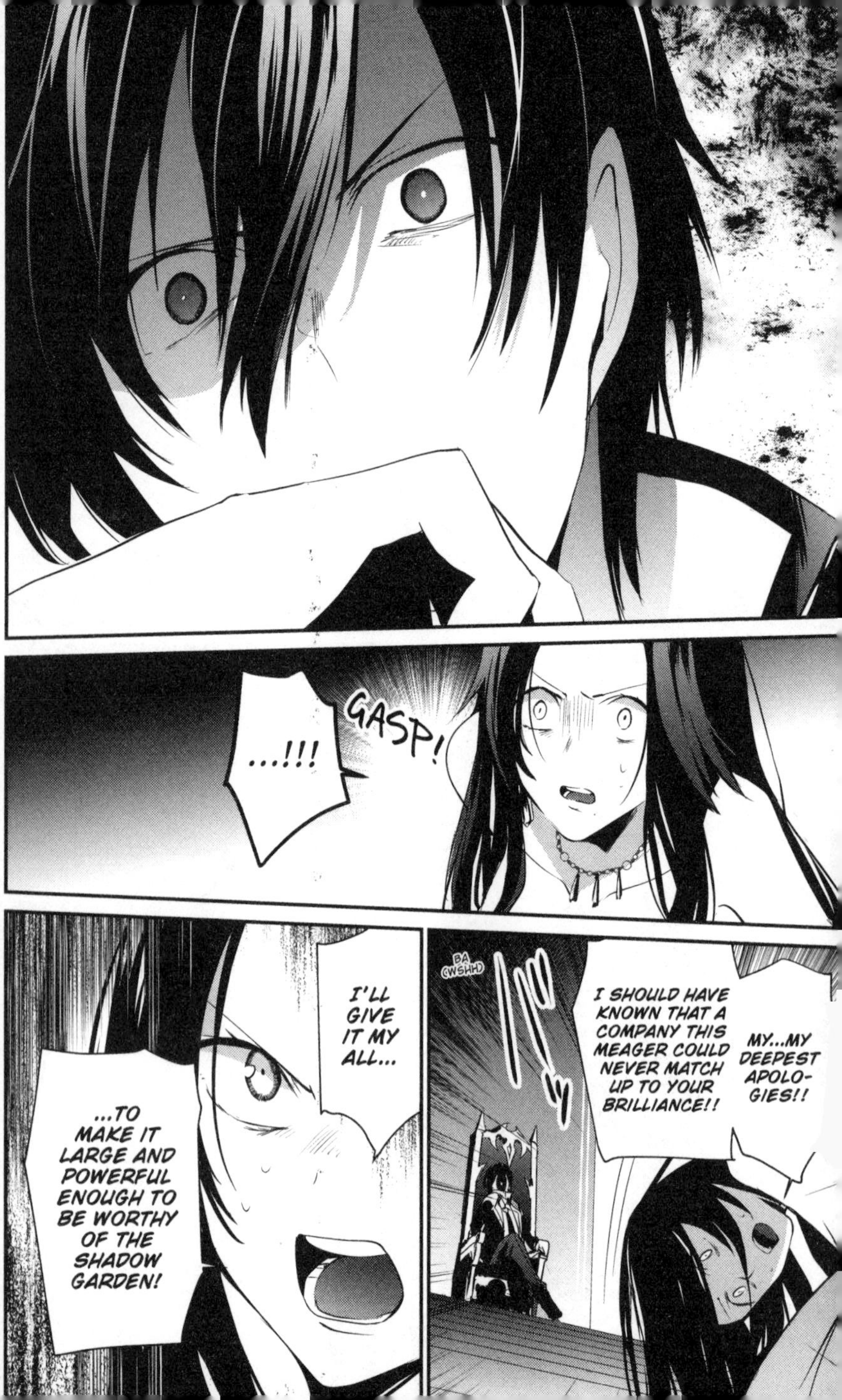
GASP!
...!!!
MY...MY DEEPEST APOLOGIES!!
I SHOULD HAVE KNOWN THAT A COMPANY THIS MEAGER COULD NEVER MATCH UP TO YOUR BRILLIANCE!!
BA (WSHH)
I'LL GIVE IT MY ALL...
...TO MAKE IT LARGE AND POWERFUL ENOUGH TO BE WORTHY OF THE SHADOW GARDEN!

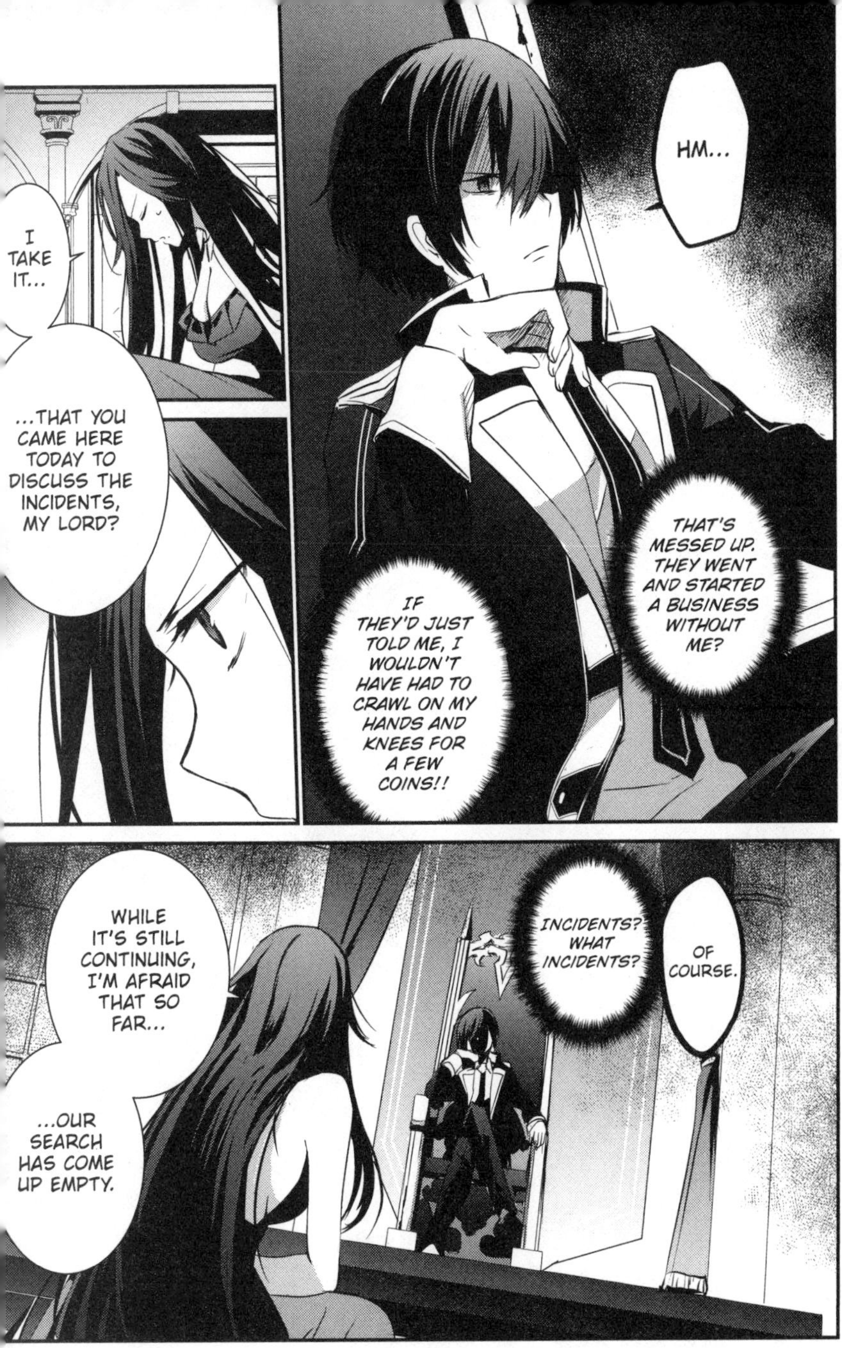
HM...
THAT'S MESSED UP. THEY WENT AND STARTED A BUSINESS WITHOUT ME?
IF THEY'D JUST TOLD ME, I WOULDN'T HAVE HAD TO CRAWL ON MY HANDS AND KNEES FOR A FEW COINS!!
I TAKE IT...
...THAT YOU CAME HERE TODAY TO DISCUSS THE INCIDENTS, MY LORD?
OF COURSE.
INCIDENTS? WHAT INCIDENTS?
WHILE IT'S STILL CONTINUING, I'M AFRAID THAT SO FAR...
...OUR SEARCH HAS COME UP EMPTY.

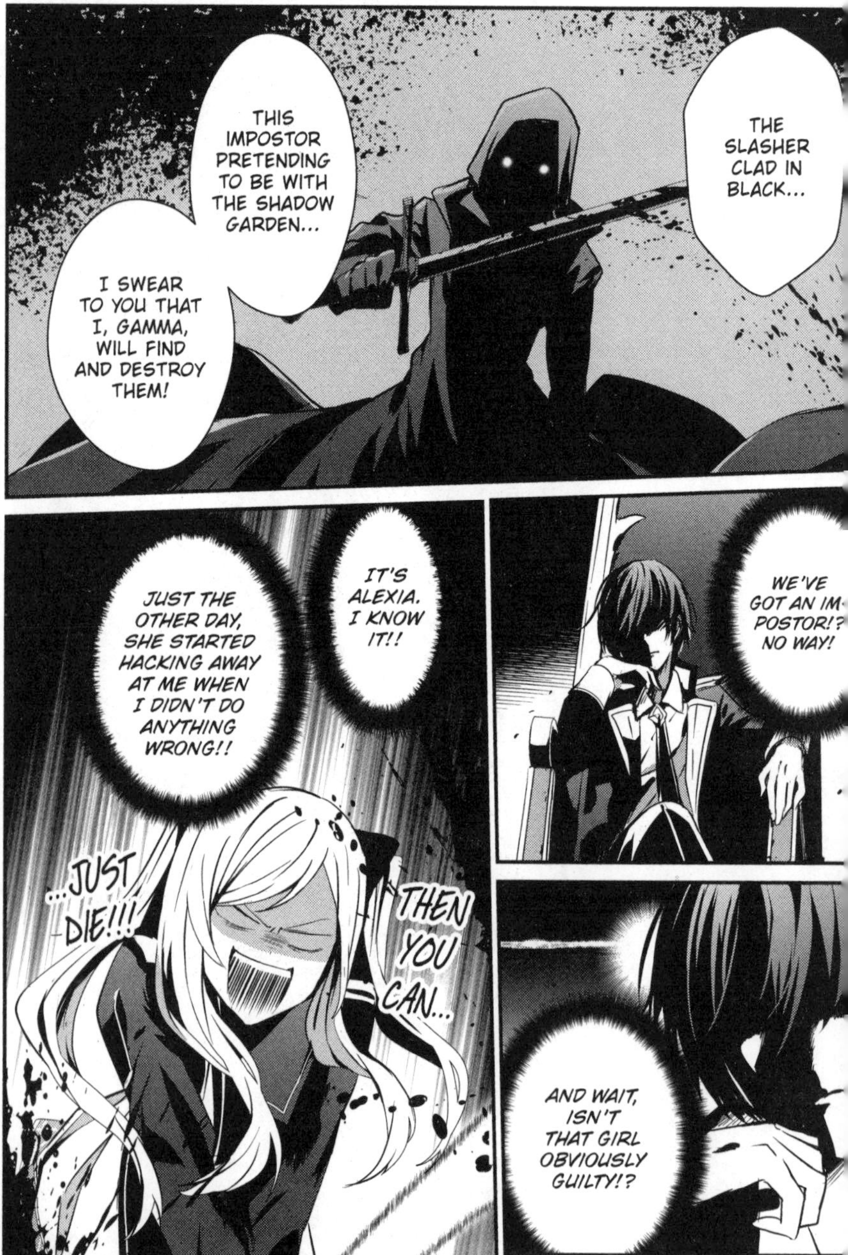
THE SLASHER CLAD IN BLACK...
THIS IMPOSTOR PRETENDING TO BE WITH THE SHADOW GARDEN...
I SWEAR TO YOU THAT I, GAMMA, WILL FIND AND DESTROY THEM!
WE'VE GOT AN IM-POSTOR!? NO WAY!
AND WAIT, ISN'T THAT GIRL OBVIOUSLY GUILTY!?
IT'S ALEXIA. I KNOW IT!!
JUST THE OTHER DAY, SHE STARTED HACKING AWAY AT ME WHEN I DIDN'T DO ANYTHING WRONG!!
THEN YOU CAN...
...JUST DIE!!!

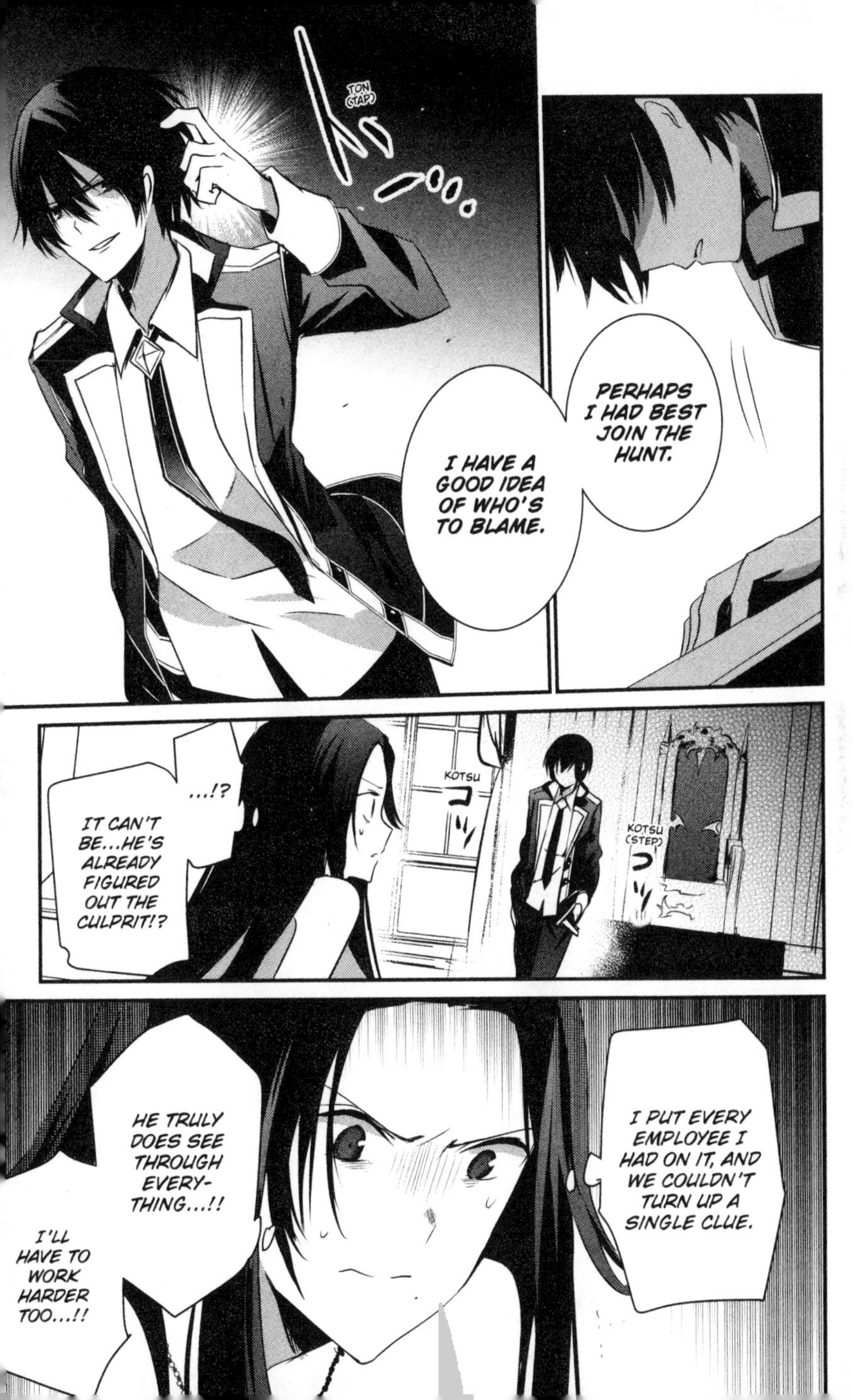
PERHAPS I HAD BEST JOIN THE HUNT.
TON (TAP)
I HAVE A GOOD IDEA OF WHO'S TO BLAME.
KOTSU (STEP)
KOTSU
...!?
IT CAN'T BE...HE'S ALREADY FIGURED OUT THE CULPRIT!?
I PUT EVERY EMPLOYEE I HAD ON IT, AND WE COULDN'T TURN UP A SINGLE CLUE.
HE TRULY DOES SEE THROUGH EVERY-THING...!!
I'LL HAVE TO WORK HARDER TOO...!!

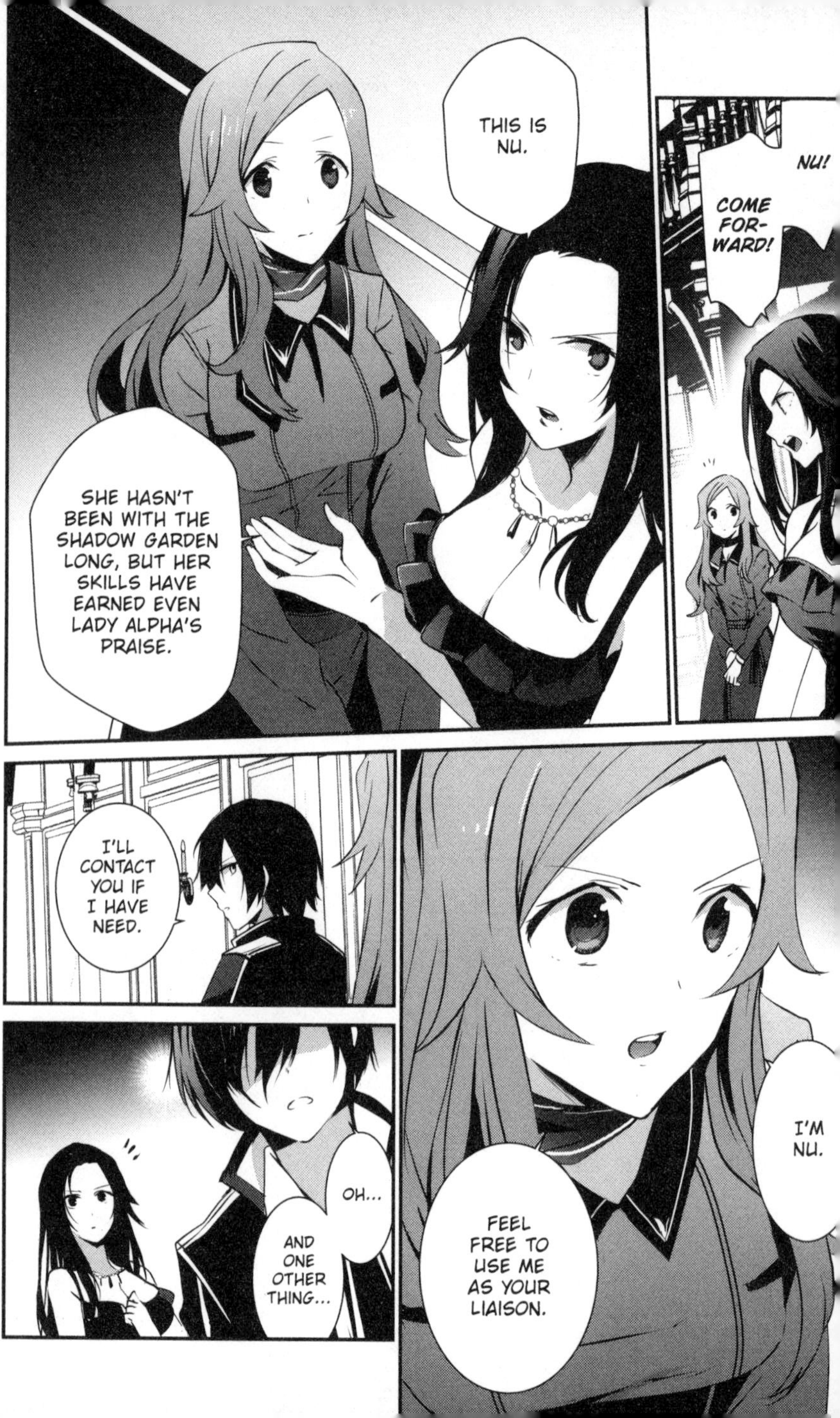
NU!
COME FORWARD!
THIS IS NU.
SHE HASN'T BEEN WITH THE SHADOW GARDEN LONG, BUT HER SKILLS HAVE EARNED EVEN LADY ALPHA'S PRAISE.
I'M NU.
FEEL FREE TO USE ME AS YOUR LIAISON.
I'LL CONTACT YOU IF I HAVE NEED.
OH...
AND ONE OTHER THING...

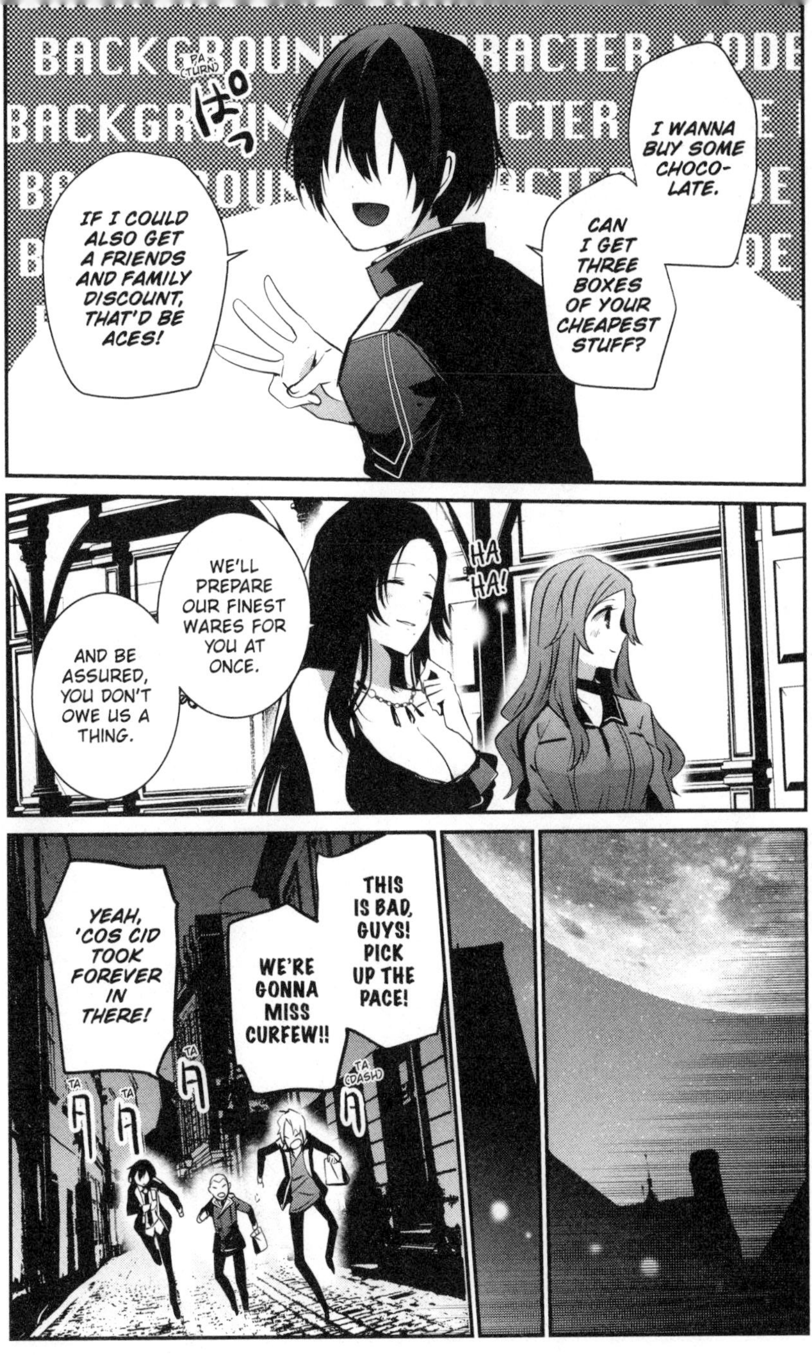

I WANNA BUY SOME CHOCO-LATE.
CAN I GET THREE BOXES OF YOUR CHEAPEST STUFF?
ぱっ PA (TURN)
IF I COULD ALSO GET A FRIENDS AND FAMILY DISCOUNT, THAT'D BE ACES!
HA HA!
WE'LL PREPARE OUR FINEST WARES FOR YOU AT ONCE.
AND BE ASSURED, YOU DON'T OWE US A THING.
THIS IS BAD, GUYS! PICK UP THE PACE!
TA (DASH)
WE'RE GONNA MISS CURFEW!!
YEAH, 'COS CID TOOK FOREVER IN THERE!
TA
TA
TA

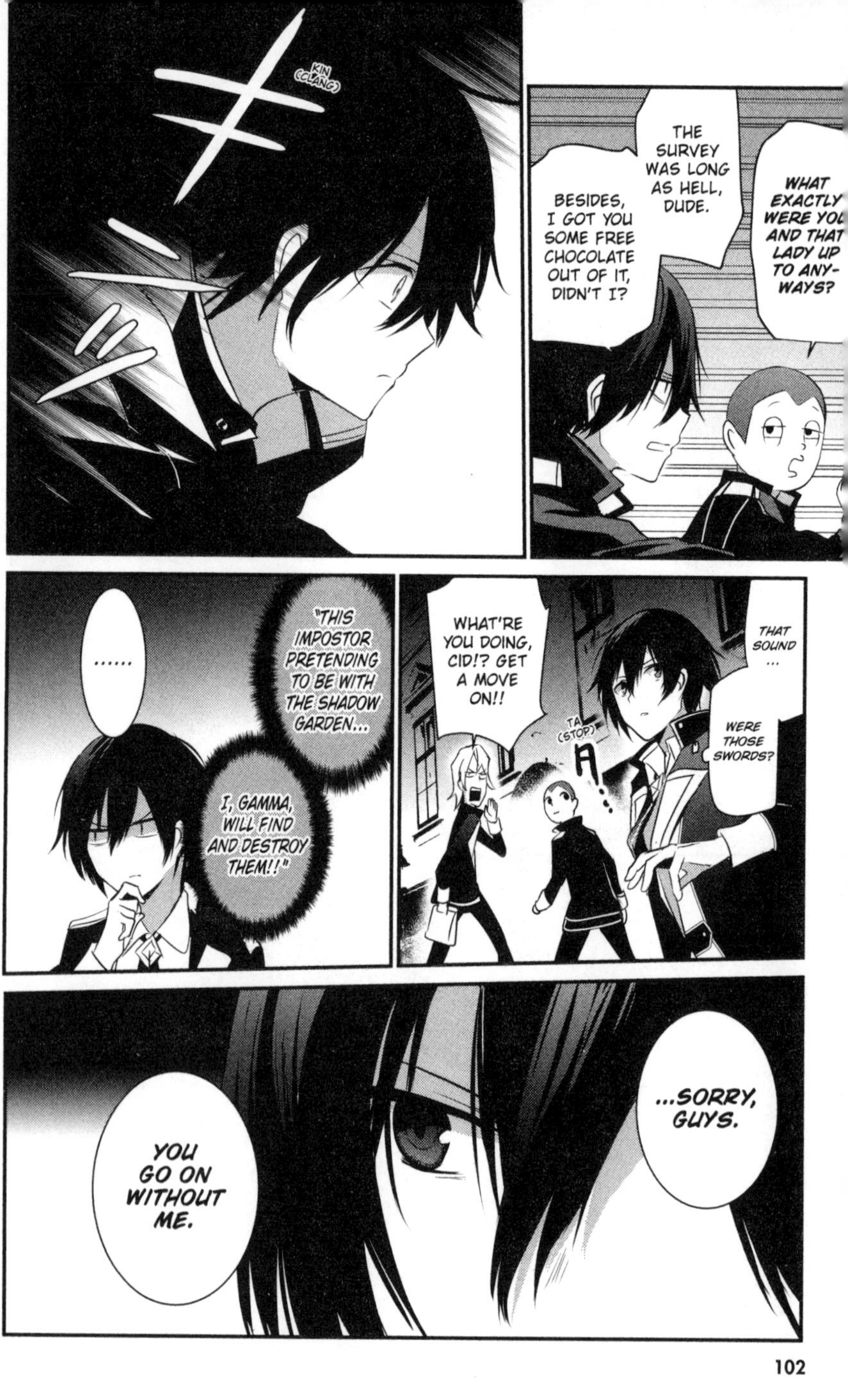
WHAT EXACTLY WERE YOU AND THAT LADY UP TO ANYWAYS?
THE SURVEY WAS LONG AS HELL, DUDE.
BESIDES, I GOT YOU SOME FREE CHOCOLATE OUT OF IT, DIDN'T I?
KIN (CLANG)
THAT SOUND ...
WERE THOSE SWORDS?
WHAT'RE YOU DOING, CID!? GET A MOVE ON!!
TA (STOP)
"THIS IMPOSTOR PRETENDING TO BE WITH THE SHADOW GARDEN...
......
I, GAMMA, WILL FIND AND DESTROY THEM!!"
...SORRY, GUYS.
YOU GO ON WITHOUT ME.

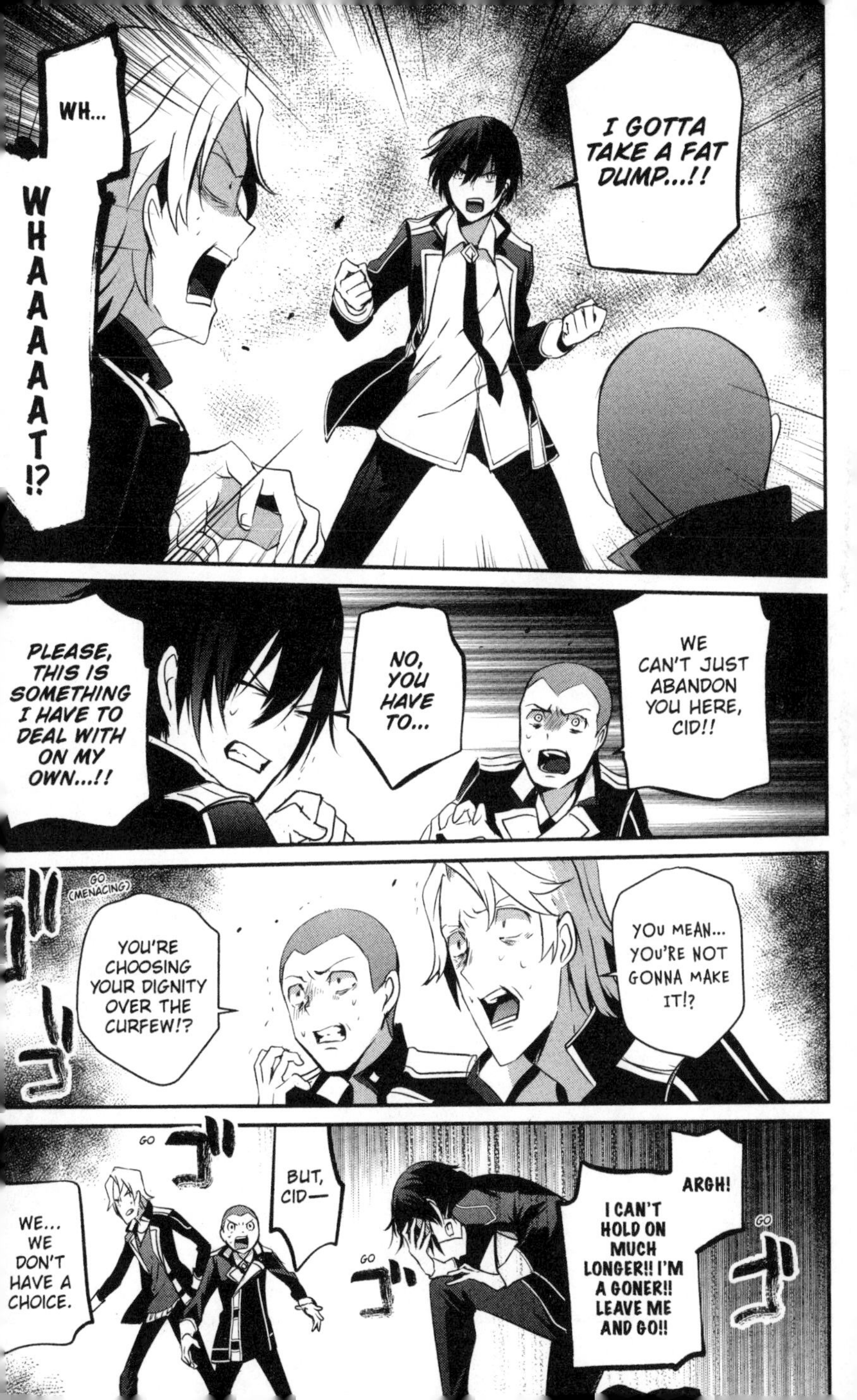

I GOTTA TAKE A FAT DUMP...!!
WH...
WHAAAAAAAT!?
WE CAN'T JUST ABANDON YOU HERE, CID!!
NO, YOU HAVE TO...
PLEASE, THIS IS SOMETHING I HAVE TO DEAL WITH ON MY OWN...!!
YOU MEAN... YOU'RE NOT GONNA MAKE IT!?
YOU'RE CHOOSING YOUR DIGNITY OVER THE CURFEW!?
GO (MENACING)
ARGH!
I CAN'T HOLD ON MUCH LONGER!! I'M A GONER!! LEAVE ME AND GO!!
GO
GO
BUT, CID—
GO
WE... WE DON'T HAVE A CHOICE.

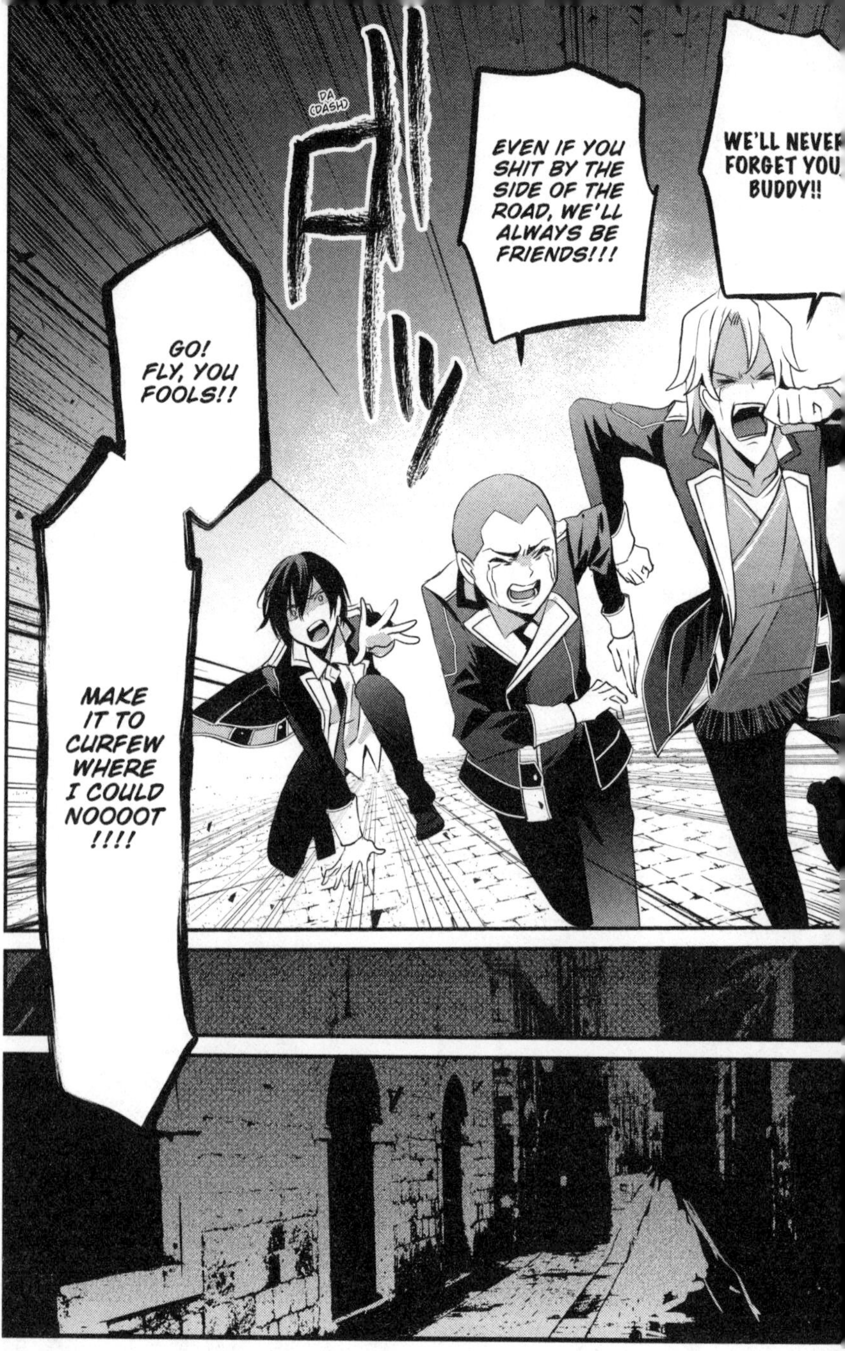
WE'LL NEVER FORGET YOU, BUDDY!!
EVEN IF YOU SHIT BY THE SIDE OF THE ROAD, WE'LL ALWAYS BE FRIENDS!!!
DA (DASH)
GO! FLY, YOU FOOLS!!
MAKE IT TO CURFEW WHERE I COULD NOOOOT!!!!

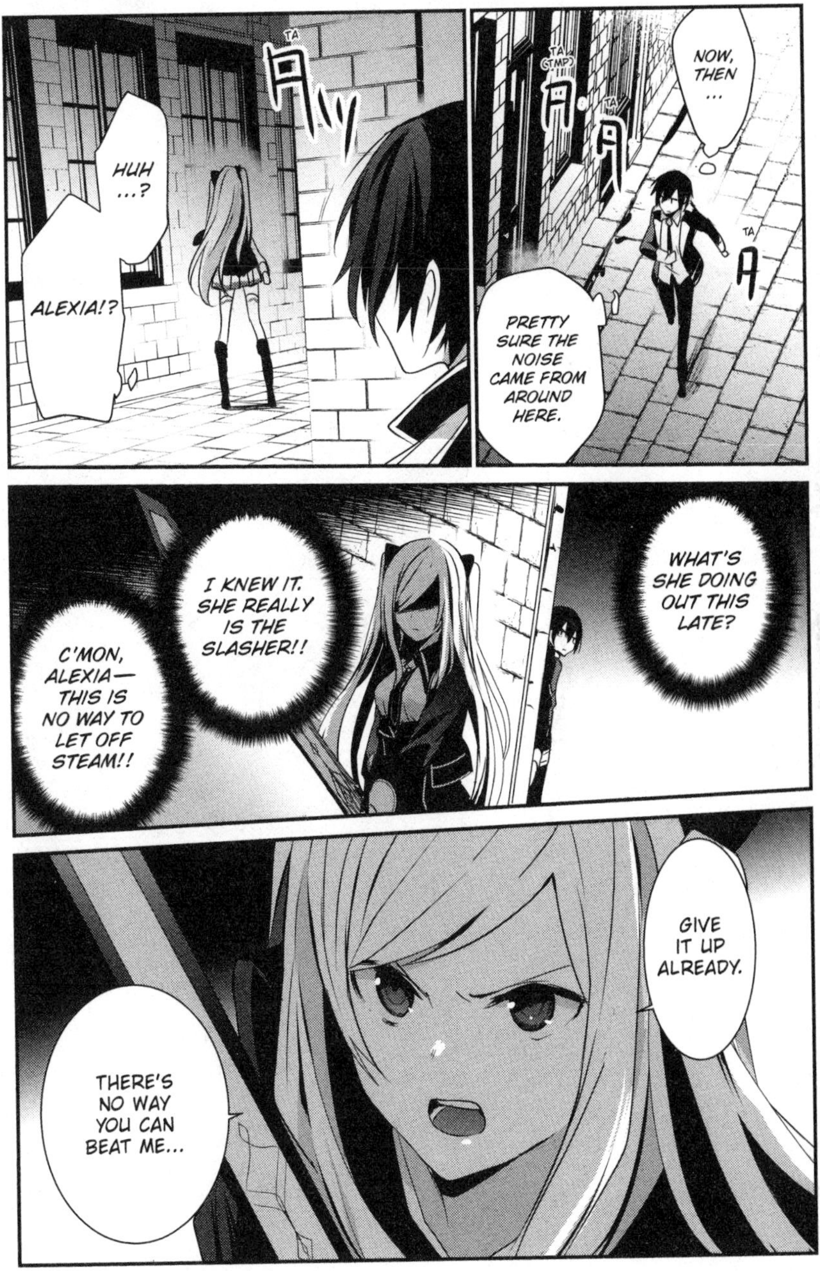
NOW, THEN ...
TA (STMP)
TA
TA
PRETTY SURE THE NOISE CAME FROM AROUND HERE.
TA
HUH ...?
ALEXIA!?
WHAT'S SHE DOING OUT THIS LATE?
I KNEW IT. SHE REALLY IS THE SLASHER!!
C'MON, ALEXIA— THIS IS NO WAY TO LET OFF STEAM!!
GIVE IT UP ALREADY.
THERE'S NO WAY YOU CAN BEAT ME...

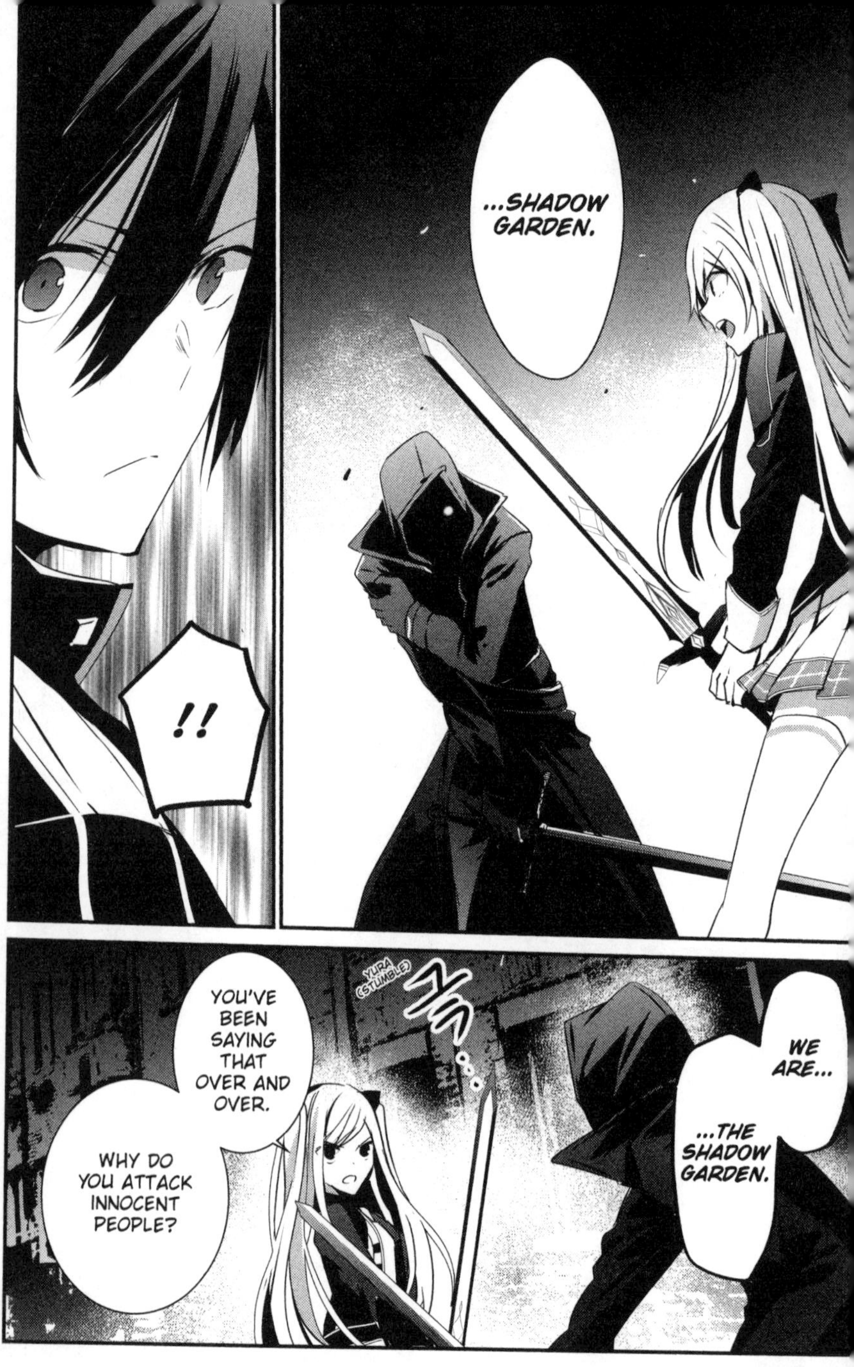
...SHADOW GARDEN.
!!
WE ARE...
...THE SHADOW GARDEN.
YURA (STUMBLE)
YOU'VE BEEN SAYING THAT OVER AND OVER.
WHY DO YOU ATTACK INNOCENT PEOPLE?

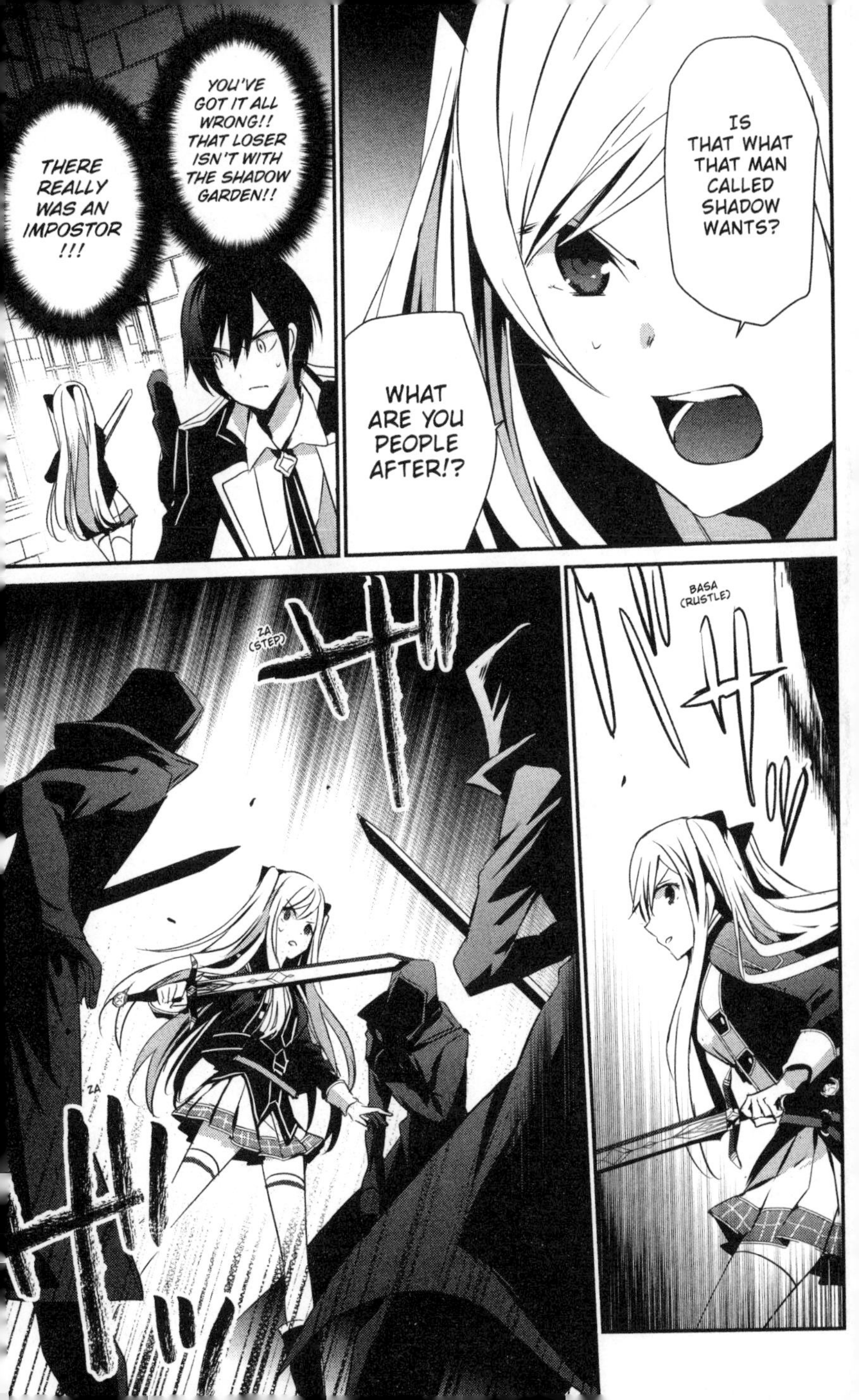
IS THAT WHAT THAT MAN CALLED SHADOW WANTS?
WHAT ARE YOU PEOPLE AFTER!?
YOU'VE GOT IT ALL WRONG!! THAT LOSER ISN'T WITH THE SHADOW GARDEN!!
THERE REALLY WAS AN IMPOSTOR !!!
BASA (RUSTLE)
ZA (STEP)
ZA

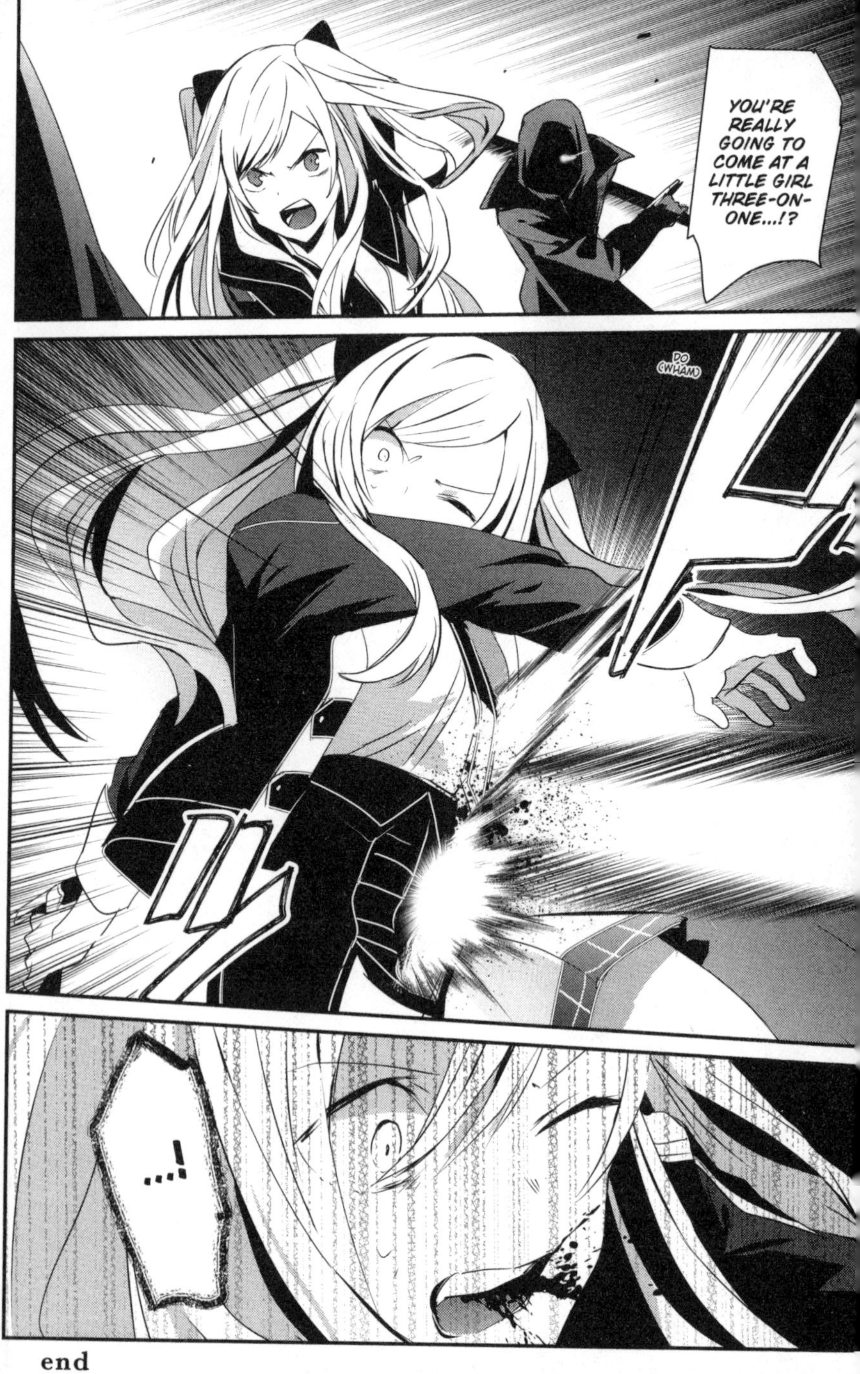
YOU'RE REALLY GOING TO COME AT A LITTLE GIRL THREE-ON-ONE...!?
DO (WHAM)
...!

end

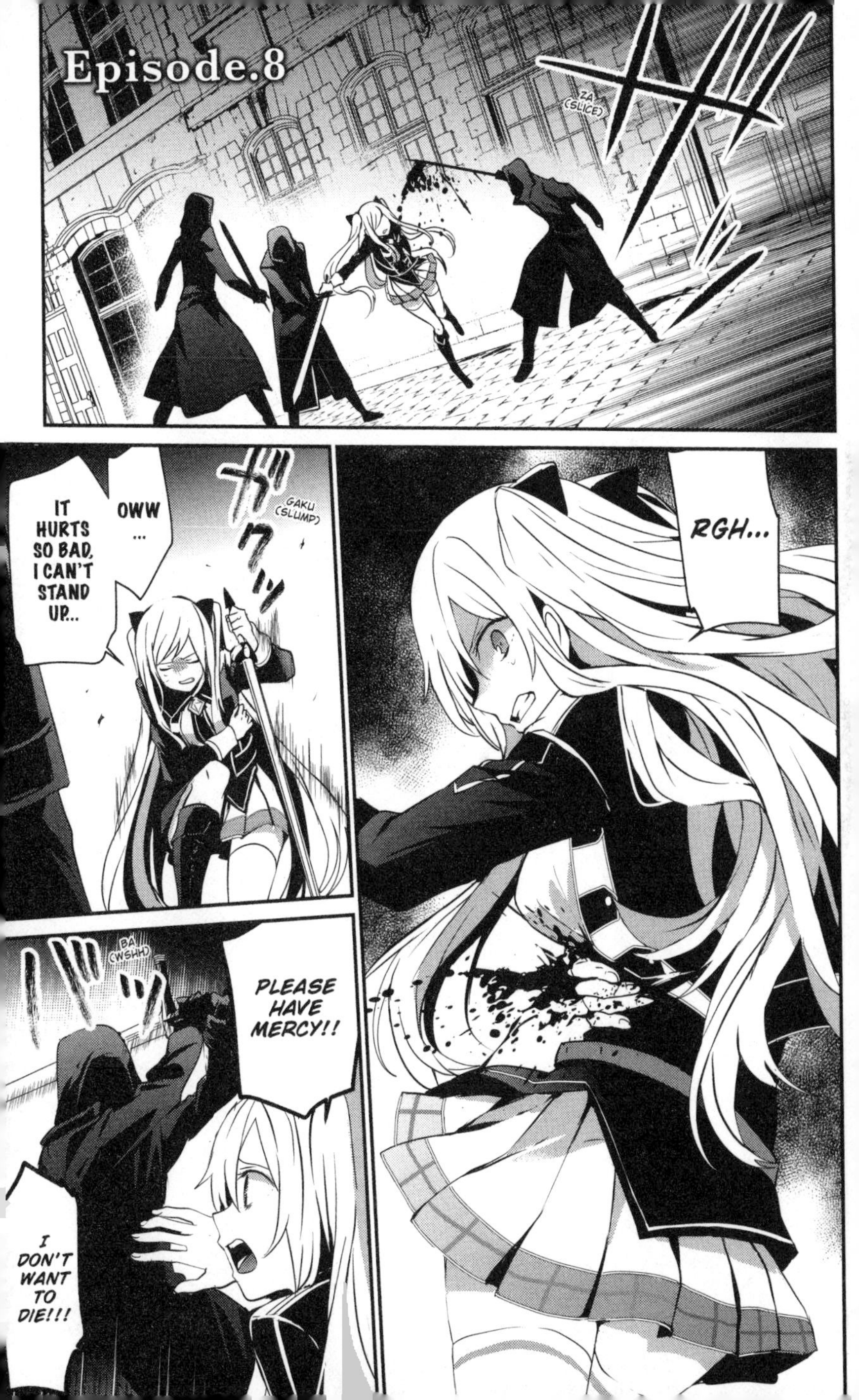

Episode.8
ZA (SLICE)
RGH...
GAKU (SLUMP)
OWW...
IT HURTS SO BAD, I CAN'T STAND UP...
BA (WSHH)
PLEASE HAVE MERCY!!
I DON'T WANT TO DIE!!!

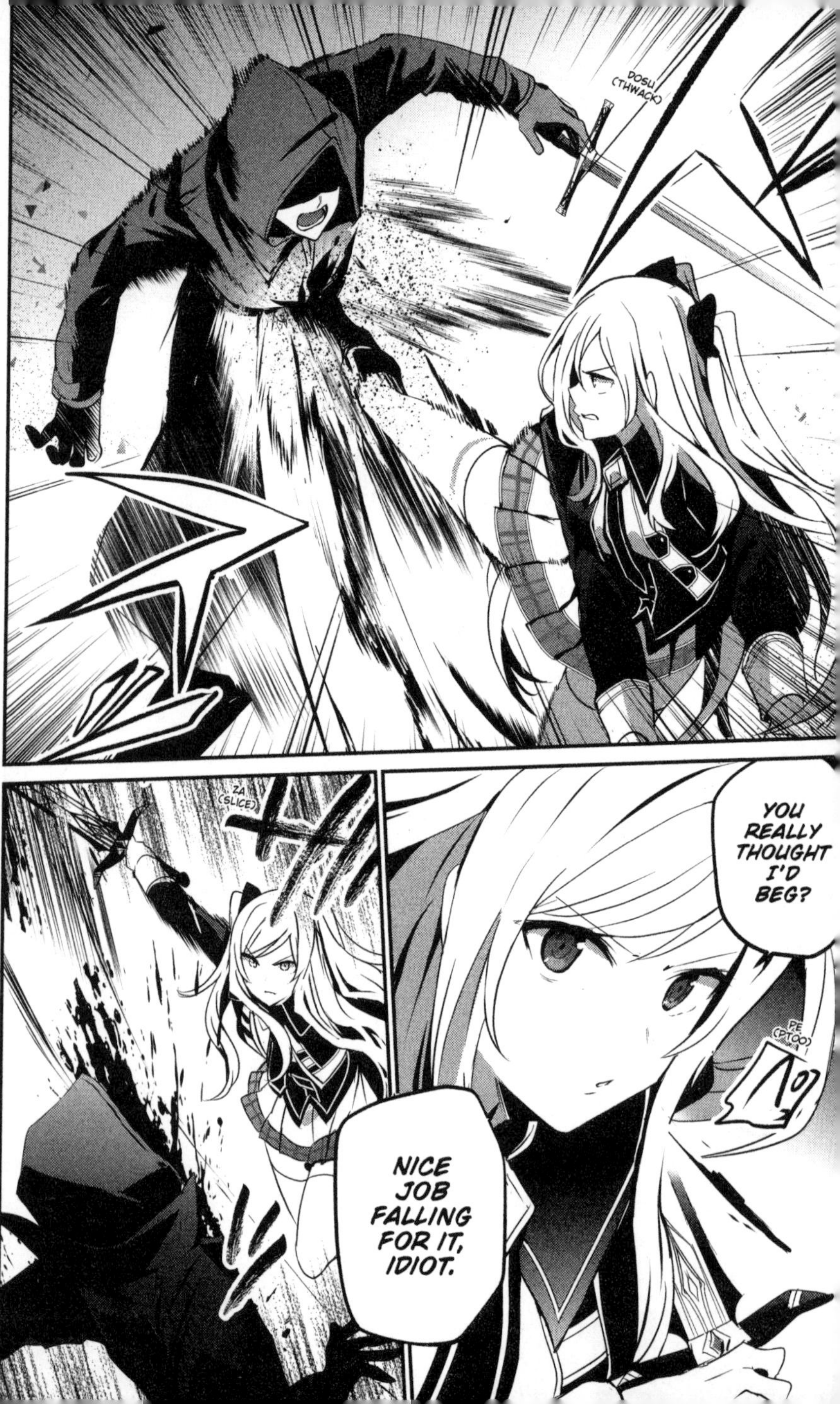
DOSU (THWACK)
YOU REALLY THOUGHT I'D BEG?
PE (PTOO)
NICE JOB FALLING FOR IT, IDIOT.
ZA (SLICE)

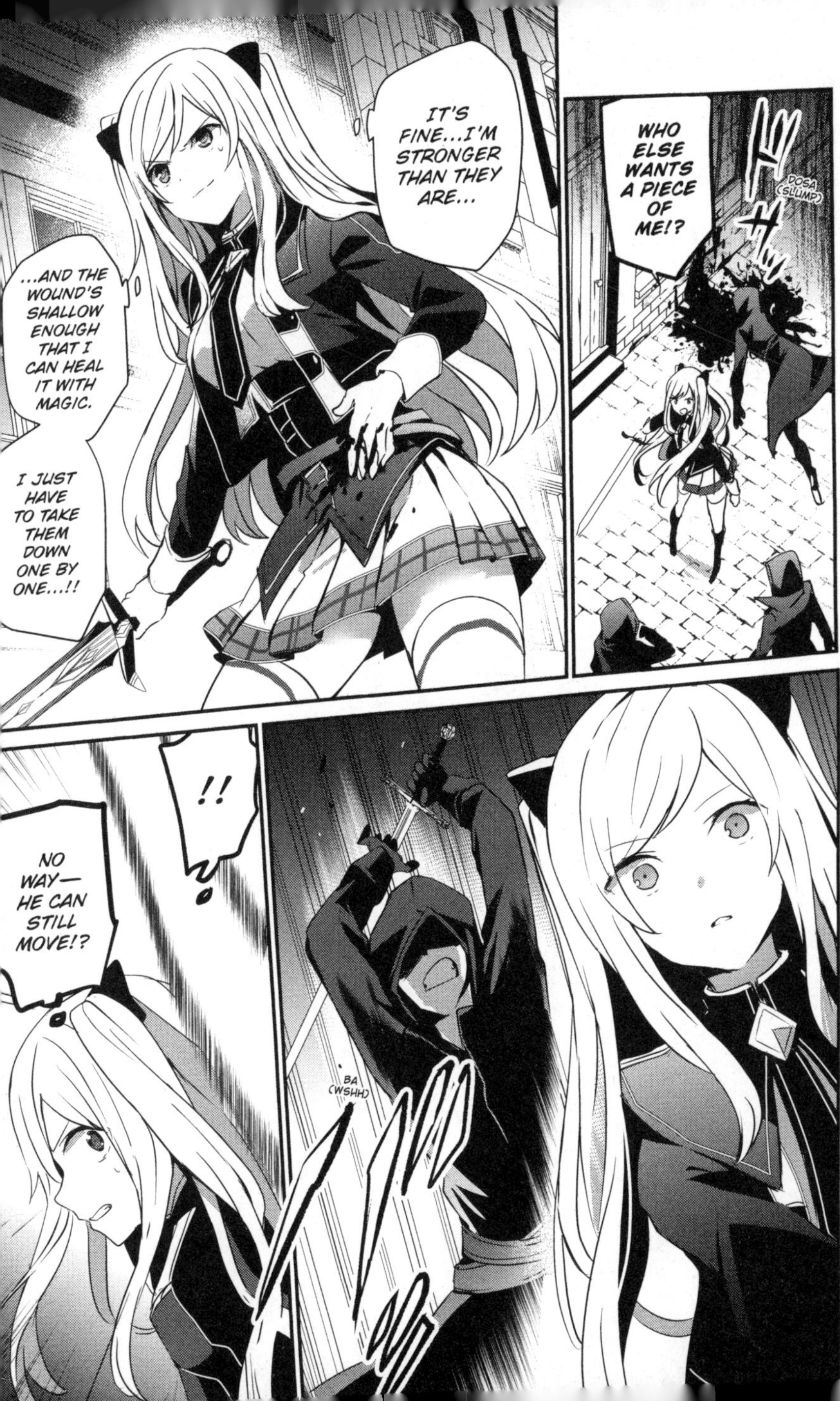
WHO ELSE WANTS A PIECE OF ME!?
DOSA (SLUMP)
IT'S FINE...I'M STRONGER THAN THEY ARE...
...AND THE WOUND'S SHALLOW ENOUGH THAT I CAN HEAL IT WITH MAGIC.
I JUST HAVE TO TAKE THEM DOWN ONE BY ONE...!!
BA (WSHH)
!!
NO WAY— HE CAN STILL MOVE!?

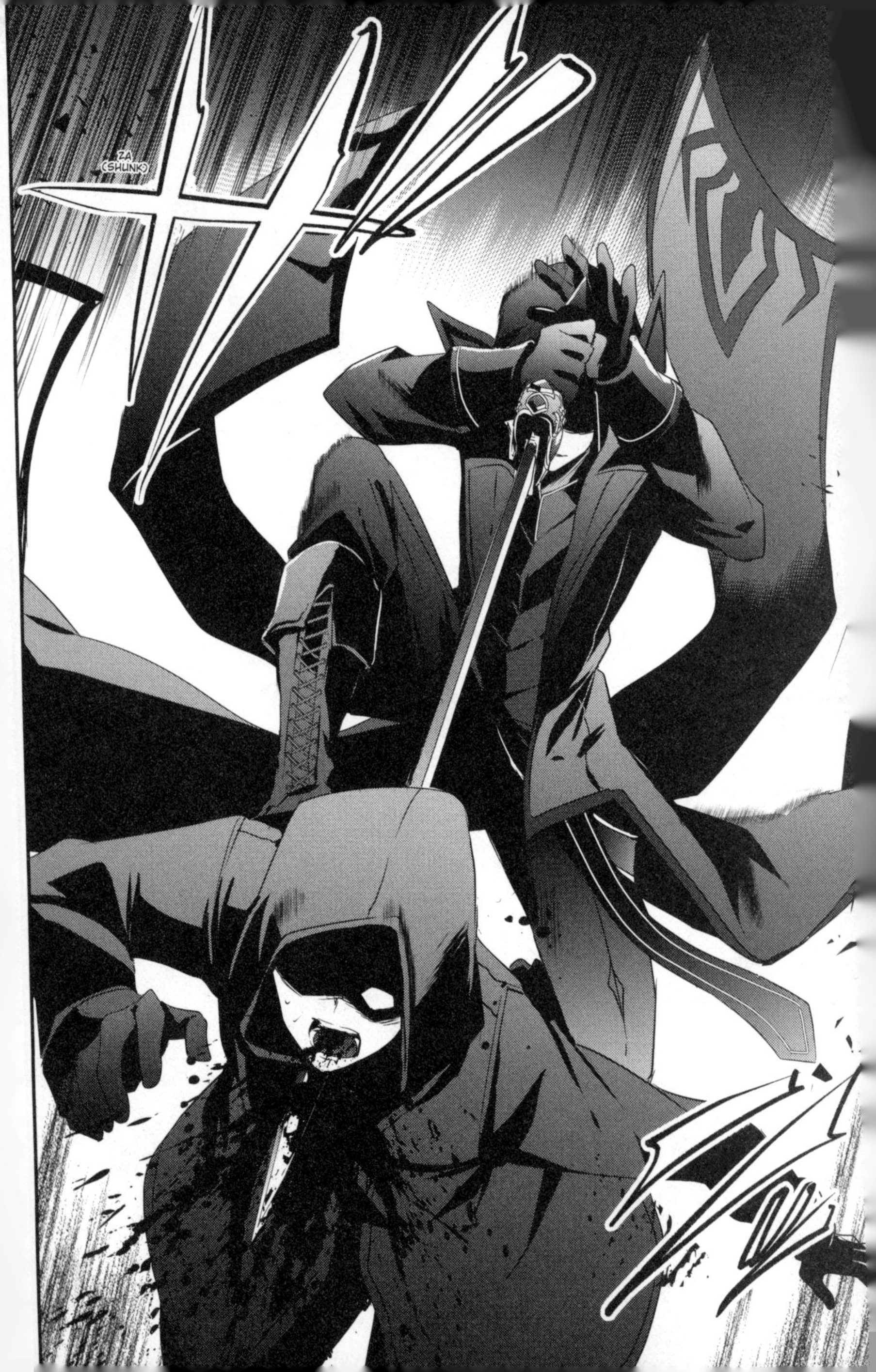
ZA
(SHUNK)

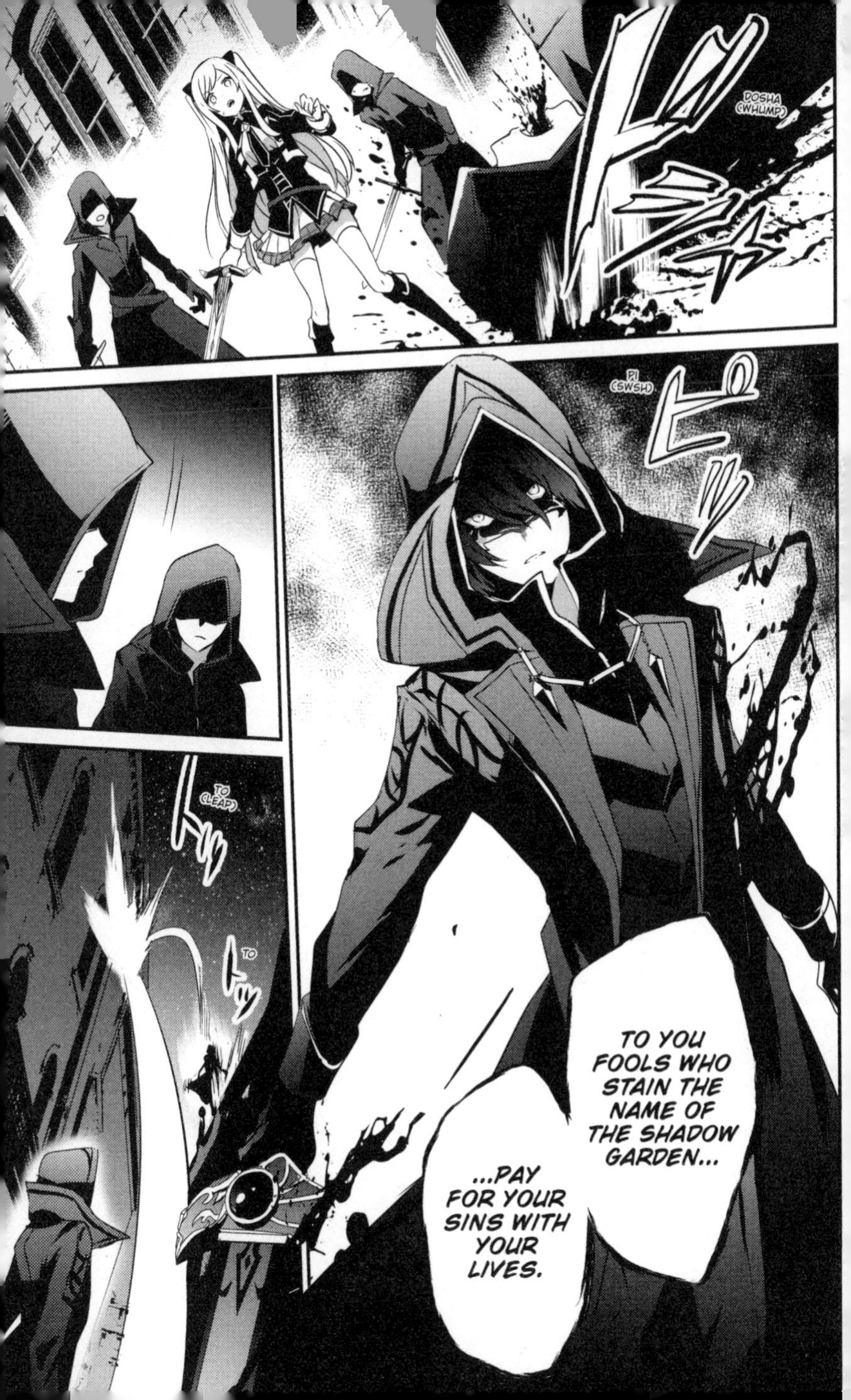
DOSHA
(WHUMP)
PI
(SWSH)
TO YOU FOOLS WHO STAIN THE NAME OF THE SHADOW GARDEN...
...PAY FOR YOUR SINS WITH YOUR LIVES.
TO
(LEAP)
TO

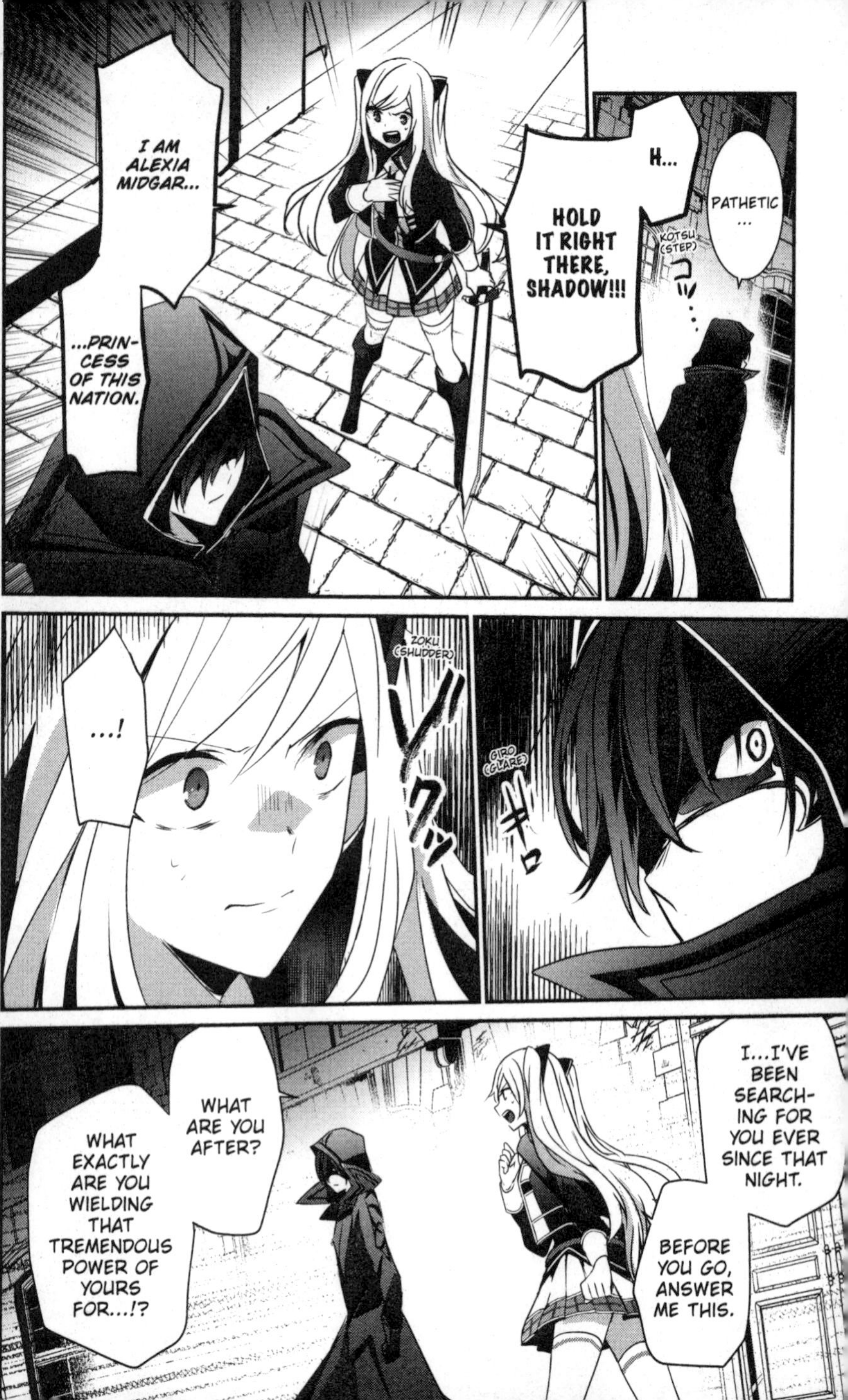
PATHETIC...
KOTSU (STEP)
H...
HOLD IT RIGHT THERE, SHADOW!!!
I AM ALEXIA MIDGAR...
...PRIN-CESS OF THIS NATION.
GIRO (GLARE)
ZOKU (SHUDDER)
...!
I...I'VE BEEN SEARCH-ING FOR YOU EVER SINCE THAT NIGHT.
BEFORE YOU GO, ANSWER ME THIS.
WHAT ARE YOU AFTER?
WHAT EXACTLY ARE YOU WIELDING THAT TREMENDOUS POWER OF YOURS FOR...!?

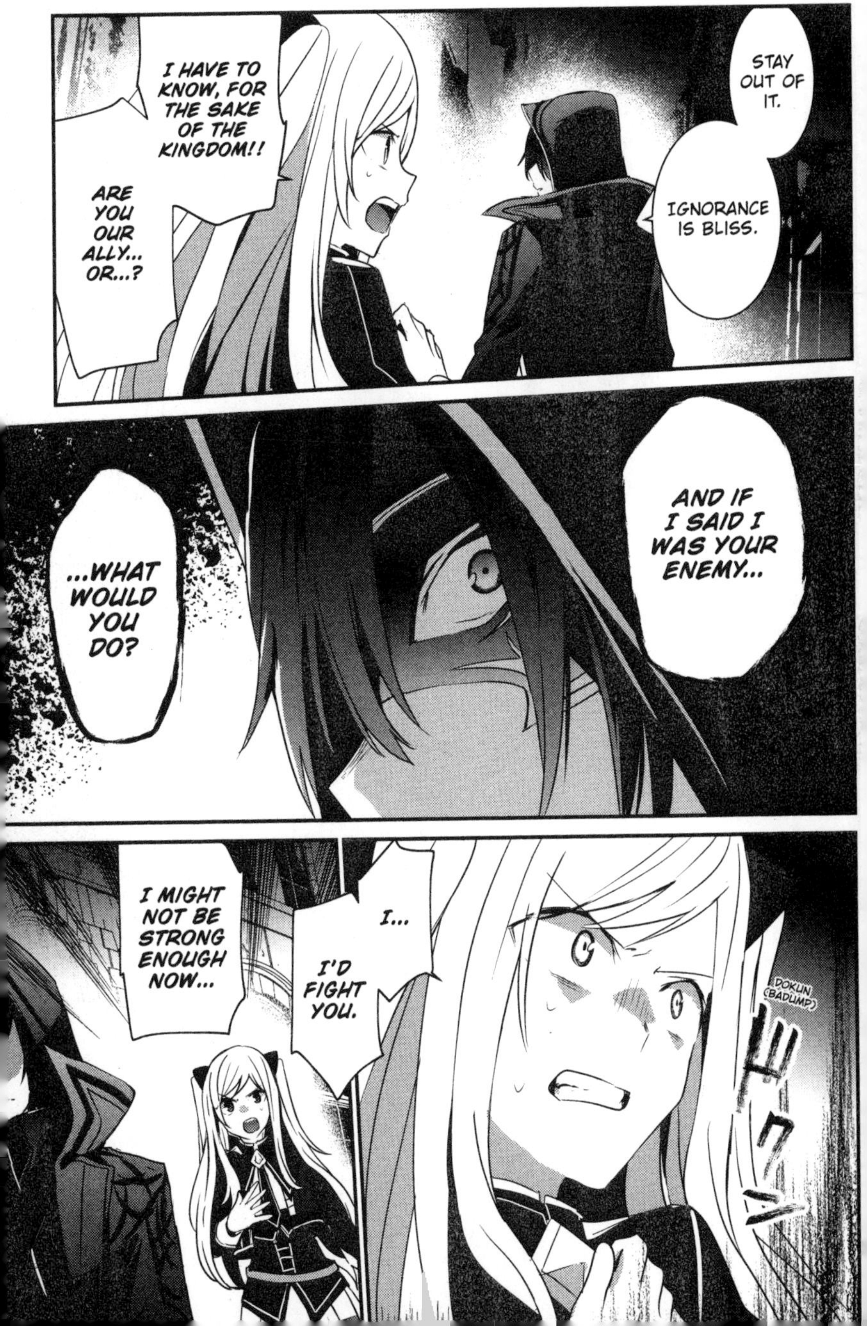
STAY OUT OF IT.
IGNORANCE IS BLISS.
I HAVE TO KNOW, FOR THE SAKE OF THE KINGDOM!!
ARE YOU OUR ALLY... OR...?
AND IF I SAID I WAS YOUR ENEMY...
...WHAT WOULD YOU DO?
DOKUN (BADUMP)
I...
I'D FIGHT YOU.
I MIGHT NOT BE STRONG ENOUGH NOW...

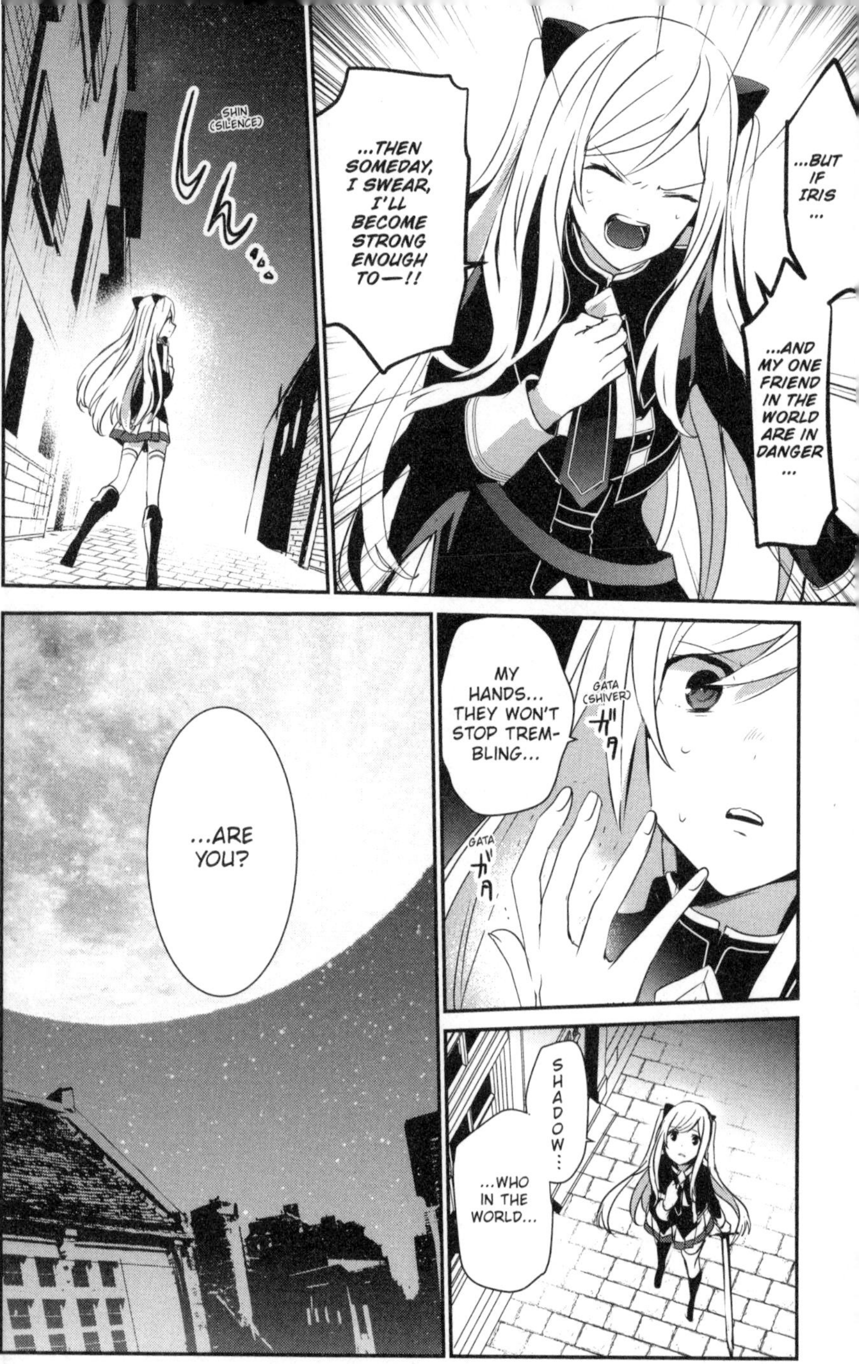
...BUT IF IRIS...
...AND MY ONE FRIEND IN THE WORLD ARE IN DANGER...
...THEN SOMEDAY, I SWEAR, I'LL BECOME STRONG ENOUGH TO—!!
SHIN (SILENCE)
MY HANDS... THEY WON'T STOP TREM-BLING...
GATA (SHIVER)
GATA
SHADOW...
...WHO IN THE WORLD...
...ARE YOU?

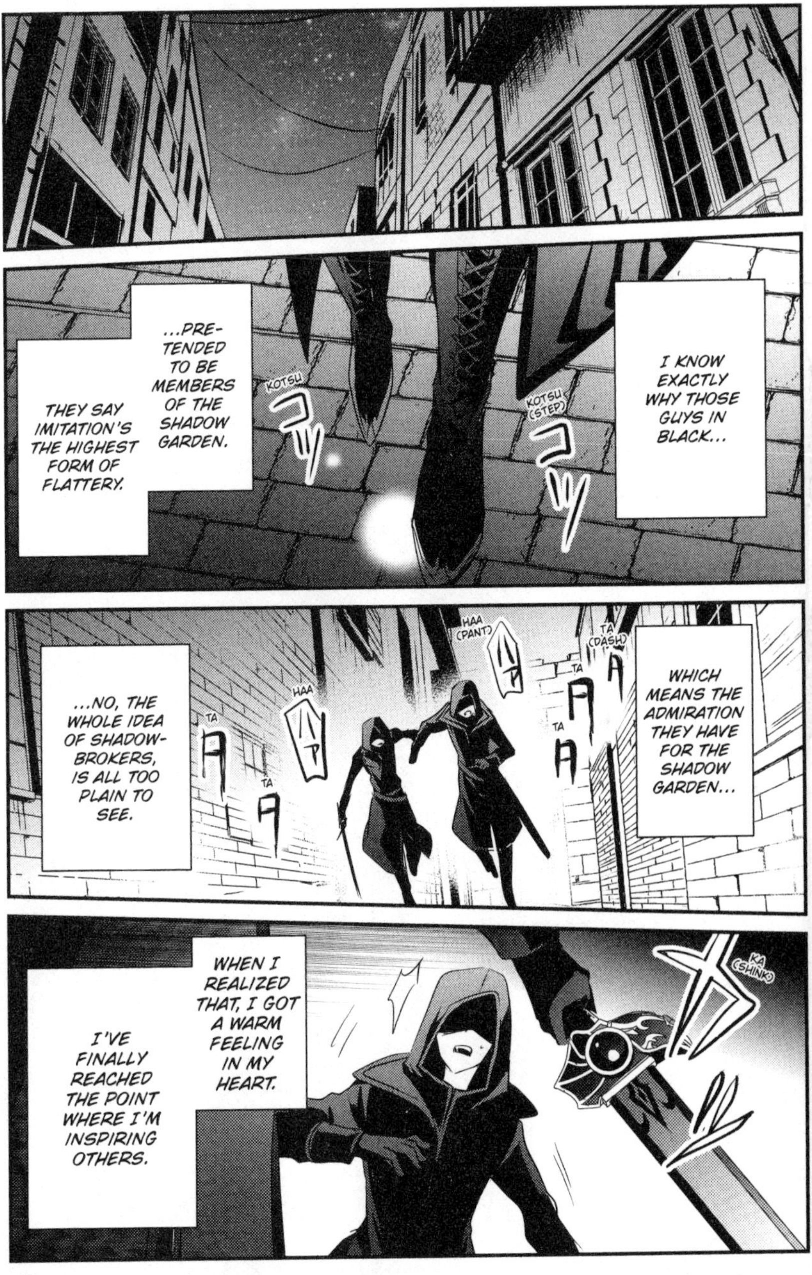
I KNOW EXACTLY WHY THOSE GUYS IN BLACK...
KOTSU (STEP)
KOTSU
...PRE-TENDED TO BE MEMBERS OF THE SHADOW GARDEN.
THEY SAY IMITATION'S THE HIGHEST FORM OF FLATTERY.
WHICH MEANS THE ADMIRATION THEY HAVE FOR THE SHADOW GARDEN...
TA (DASH)
TA
TA
HAA (PANT)
HAA
TA
TA
...NO, THE WHOLE IDEA OF SHADOW-BROKERS, IS ALL TOO PLAIN TO SEE.
KA (SHINK)
WHEN I REALIZED THAT, I GOT A WARM FEELING IN MY HEART.
I'VE FINALLY REACHED THE POINT WHERE I'M INSPIRING OTHERS.

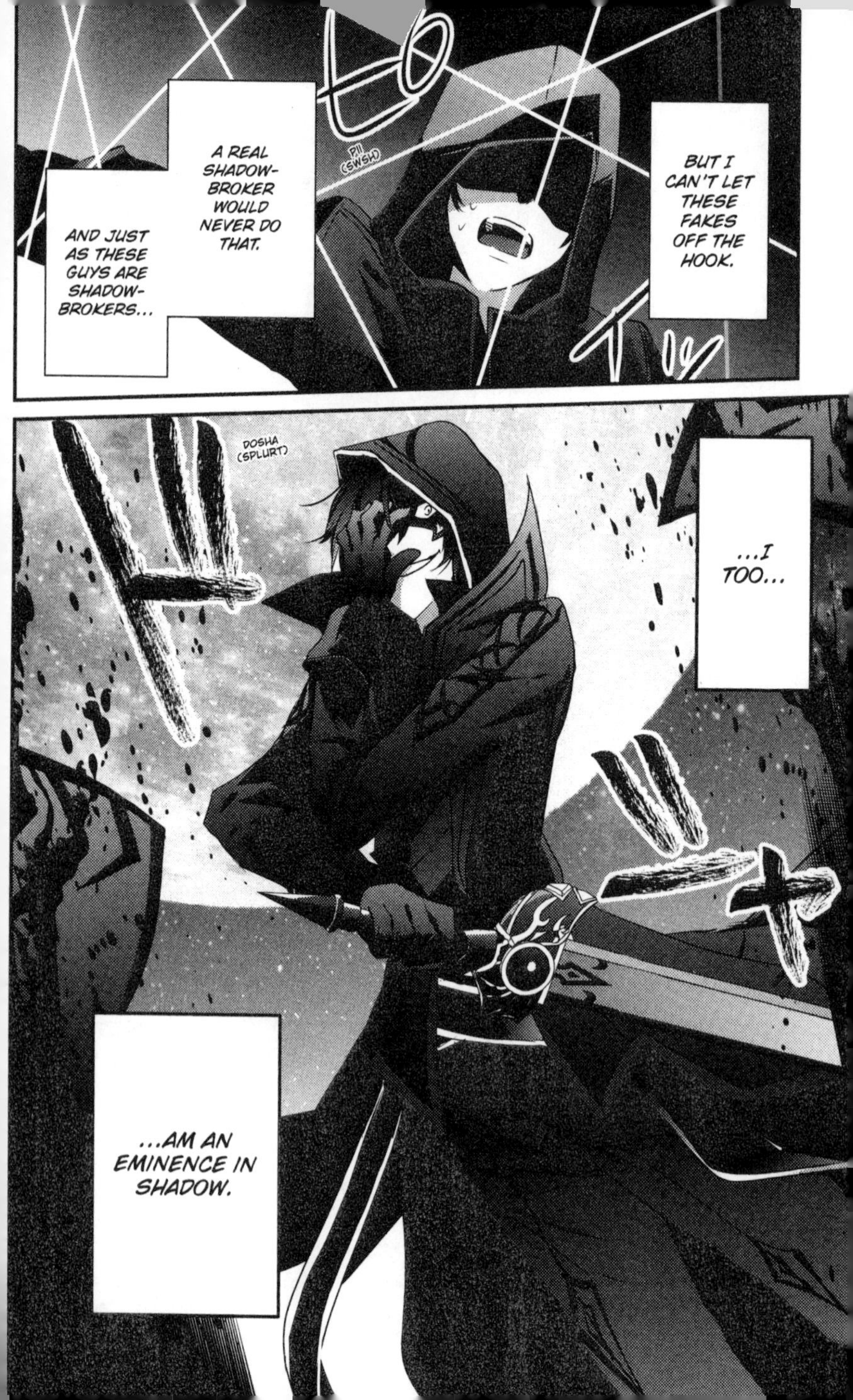
BUT I CAN'T LET THESE FAKES OFF THE HOOK.
PII (SWSH)
A REAL SHADOW-BROKER WOULD NEVER DO THAT.
AND JUST AS THESE GUYS ARE SHADOW-BROKERS...
DOSHA (SPLURT)
...I TOO...
...AM AN EMINENCE IN SHADOW.

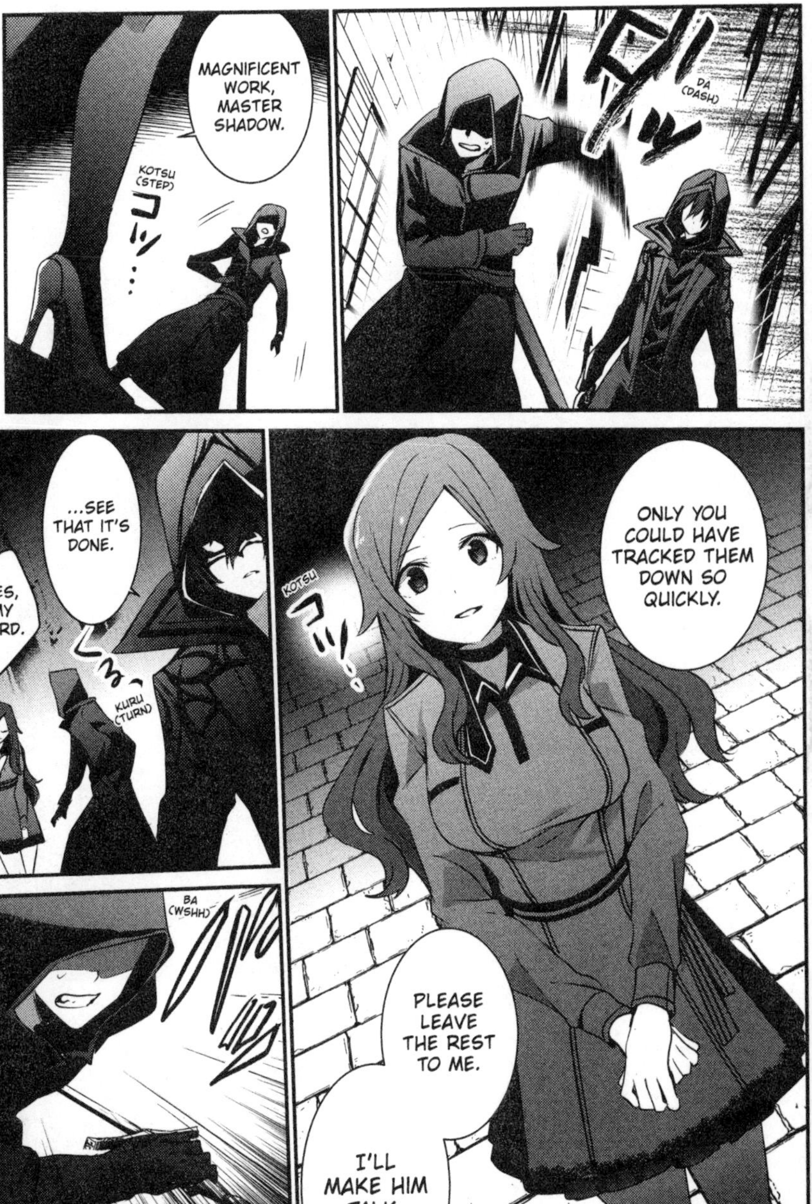
DA (DASH)
MAGNIFICENT WORK, MASTER SHADOW.
KOTSU (STEP)
ONLY YOU COULD HAVE TRACKED THEM DOWN SO QUICKLY.
KOTSU
PLEASE LEAVE THE REST TO ME.
I'LL MAKE HIM TALK.
...SEE THAT IT'S DONE.
YES, MY LORD.
KURU (TURN)
BA (WSHH)

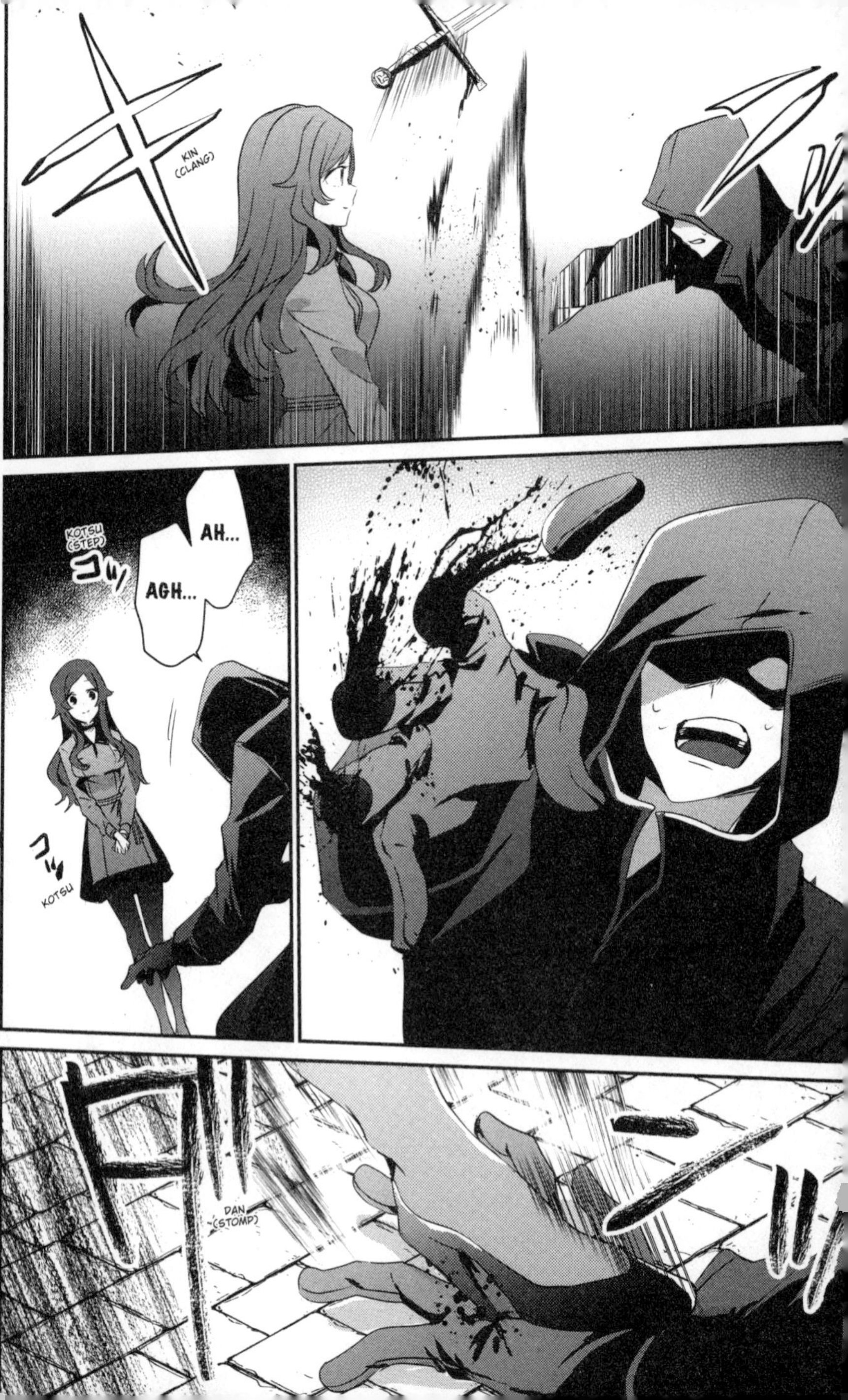
KIN (CLANG)
AH... AGH...
KOTSU (STEP)
コツ
コツ
KOTSU
DAN (STOMP)

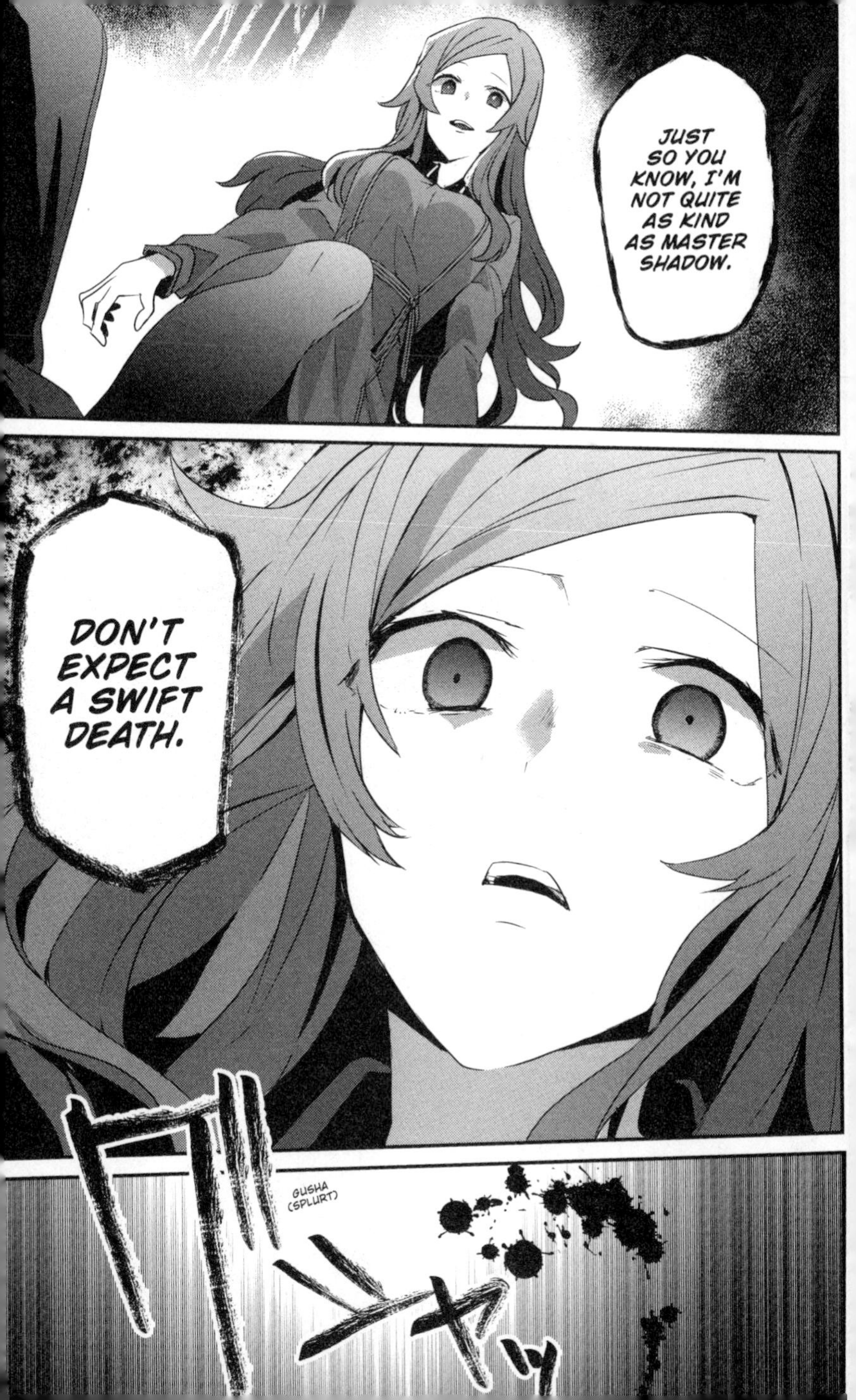
JUST SO YOU KNOW, I'M NOT QUITE AS KIND AS MASTER SHADOW.
DON'T EXPECT A SWIFT DEATH.
GUSHA (SPLURT)

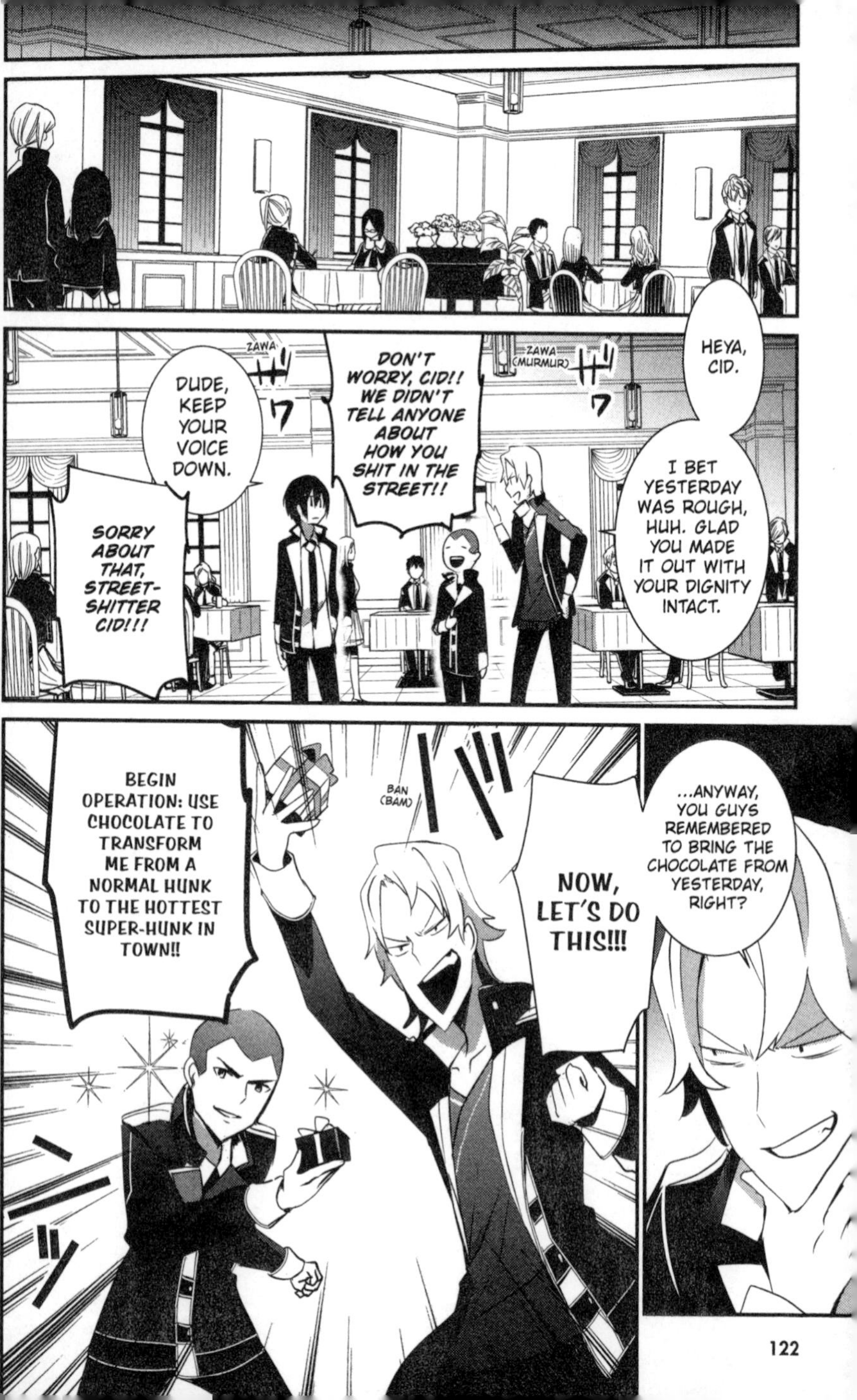
HEYA, CID.
I BET YESTERDAY WAS ROUGH, HUH. GLAD YOU MADE IT OUT WITH YOUR DIGNITY INTACT.
ZAWA (MURMUR)
DON'T WORRY, CID!! WE DIDN'T TELL ANYONE ABOUT HOW YOU SHIT IN THE STREET!!
ZAWA
DUDE, KEEP YOUR VOICE DOWN.
SORRY ABOUT THAT, STREET-SHITTER CID!!!
...ANYWAY, YOU GUYS REMEMBERED TO BRING THE CHOCOLATE FROM YESTERDAY, RIGHT?
NOW, LET'S DO THIS!!!
BAN (BAM)
BEGIN OPERATION: USE CHOCOLATE TO TRANSFORM ME FROM A NORMAL HUNK TO THE HOTTEST SUPER-HUNK IN TOWN!!

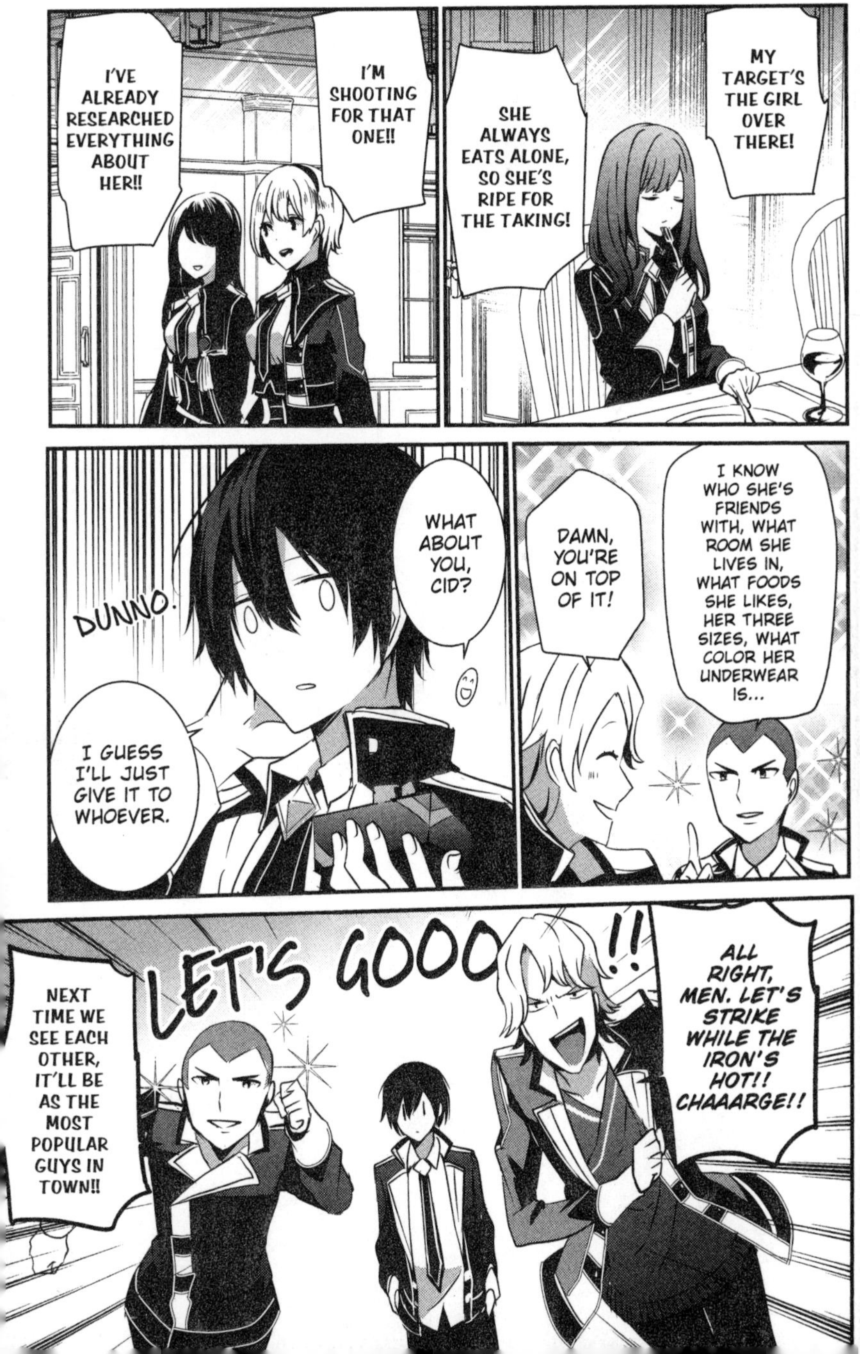
MY TARGET'S THE GIRL OVER THERE!
SHE ALWAYS EATS ALONE, SO SHE'S RIPE FOR THE TAKING!
I'M SHOOTING FOR THAT ONE!!
I'VE ALREADY RESEARCHED EVERYTHING ABOUT HER!!
I KNOW WHO SHE'S FRIENDS WITH, WHAT ROOM SHE LIVES IN, WHAT FOODS SHE LIKES, HER THREE SIZES, WHAT COLOR HER UNDERWEAR IS...
DAMN, YOU'RE ON TOP OF IT!
WHAT ABOUT YOU, CID?
DUNNO.
I GUESS I'LL JUST GIVE IT TO WHOEVER.
ALL RIGHT, MEN. LET'S STRIKE WHILE THE IRON'S HOT!! CHAAARGE!!
LET'S GOOO!!
NEXT TIME WE SEE EACH OTHER, IT'LL BE AS THE MOST POPULAR GUYS IN TOWN!!

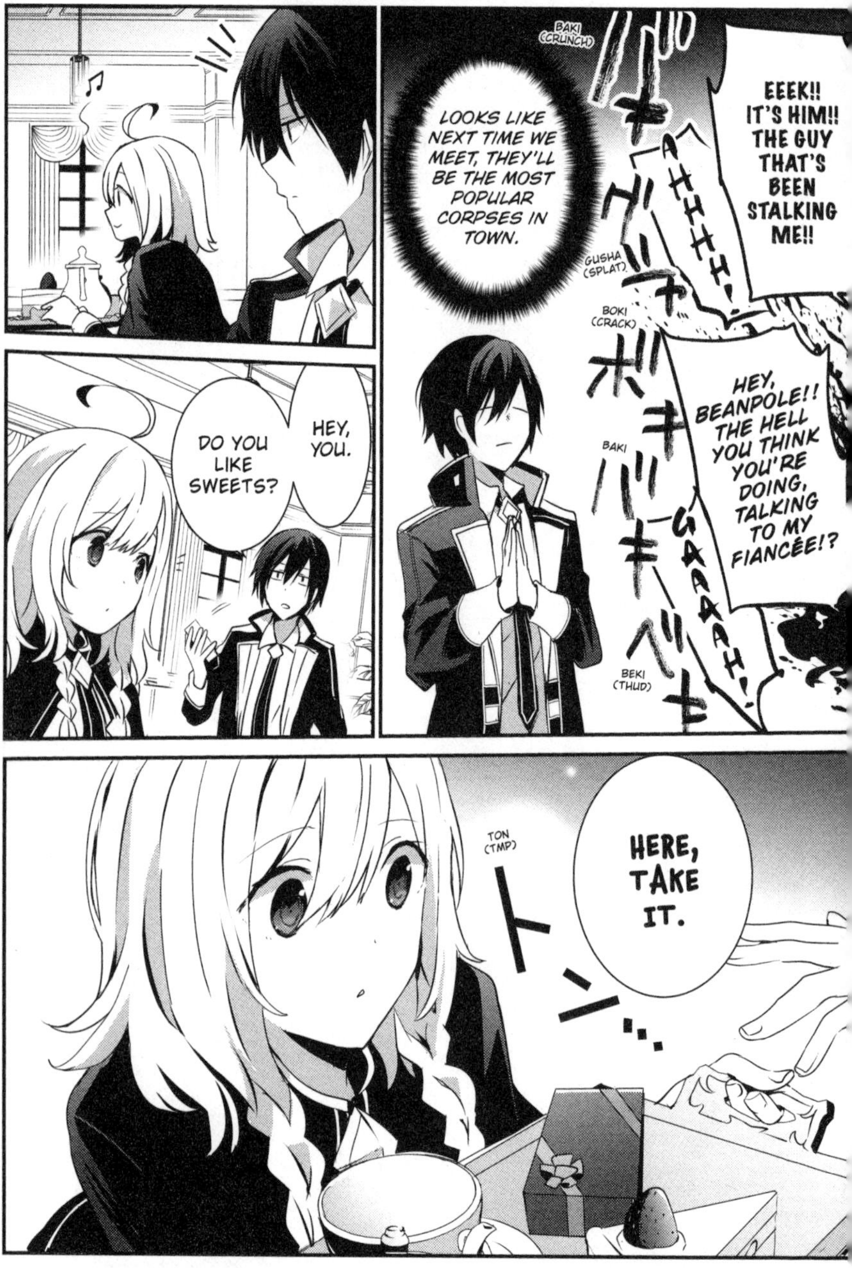
EEEK!! IT'S HIM!! THE GUY THAT'S BEEN STALKING ME!!
BAKI (CRUNCH)
LOOKS LIKE NEXT TIME WE MEET, THEY'LL BE THE MOST POPULAR CORPSES IN TOWN.
AHHHHH!
GUSHA (SPLAT)
BOKI (CRACK)
HEY, BEANPOLE!! THE HELL YOU THINK YOU'RE DOING, TALKING TO MY FIANCÉE!?
BAKI
GAAAAAH!
BEKI (THUD)
HEY, YOU.
DO YOU LIKE SWEETS?
HERE, TAKE IT.
TON (TMP)

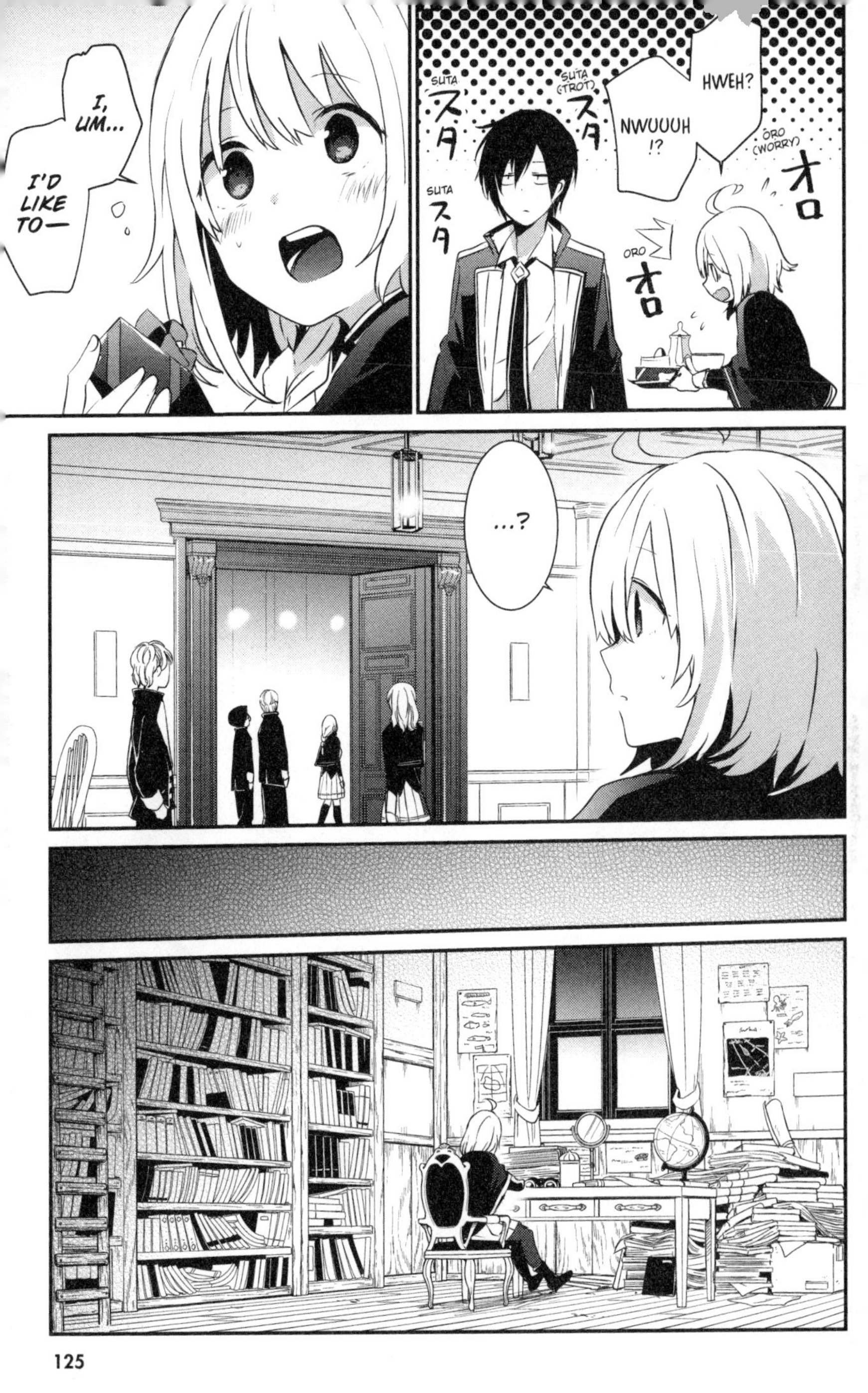
HWEH?
NWUUUH !?
ORO (WORRY)
オロ
SUTA (TROT)
スタ
SUTA
スタ
SUTA
スタ
ORO
オロ
I, UM...
I'D LIKE TO—
...?

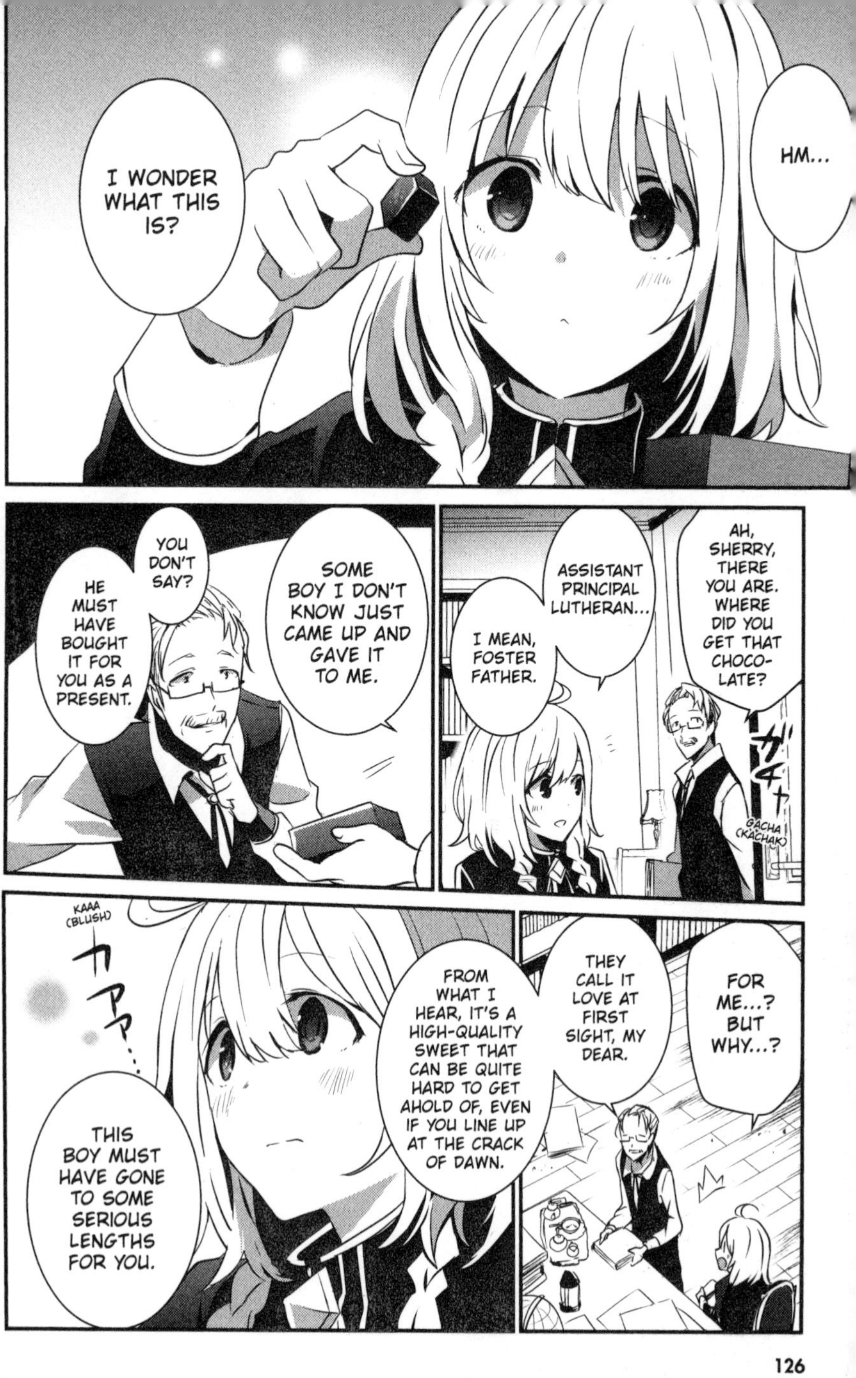
HM...
I WONDER WHAT THIS IS?
AH, SHERRY, THERE YOU ARE. WHERE DID YOU GET THAT CHOCO-LATE?
GACHA (KACHAK)
ASSISTANT PRINCIPAL LUTHERAN...
I MEAN, FOSTER FATHER.
SOME BOY I DON'T KNOW JUST CAME UP AND GAVE IT TO ME.
YOU DON'T SAY?
HE MUST HAVE BOUGHT IT FOR YOU AS A PRESENT.
FOR ME...? BUT WHY...?
THEY CALL IT LOVE AT FIRST SIGHT, MY DEAR.
FROM WHAT I HEAR, IT'S A HIGH-QUALITY SWEET THAT CAN BE QUITE HARD TO GET AHOLD OF, EVEN IF YOU LINE UP AT THE CRACK OF DAWN.
KAAA (BLUSH)
THIS BOY MUST HAVE GONE TO SOME SERIOUS LENGTHS FOR YOU.

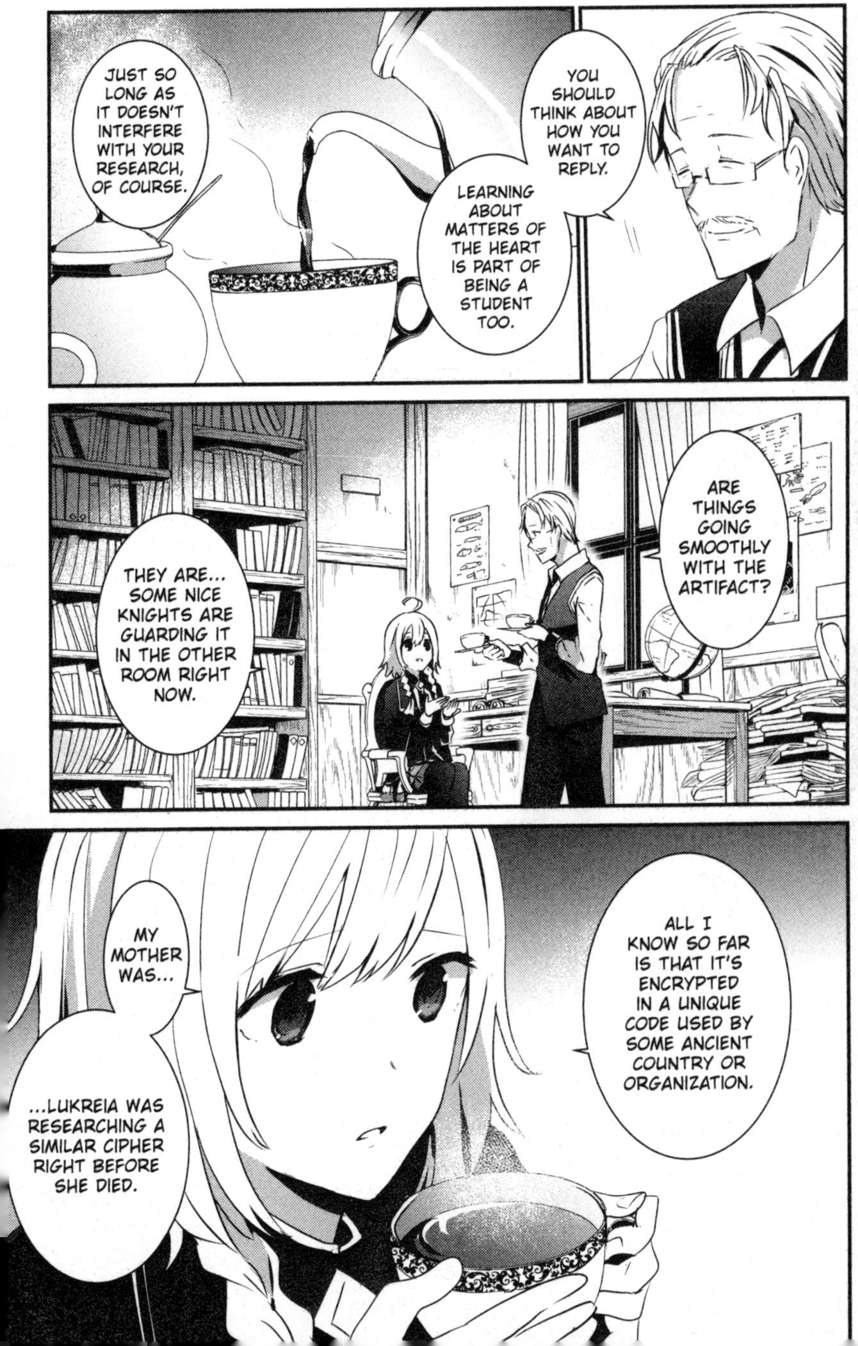
YOU SHOULD THINK ABOUT HOW YOU WANT TO REPLY.
LEARNING ABOUT MATTERS OF THE HEART IS PART OF BEING A STUDENT TOO.
JUST SO LONG AS IT DOESN'T INTERFERE WITH YOUR RESEARCH, OF COURSE.
ARE THINGS GOING SMOOTHLY WITH THE ARTIFACT?
THEY ARE... SOME NICE KNIGHTS ARE GUARDING IT IN THE OTHER ROOM RIGHT NOW.
ALL I KNOW SO FAR IS THAT IT'S ENCRYPTED IN A UNIQUE CODE USED BY SOME ANCIENT COUNTRY OR ORGANIZATION.
MY MOTHER WAS...
...LUKREIA WAS RESEARCHING A SIMILAR CIPHER RIGHT BEFORE SHE DIED.

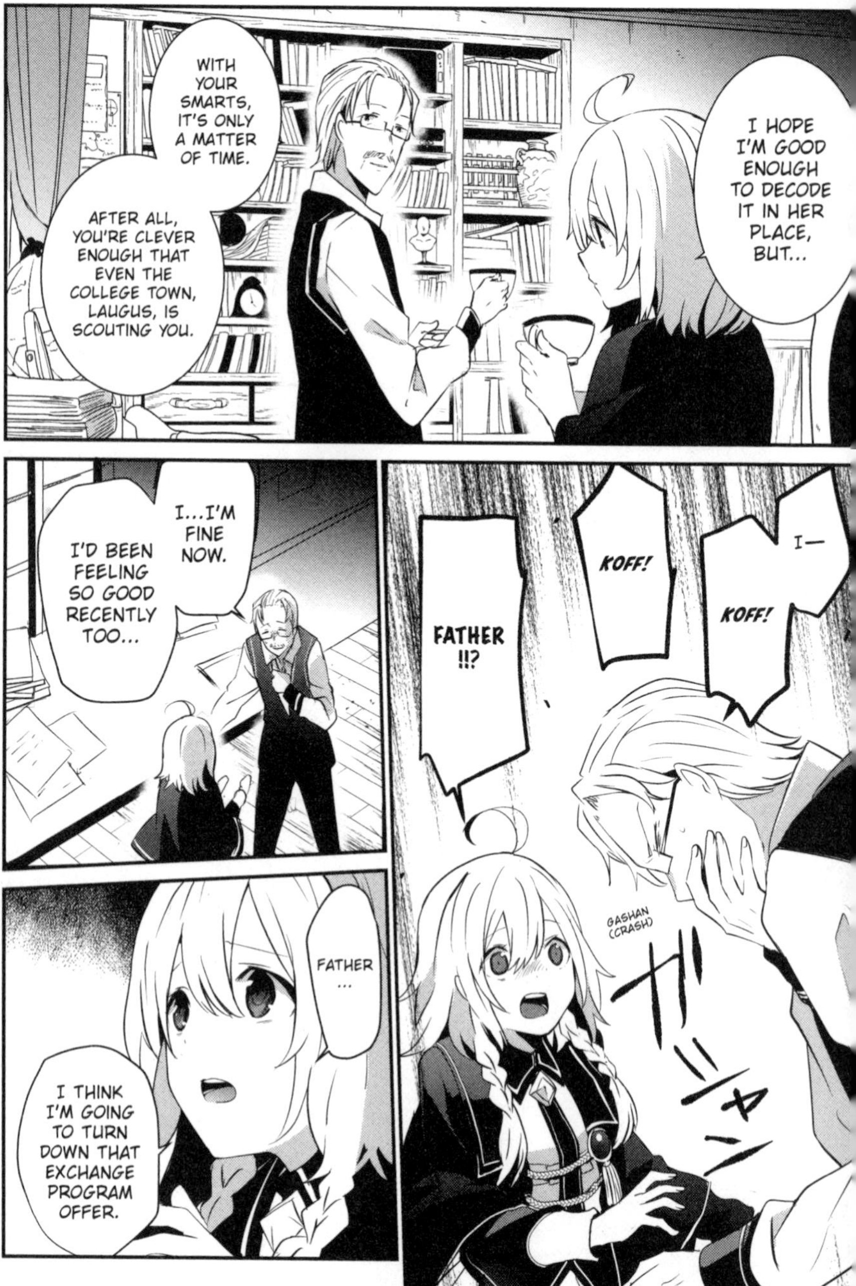
I HOPE I'M GOOD ENOUGH TO DECODE IT IN HER PLACE, BUT...
WITH YOUR SMARTS, IT'S ONLY A MATTER OF TIME.
AFTER ALL, YOU'RE CLEVER ENOUGH THAT EVEN THE COLLEGE TOWN, LAUGUS, IS SCOUTING YOU.
I—
KOFF!
KOFF!
FATHER !!?
GASHAN (CRASH)
I...I'M FINE NOW.
I'D BEEN FEELING SO GOOD RECENTLY TOO...
FATHER...
I THINK I'M GOING TO TURN DOWN THAT EXCHANGE PROGRAM OFFER.

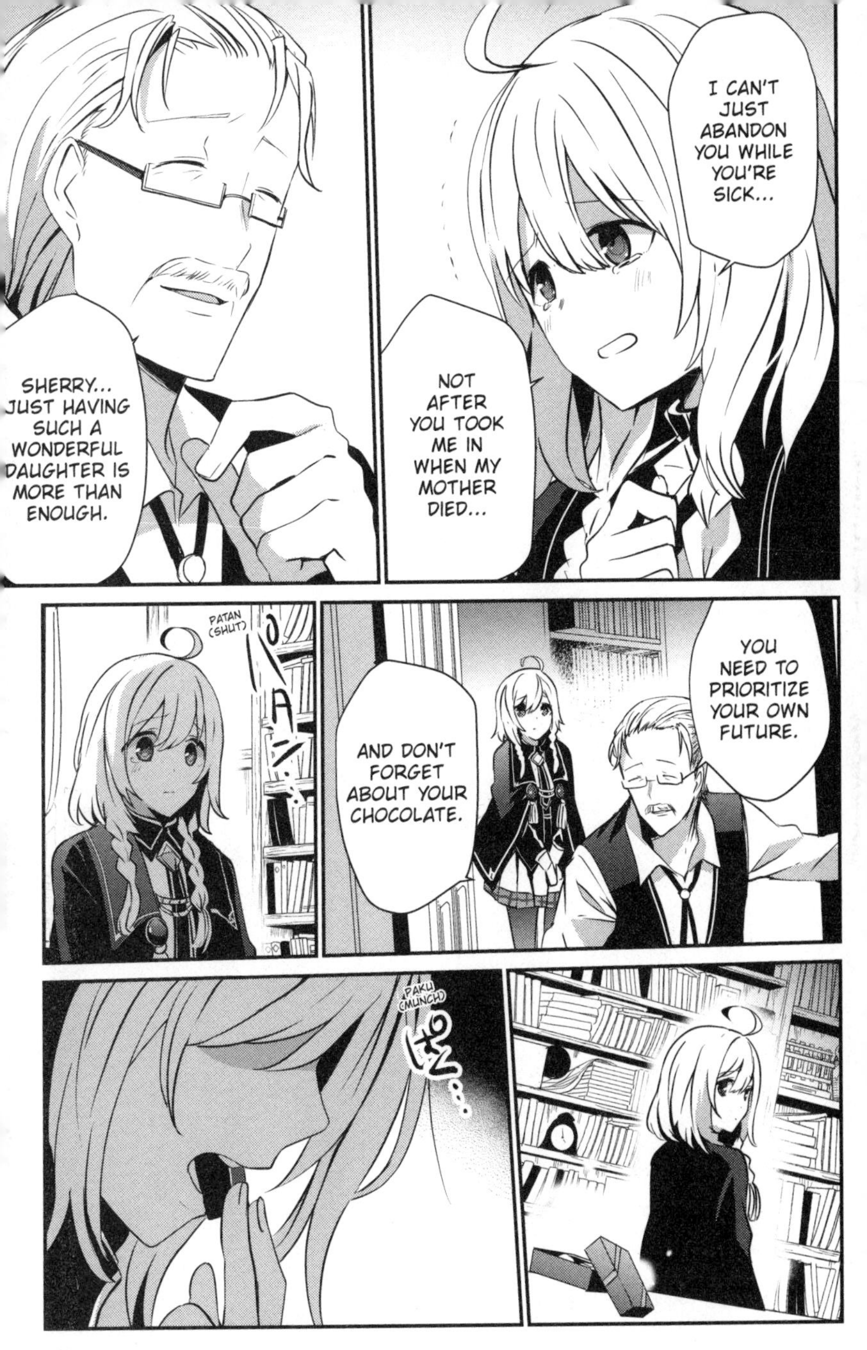
I CAN'T JUST ABANDON YOU WHILE YOU'RE SICK...
NOT AFTER YOU TOOK ME IN WHEN MY MOTHER DIED...
SHERRY... JUST HAVING SUCH A WONDERFUL DAUGHTER IS MORE THAN ENOUGH.
YOU NEED TO PRIORITIZE YOUR OWN FUTURE.
AND DON'T FORGET ABOUT YOUR CHOCOLATE.
PATAN (SHUT)
パタン…
PAKU (MUNCH)
ぱく…

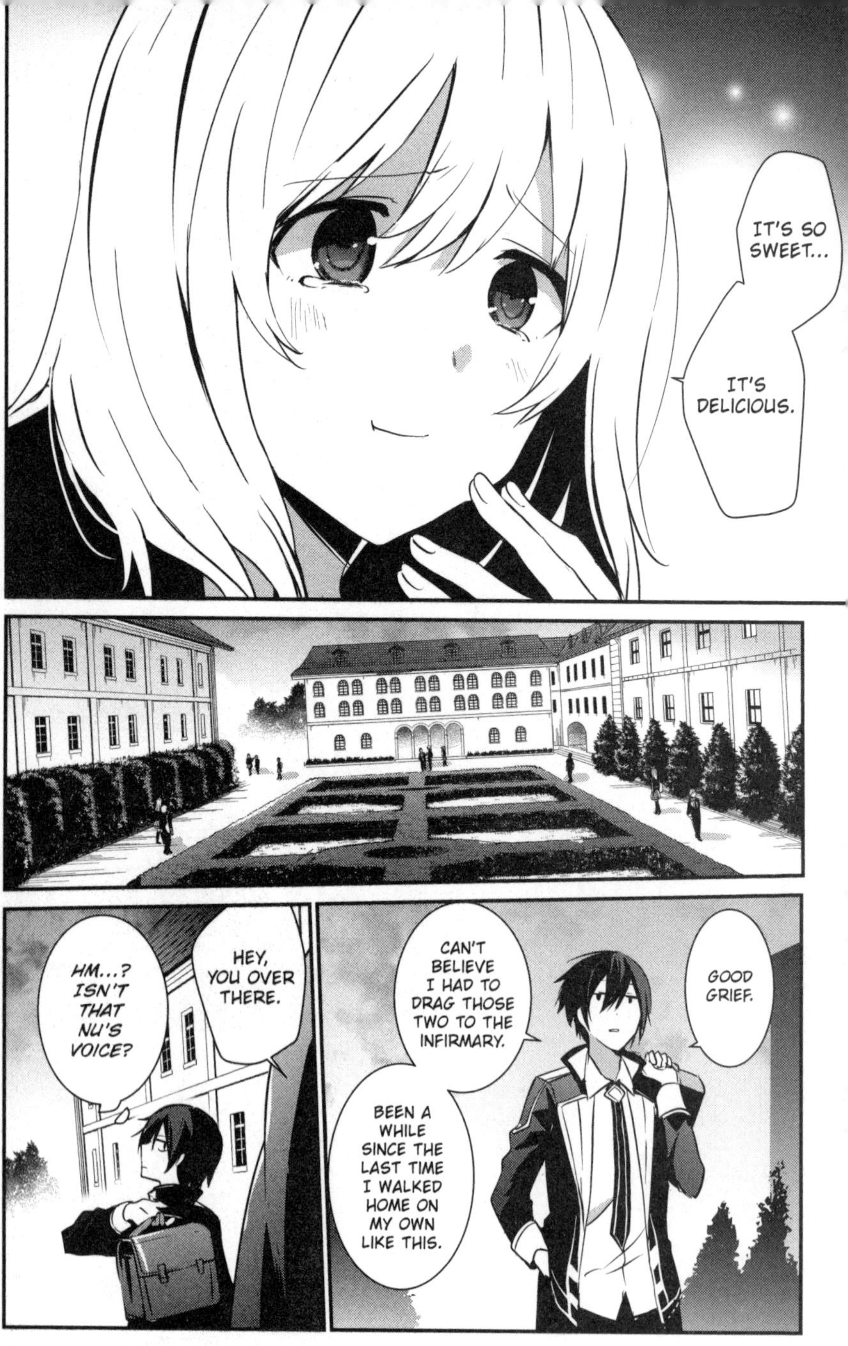
IT'S SO SWEET...
IT'S DELICIOUS.
GOOD GRIEF.
CAN'T BELIEVE I HAD TO DRAG THOSE TWO TO THE INFIRMARY.
BEEN A WHILE SINCE THE LAST TIME I WALKED HOME ON MY OWN LIKE THIS.
HEY, YOU OVER THERE.
HM...? ISN'T THAT NU'S VOICE?

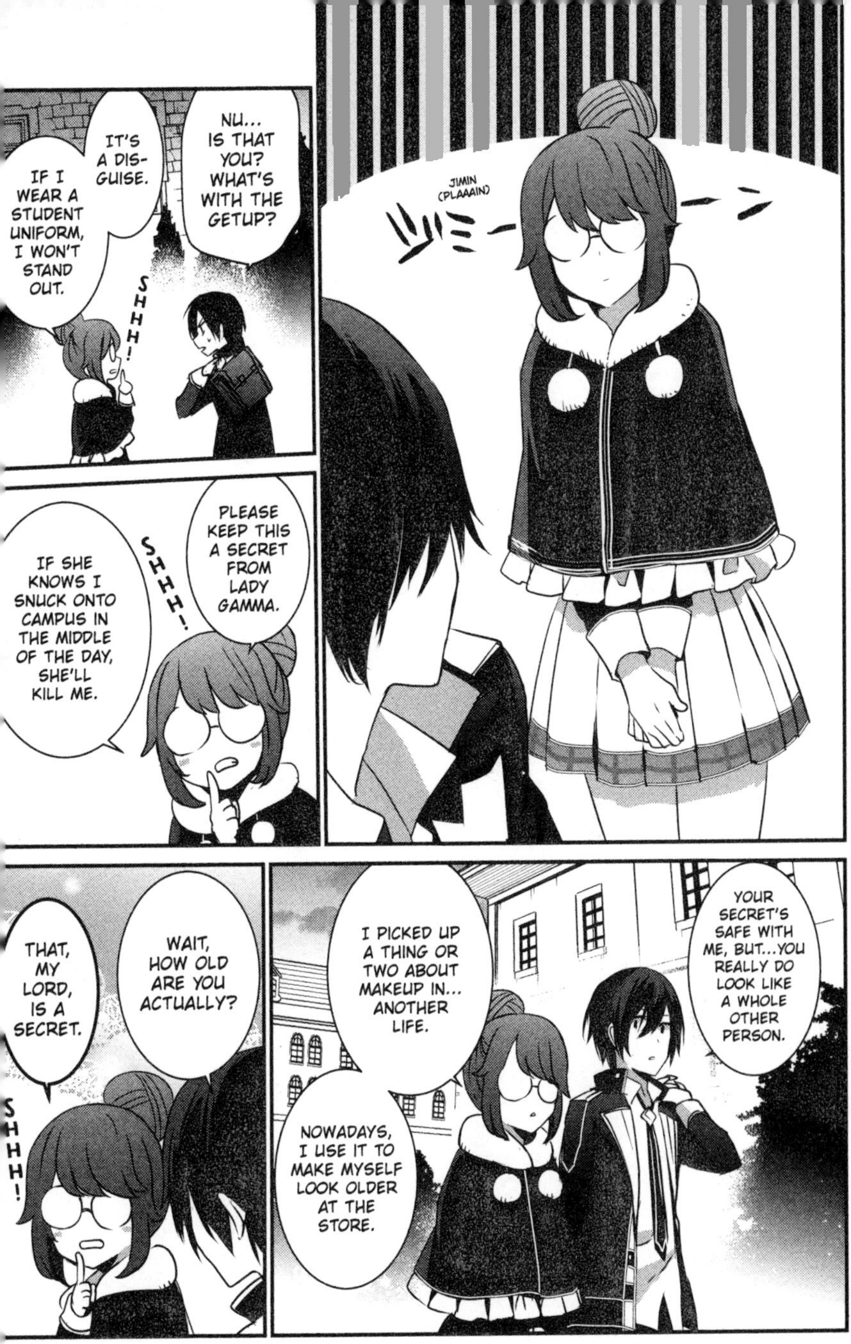
JIMIN (PLAAAIN)
NU... IS THAT YOU? WHAT'S WITH THE GETUP?
IT'S A DISGUISE.
IF I WEAR A STUDENT UNIFORM, I WON'T STAND OUT.
SHHH!
PLEASE KEEP THIS A SECRET FROM LADY GAMMA.
SHHH!
IF SHE KNOWS I SNUCK ONTO CAMPUS IN THE MIDDLE OF THE DAY, SHE'LL KILL ME.
YOUR SECRET'S SAFE WITH ME, BUT...YOU REALLY DO LOOK LIKE A WHOLE OTHER PERSON.
I PICKED UP A THING OR TWO ABOUT MAKEUP IN... ANOTHER LIFE.
NOWADAYS, I USE IT TO MAKE MYSELF LOOK OLDER AT THE STORE.
WAIT, HOW OLD ARE YOU ACTUALLY?
THAT, MY LORD, IS A SECRET.
SHHH!

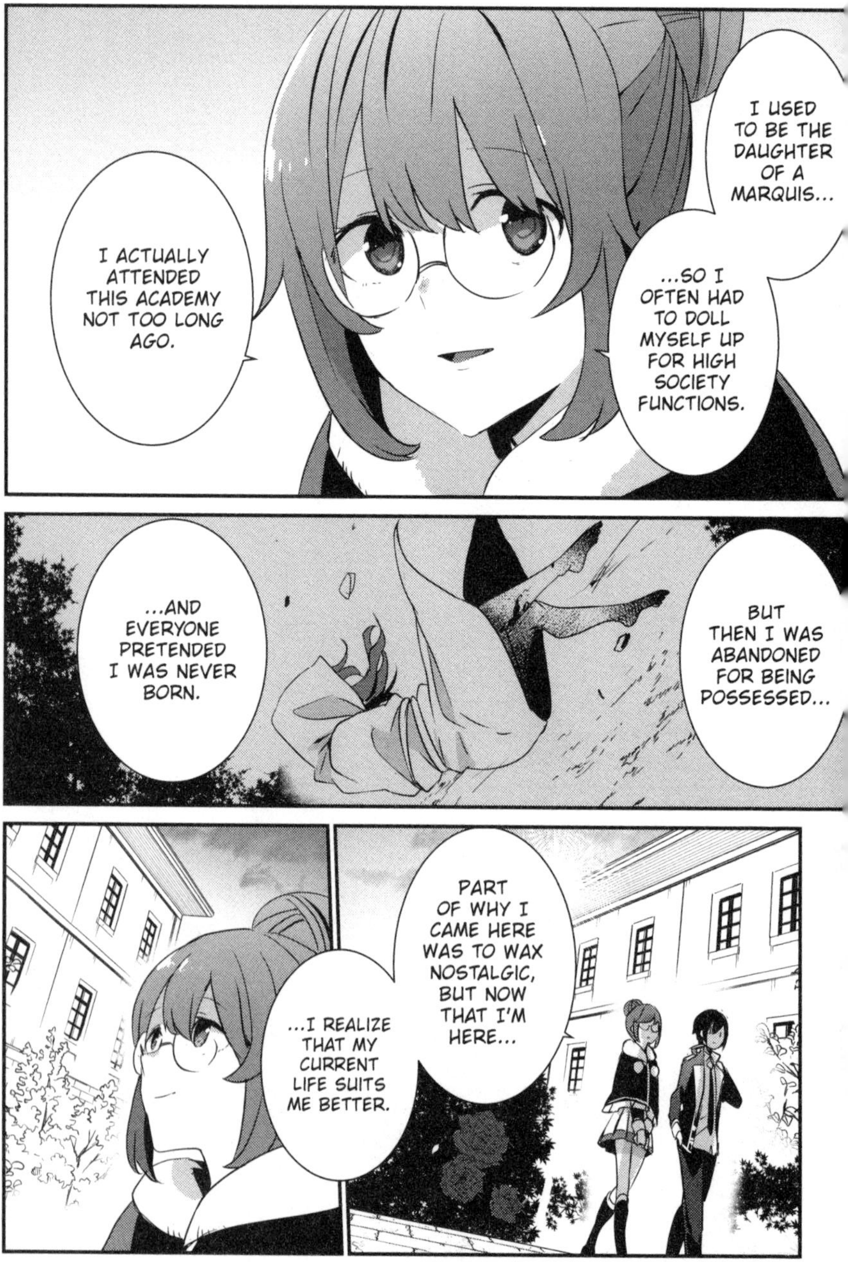
I USED TO BE THE DAUGHTER OF A MARQUIS...
...SO I OFTEN HAD TO DOLL MYSELF UP FOR HIGH SOCIETY FUNCTIONS.
I ACTUALLY ATTENDED THIS ACADEMY NOT TOO LONG AGO.
BUT THEN I WAS ABANDONED FOR BEING POSSESSED...
...AND EVERYONE PRETENDED I WAS NEVER BORN.
PART OF WHY I CAME HERE WAS TO WAX NOSTALGIC, BUT NOW THAT I'M HERE...
...I REALIZE THAT MY CURRENT LIFE SUITS ME BETTER.

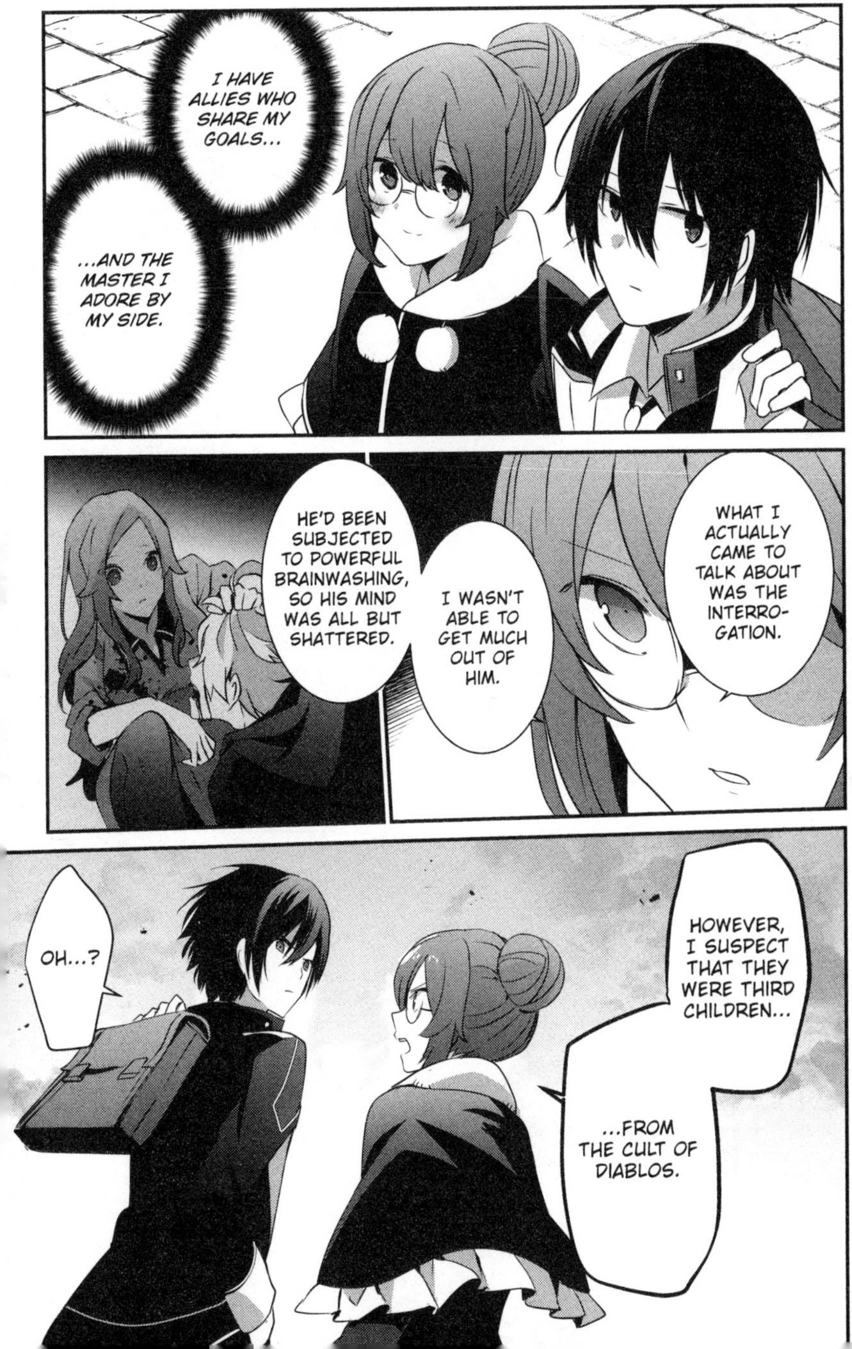
I HAVE ALLIES WHO SHARE MY GOALS...
...AND THE MASTER I ADORE BY MY SIDE.
WHAT I ACTUALLY CAME TO TALK ABOUT WAS THE INTERRO-GATION.
I WASN'T ABLE TO GET MUCH OUT OF HIM.
HE'D BEEN SUBJECTED TO POWERFUL BRAINWASHING, SO HIS MIND WAS ALL BUT SHATTERED.
HOWEVER, I SUSPECT THAT THEY WERE THIRD CHILDREN...
...FROM THE CULT OF DIABLOS.
OH...?

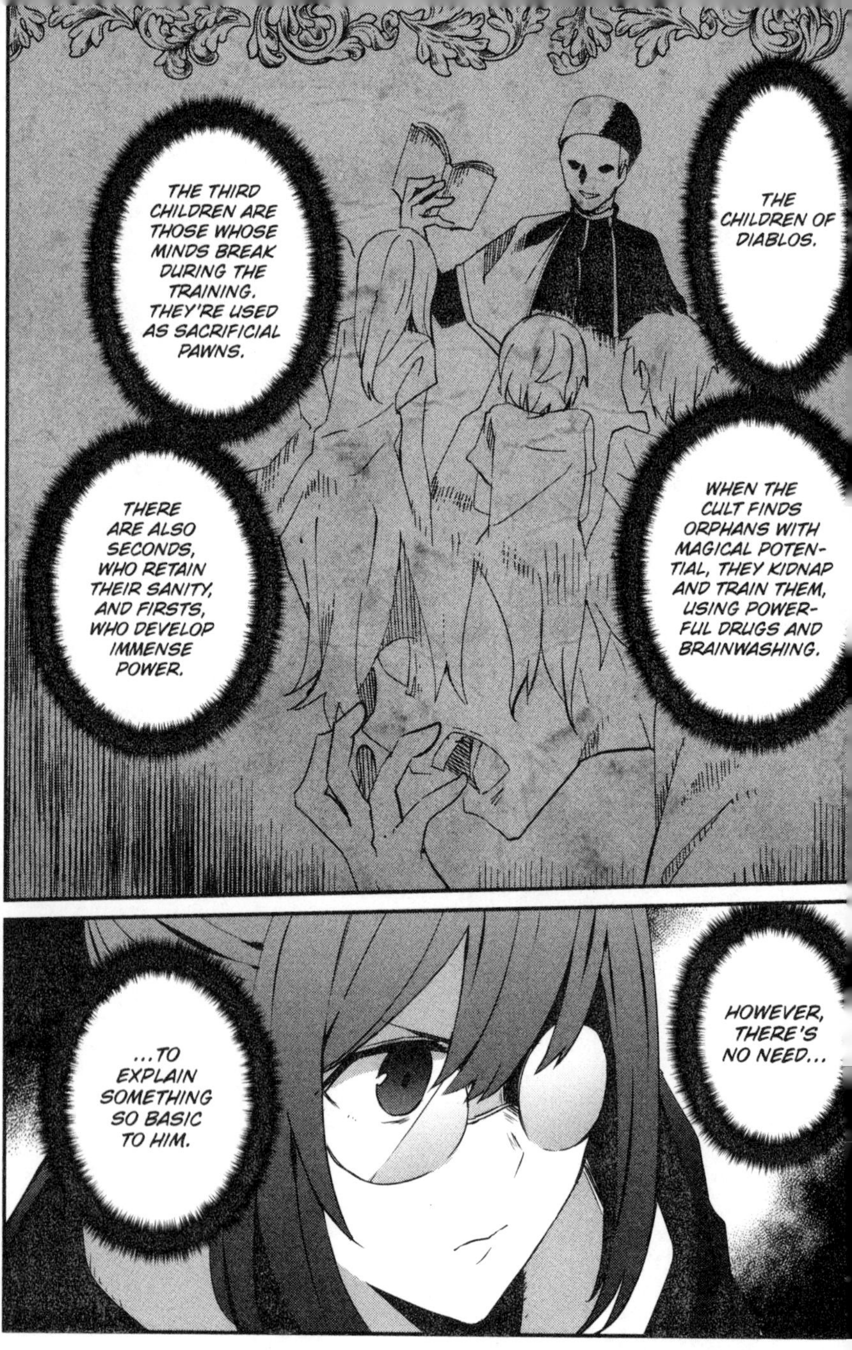
THE CHILDREN OF DIABLOS.
WHEN THE CULT FINDS ORPHANS WITH MAGICAL POTEN-TIAL, THEY KIDNAP AND TRAIN THEM, USING POWER-FUL DRUGS AND BRAINWASHING.
THE THIRD CHILDREN ARE THOSE WHOSE MINDS BREAK DURING THE TRAINING. THEY'RE USED AS SACRIFICIAL PAWNS.
THERE ARE ALSO SECONDS, WHO RETAIN THEIR SANITY, AND FIRSTS, WHO DEVELOP IMMENSE POWER.
HOWEVER, THERE'S NO NEED...
...TO EXPLAIN SOMETHING SO BASIC TO HIM.

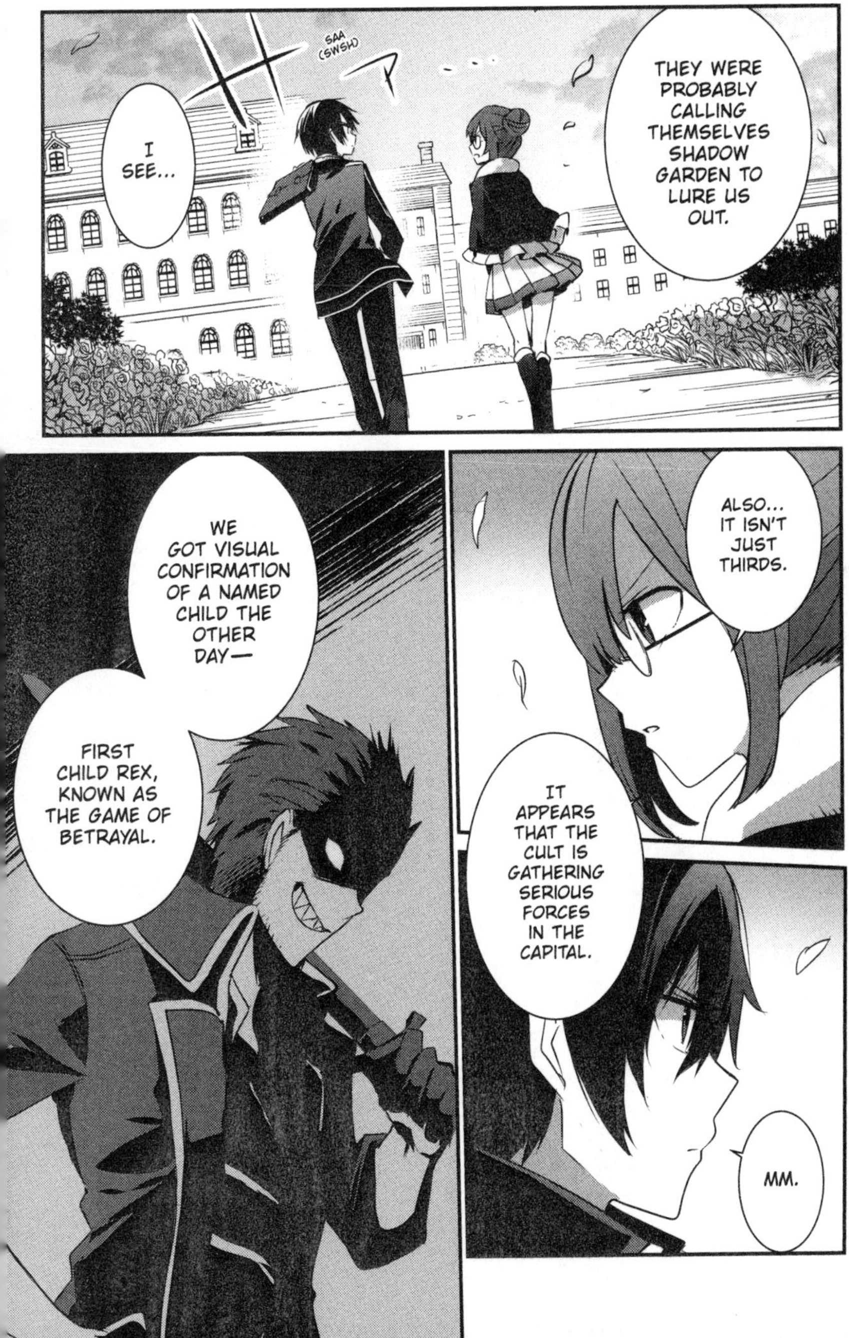
THEY WERE PROBABLY CALLING THEMSELVES SHADOW GARDEN TO LURE US OUT.
SAA (SWSH)
I SEE...
ALSO... IT ISN'T JUST THIRDS.
IT APPEARS THAT THE CULT IS GATHERING SERIOUS FORCES IN THE CAPITAL.
MM.
WE GOT VISUAL CONFIRMATION OF A NAMED CHILD THE OTHER DAY—
FIRST CHILD REX, KNOWN AS THE GAME OF BETRAYAL.

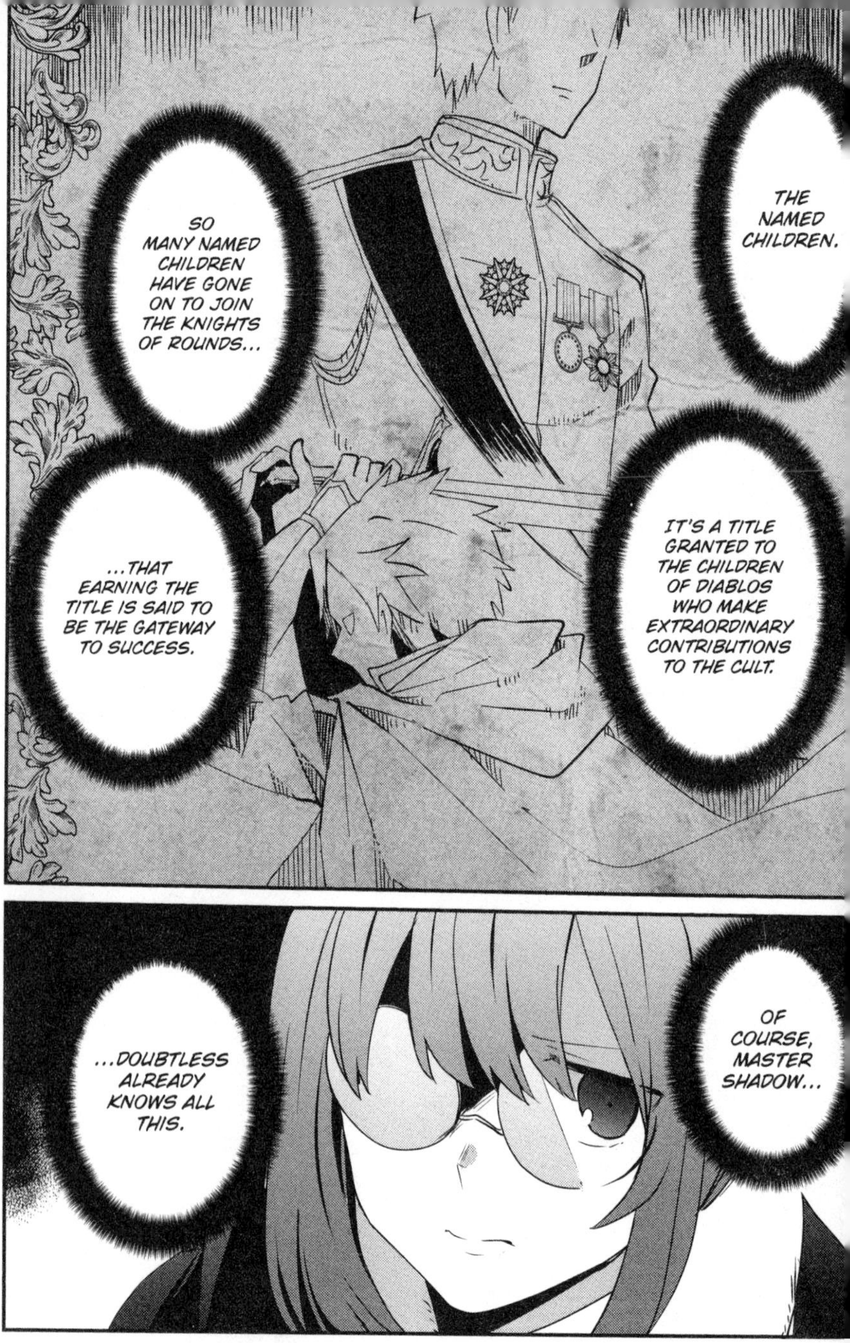
THE NAMED CHILDREN.
IT'S A TITLE GRANTED TO THE CHILDREN OF DIABLOS WHO MAKE EXTRAORDINARY CONTRIBUTIONS TO THE CULT.
SO MANY NAMED CHILDREN HAVE GONE ON TO JOIN THE KNIGHTS OF ROUNDS...
...THAT EARNING THE TITLE IS SAID TO BE THE GATEWAY TO SUCCESS.
OF COURSE, MASTER SHADOW...
...DOUBTLESS ALREADY KNOWS ALL THIS.

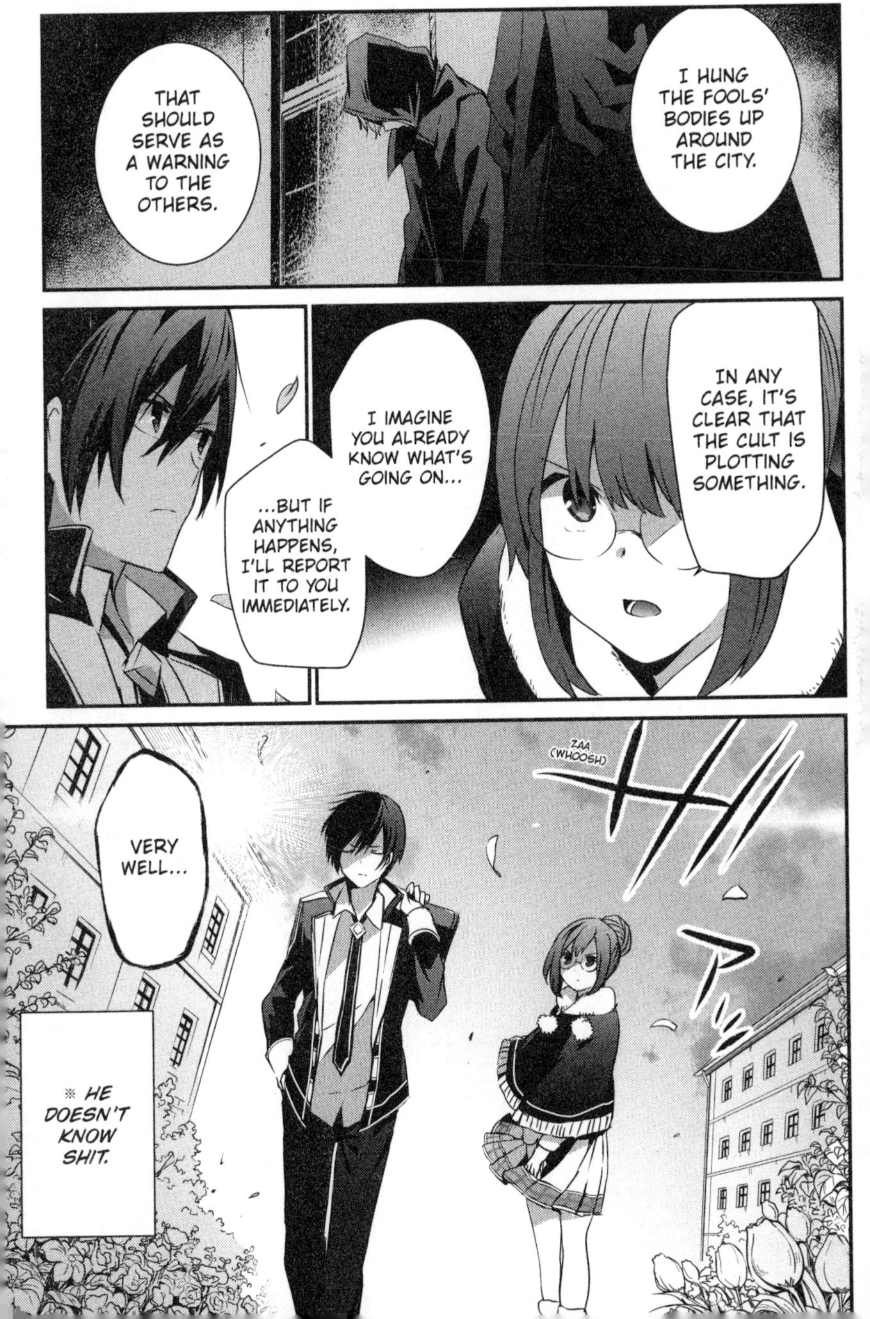
I HUNG THE FOOLS' BODIES UP AROUND THE CITY.
THAT SHOULD SERVE AS A WARNING TO THE OTHERS.
IN ANY CASE, IT'S CLEAR THAT THE CULT IS PLOTTING SOMETHING.
I IMAGINE YOU ALREADY KNOW WHAT'S GOING ON...
...BUT IF ANYTHING HAPPENS, I'LL REPORT IT TO YOU IMMEDIATELY.
ZAA (WHOOSH)
VERY WELL...
※ HE DOESN'T KNOW SHIT.

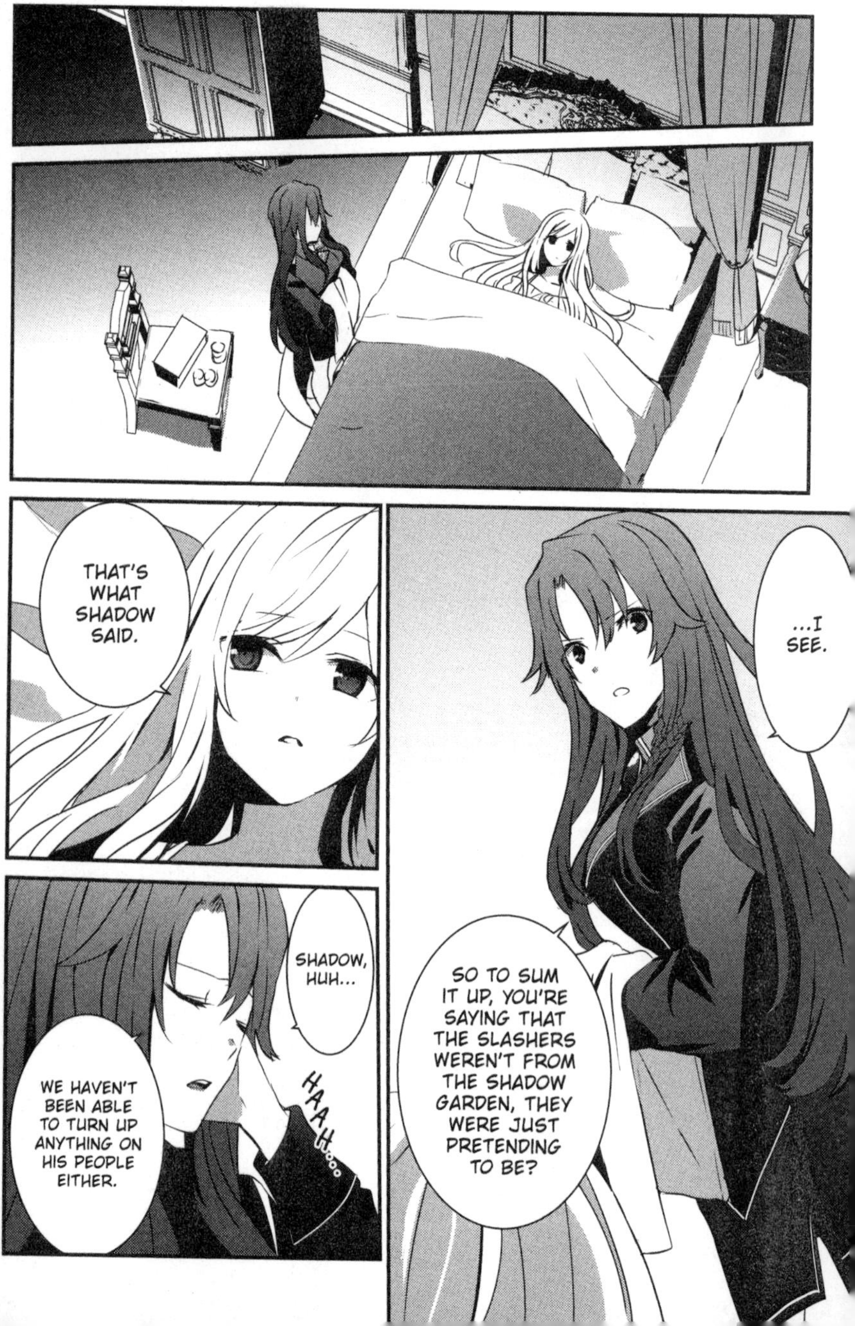
...I SEE.
SO TO SUM IT UP, YOU'RE SAYING THAT THE SLASHERS WEREN'T FROM THE SHADOW GARDEN, THEY WERE JUST PRETENDING TO BE?
THAT'S WHAT SHADOW SAID.
SHADOW, HUH...
HAAAH...
WE HAVEN'T BEEN ABLE TO TURN UP ANYTHING ON HIS PEOPLE EITHER.

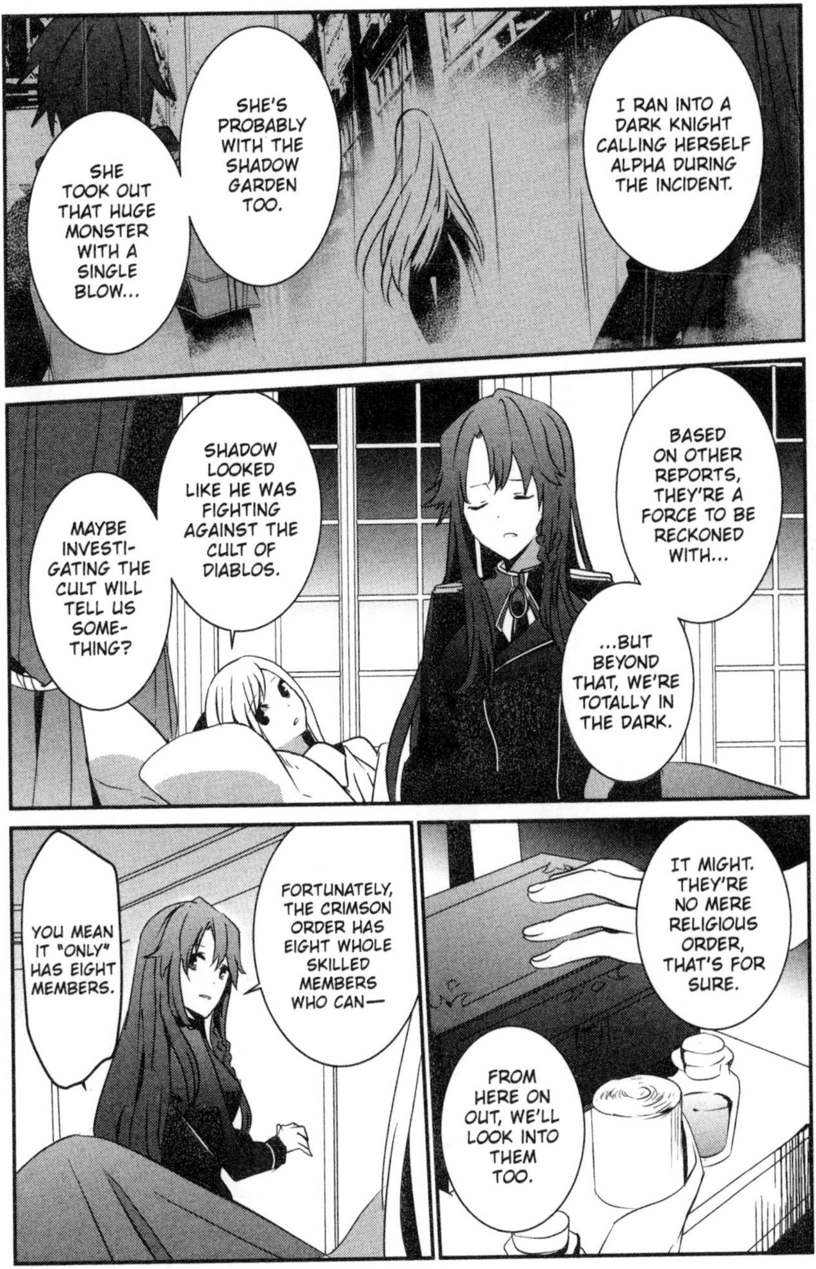
I RAN INTO A DARK KNIGHT CALLING HERSELF ALPHA DURING THE INCIDENT.
SHE'S PROBABLY WITH THE SHADOW GARDEN TOO.
SHE TOOK OUT THAT HUGE MONSTER WITH A SINGLE BLOW...
BASED ON OTHER REPORTS, THEY'RE A FORCE TO BE RECKONED WITH...
...BUT BEYOND THAT, WE'RE TOTALLY IN THE DARK.
SHADOW LOOKED LIKE HE WAS FIGHTING AGAINST THE CULT OF DIABLOS.
MAYBE INVESTIGATING THE CULT WILL TELL US SOMETHING?
IT MIGHT. THEY'RE NO MERE RELIGIOUS ORDER, THAT'S FOR SURE.
FROM HERE ON OUT, WE'LL LOOK INTO THEM TOO.
FORTUNATELY, THE CRIMSON ORDER HAS EIGHT WHOLE SKILLED MEMBERS WHO CAN—
YOU MEAN IT "ONLY" HAS EIGHT MEMBERS.

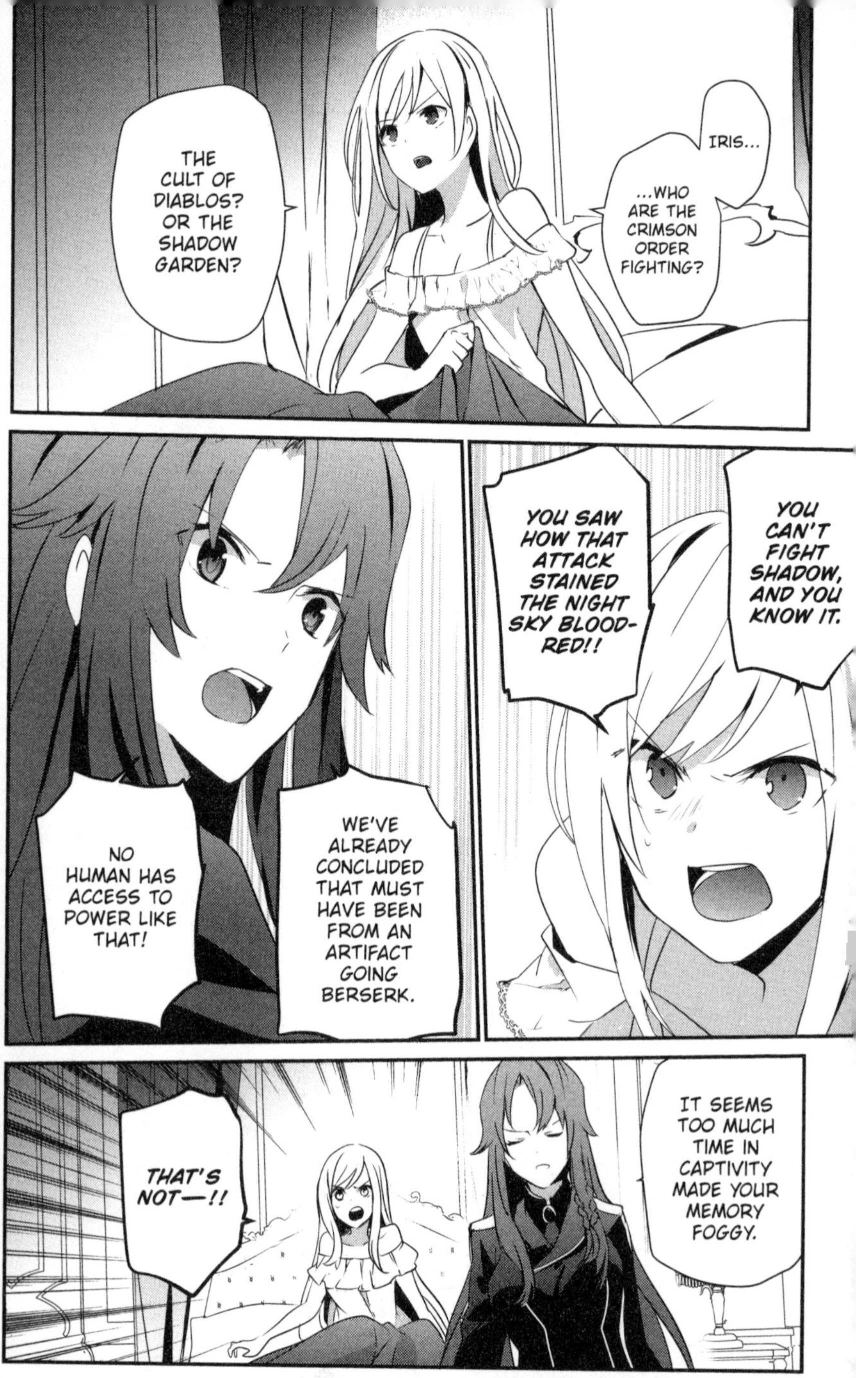
IRIS...
...WHO ARE THE CRIMSON ORDER FIGHTING?
THE CULT OF DIABLOS? OR THE SHADOW GARDEN?
YOU CAN'T FIGHT SHADOW, AND YOU KNOW IT.
YOU SAW HOW THAT ATTACK STAINED THE NIGHT SKY BLOOD-RED!!
WE'VE ALREADY CONCLUDED THAT MUST HAVE BEEN FROM AN ARTIFACT GOING BERSERK.
NO HUMAN HAS ACCESS TO POWER LIKE THAT!
IT SEEMS TOO MUCH TIME IN CAPTIVITY MADE YOUR MEMORY FOGGY.
THAT'S NOT—!!

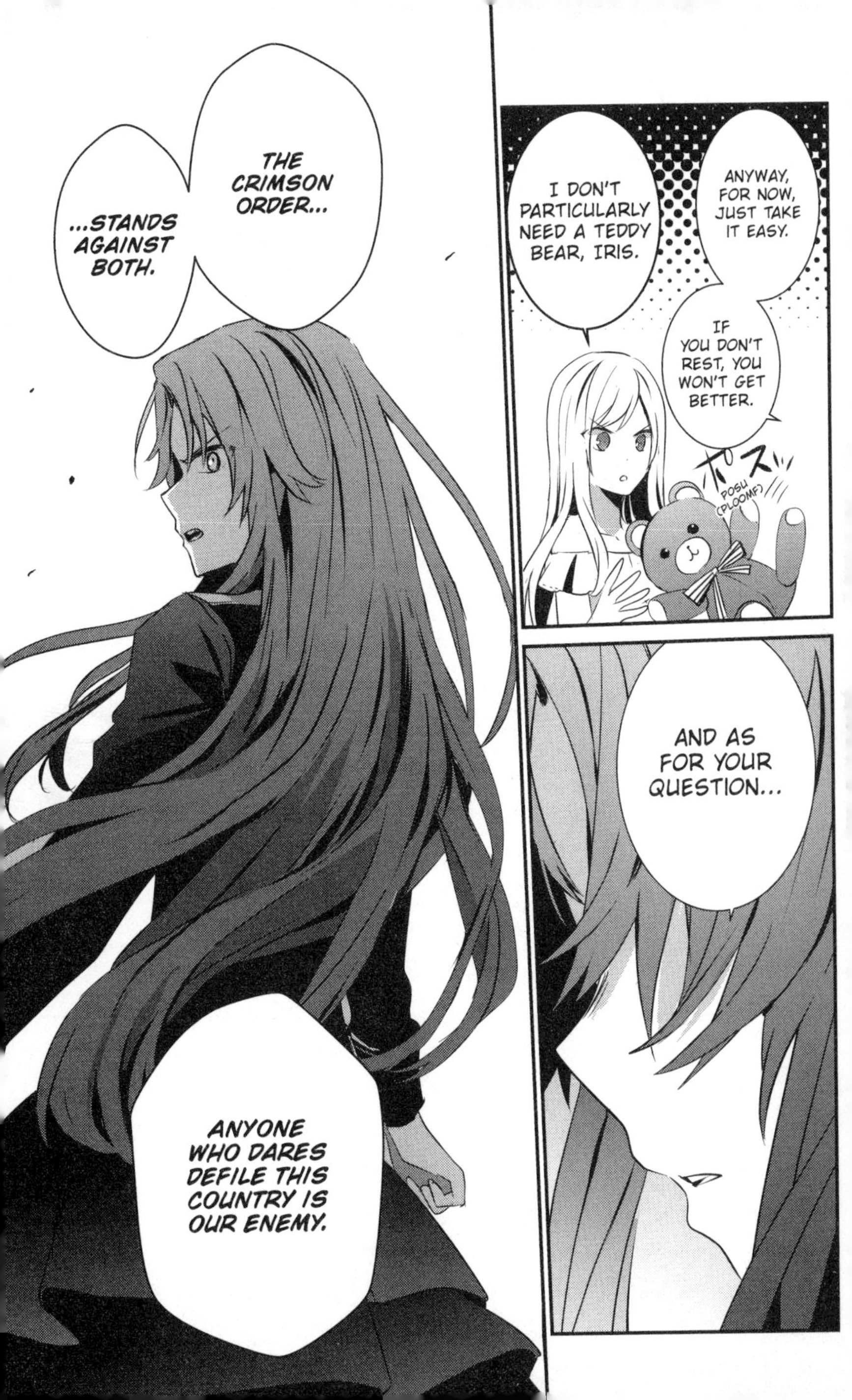
ANYWAY, FOR NOW, JUST TAKE IT EASY.
IF YOU DON'T REST, YOU WON'T GET BETTER.
POSU (PLOOMF)
I DON'T PARTICULARLY NEED A TEDDY BEAR, IRIS.
AND AS FOR YOUR QUESTION...
THE CRIMSON ORDER...
...STANDS AGAINST BOTH.
ANYONE WHO DARES DEFILE THIS COUNTRY IS OUR ENEMY.

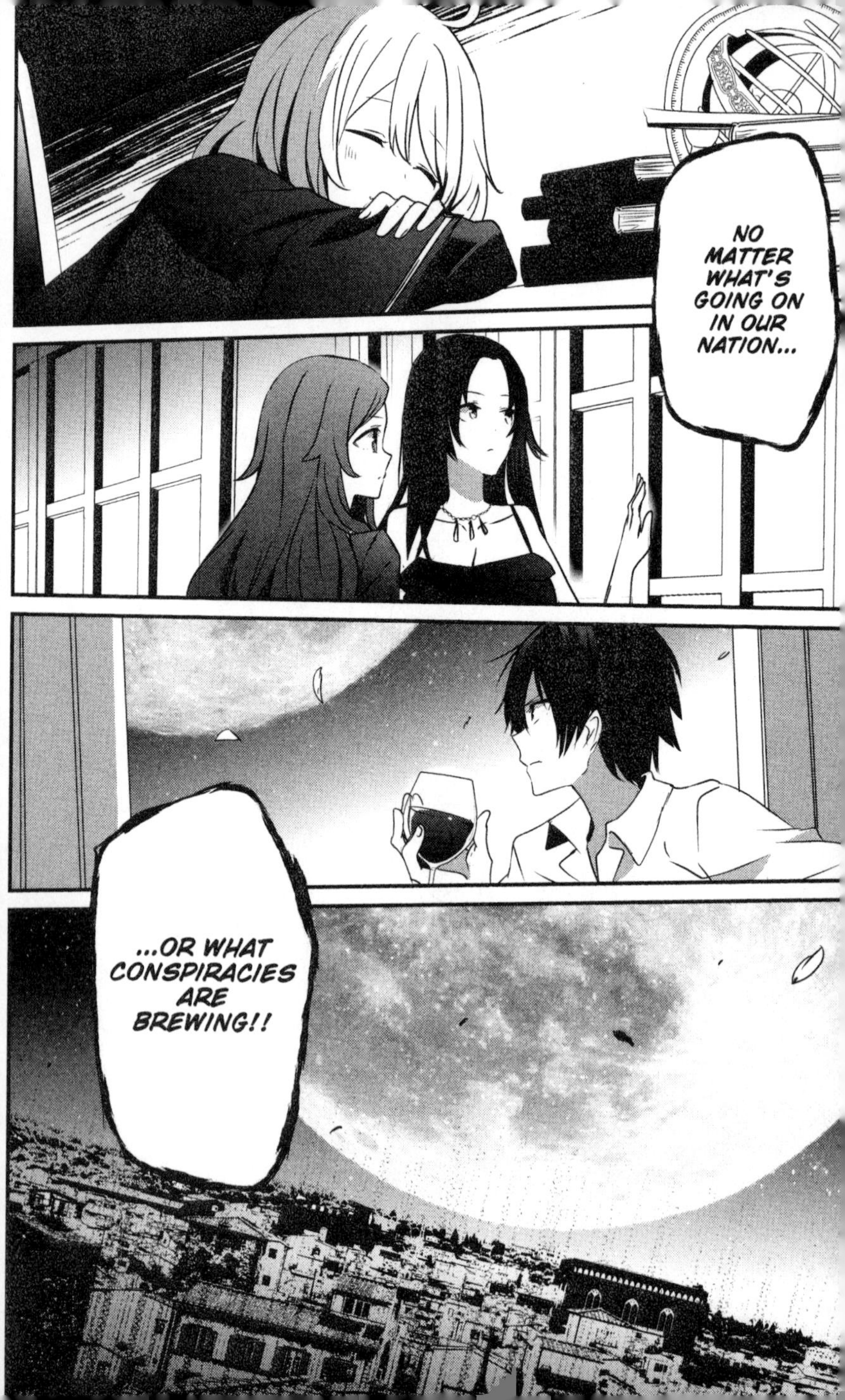
NO MATTER WHAT'S GOING ON IN OUR NATION...
...OR WHAT CONSPIRACIES ARE BREWING!!

To be continued in *The Eminence in Shadow*, Vol. 3

Art
Anri Sakano
Original Story
Daisuke Aizawa
Character Design
Touzai

The Eminence in Shadow 2

LETTERING: Phil Christie

TRANSLATION: Nathaniel Hiroshi Thrasher

KAGE NO JITSURYOKUSHA
NI NARITAKUTE! Volume 2
©Anri Sakano 2019
©Daisuke Aizawa 2019
©Touzai 2019
First published in Japan in 2019 by
KADOKAWA CORPORATION, Tokyo.
English translation rights arranged
with KADOKAWA CORPORATION, Tokyo
through Tuttle-Mori Agency, Inc., Tokyo.

English translation © 2021 by
Yen Press, LLC

Yen Press
150 West 30th Street
19th Floor
New York, NY 10001

Visit us at yenpress.com
facebook.com/yenpress
twitter.com/yenpress
yenpress.tumblr.com
instagram.com/yenpress

First Yen Press Edition: November 2021

Yen Press is an imprint of
Yen Press, LLC.
The Yen Press name and logo are
trademarks of Yen Press, LLC.

The publisher is not responsible for websites (or their content) that are not owned by the publisher.

Library of Congress Control Number:
2021935892

ISBNs: 978-1-9753-2520-6 (paperback)
       978-1-9753-2521-3 (ebook)

10 9 8 7 6 5 4 3 2 1

LSC-C

Printed in the United States of America